Entangled: Exploring Global Citizenship through the Lens of Quantum Physics

By Sandra Ferreira, MA, MS, LMHC, LPCC
2024

Entangled   Sandra Ferreira

<u>Index</u>

Introduction
A Quantum World, A Global Society

In a world that's increasingly interconnected, the concept of citizenship is evolving. Traditional citizenship is tied to one's country of origin, a bond based on birthplace or legal processes that tie us to one nation. But what if our citizenship extended beyond our borders, our governments, and our national identities? What if we considered ourselves not only citizens of one country but of the world? For those of us who, like me, have lived in different parts of the world, this concept is much easier to understand. Our perspective on life, cultures, others and ourselves changes radically as we immerse ourselves in different cultural realities when living in other countries. All the prejudices, superficial views and values that we carry from our local upbringing, which distance us from everyone else, fall away. Our horizons expand, allowing us to see, understand and feel our common humanity with other citizens around the world. At first, the idea may seem disturbing, but if we experience it with maturity, it becomes extremely enriching. It is, in fact, the understanding of a reality that exists beforehand, regardless of whether we are aware of it or not.

The purpose of this book is to share this magnificent and enriching learning experience with you, inviting you to embark on this adventure that broadens our horizons, strengthens us individually and collectively as a species and, consequently, allows us to create a better reality for all of us, nature and humans. Let us explore together the reality that we are all members of a larger global community. Being a global citizen means understanding and embracing diversity, recognizing our shared humanity, and taking responsibility for the planet and its people.

This expanded view of the world and our role in it reflects and triggers higher levels of knowledge, cognition, intelligence, and spiritual development, as new scientific findings will demonstrate. This book takes you through what it means to be a global citizen in the 21st century, why it matters, and how each of us can play a part in shaping a better, more inclusive world.

We live in a world shaped by forces both seen and unseen. Just as quantum physics reveals a universe that defies our intuitive sense of reality—where particles are entangled across vast distances, and observation changes outcomes—our society is becoming more complex, interconnected, and in need of a fresh perspective. What if the principles of quantum physics could help us understand and embrace the concept of global citizenship?

Entangled: Exploring Global Citizenship through the Lens of Quantum Physics invites readers to explore the world as a quantum phenomenon, where actions resonate across borders, and interconnections shape our shared destiny. Drawing parallels between the findings of the quantum world and the values of global citizenship, this book offers a new approach to seeing ourselves as integral parts of a larger whole. It's an invitation to embrace both the science of the infinitely small and the social potential of the infinitely connected.

As this refers to finding more definite solutions to problems that pertains to all of us, without exception, I am excited to have you on board!

Chapter 1
Understanding Global Citizenship

In a world that's expanding its interdependence, the concept of citizenship is becoming the new trend. As mentioned in the introduction, traditional citizenship is tied to one's country of origin, a bond based on birthplace or legal processes that tie us to one nation. But what if our citizenship extended beyond our borders, our governments, and our national identities? What if we considered ourselves not only citizens of one country but of the world?

Here we explore the concept that we are all members of a larger, global community. Being a global citizen is about understanding and embracing diversity, recognizing our shared humanity, and taking responsibility for the planet and its people. This book takes you through what it means to be a global citizen in the 21st century, why it matters, and how each of us can play a part in shaping a better, more inclusive world.

What is global citizenship, and why does it matter? This chapter introduces the concept, tracing its roots to early philosophers and thinkers who believed in a universal human connection. Through historical examples and modern-day definitions, readers will come to understand global citizenship as more than a political idea—it's a way of life, an approach to understanding our interdependent world.

The Philosophical Roots of Global Citizenship

Global citizenship, the idea that individuals are members of a worldwide community with shared responsibilities, has gained increasing relevance in our complex world. Its roots, however, trace back to ancient and modern philosophical traditions that emphasize universalism, human equality, and ethical responsibility across borders. This essay explores the philosophical origins of global citizenship by examining contributions from Stoicism, Enlightenment thinkers, and modern cosmopolitanism, showing how these ideas have shaped our understanding of global interdependence and moral obligation.

Stoicism and Early Universalism

The concept of global citizenship can be traced back to the ancient Stoics, particularly philosophers like Zeno of Citium, Epictetus, and Marcus Aurelius. Stoicism emphasized the idea of a universal human community bound by a shared capacity for reason and virtue. According to the Stoics, all humans are part of a "cosmopolis," or universal city, governed by natural law rather than arbitrary divisions of race, class, or nationality.

One of the Stoics' key principles was the concept of *oikeiosis*, or the idea of recognizing oneself as part of a larger community that includes all humanity. This notion challenged the prevailing tribalism of their time, encouraging individuals to see beyond their immediate social and political affiliations. As Marcus Aurelius wrote in his *Meditations*, "You are a citizen of the universe." Such statements reflect a profound sense of interconnectedness, which serves as a philosophical foundation for modern ideas of global citizenship.

Stoicism also advanced the idea of moral responsibility. For the Stoics, virtue was the highest good, and living virtuously meant acting in accordance with reason and natural law. This included treating others justly, regardless of their origin. By advocating for the equality of all humans under a universal moral framework, the Stoics laid the groundwork for later discussions of global ethics.

Enlightenment and the Expansion of Cosmopolitanism

The Enlightenment era further developed the principles of global citizenship through the works of philosophers like Immanuel Kant, Jean-Jacques Rousseau, and Adam Smith. These thinkers expanded on Stoic ideas of universalism by grounding them in reason, individual rights, and the pursuit of a just society.

Immanuel Kant, in particular, made significant contributions to the philosophy of global citizenship. In his essay *Perpetual Peace: A Philosophical Sketch*, Kant argued for a world order based on international cooperation, republican governance, and respect for human rights. He introduced the concept of a "universal hospitality," asserting that individuals have the right to be treated with dignity wherever they go. Kant's vision of a cosmopolitan world, where moral and legal principles transcend national borders, resonates strongly with contemporary global citizenship movements.

Similarly, Rousseau's emphasis on the social contract and the collective good underscores the interconnectedness of individuals within society. While Rousseau primarily focused on the nation-state, his ideas about collective responsibility can be extended to a global scale, highlighting the ethical obligations individuals have toward humanity as a whole.

Adam Smith's work, particularly *The Theory of Moral Sentiments*, also contributes to the philosophy of global citizenship. Smith emphasized the importance of empathy and the moral imagination in understanding and responding to the needs of others. This perspective aligns with the idea that global citizens should cultivate a sense of solidarity and compassion toward people from diverse cultural and geographical backgrounds.

Modern Cosmopolitanism and Global Ethics

In the 20th and 21st centuries, the idea of global citizenship has been further refined through modern cosmopolitanism. Philosophers like Martha Nussbaum, Kwame Anthony Appiah, and Peter Singer have expanded on earlier ideas, emphasizing the ethical dimensions of global interdependence in an increasingly interconnected world.

Martha Nussbaum advocates for the development of "world citizenship" through education. In her essay *Patriotism and Cosmopolitanism*, Nussbaum argues that education should prioritize the cultivation of a global perspective, encouraging students to see themselves as citizens of the world. She critiques narrow nationalistic thinking, asserting that a cosmopolitan education fosters empathy, critical thinking, and a commitment to justice on a global scale.

Kwame Anthony Appiah's concept of "cosmopolitan patriotism" provides a nuanced approach to global citizenship. While acknowledging the importance of local and national identities, Appiah argues that these identities should coexist with a commitment to universal values. According to Appiah, global citizenship is not about abandoning one's roots but about recognizing shared humanity and embracing cultural diversity.

Peter Singer's work on global ethics further underscores the moral responsibilities of global citizens. In *The Life You Can Save*, Singer makes a compelling case for individuals' ethical obligation to alleviate global poverty. His utilitarian approach challenges people to think beyond their immediate communities and act in ways that maximize well-being for the greatest number of people, regardless of geographic or cultural boundaries.

Challenges and Critiques of Global Citizenship

While the philosophical roots of global citizenship are rich and inspiring, the concept is not without challenges and critiques. One major critique comes from communitarian philosophers, who argue that global citizenship risks undermining local identities and loyalties. Michael Walzer, for example, contends that meaningful moral obligations arise from specific cultural and political communities rather than abstract universal principles.

Additionally, some critics argue that global citizenship can be overly idealistic, failing to account for the power imbalances and structural inequalities that shape global relations. They caution against a form of global citizenship that is detached from the realities of political and economic oppression, emphasizing the need for a more grounded approach that addresses systemic injustices.

Despite these critiques, the philosophical foundations of global citizenship provide a valuable framework for addressing contemporary global challenges. Climate change, pandemics, and social inequality all demand collective action and a sense of shared responsibility that transcends national borders. By drawing on the insights of Stoicism, Enlightenment thinkers, and modern cosmopolitanism, global citizenship offers a way to navigate these challenges with ethical clarity and purpose.

The philosophical roots of global citizenship highlight a long-standing tradition of universalism, ethical responsibility, and interconnectedness. From the Stoics' vision of a universal community to Enlightenment ideals of human rights and modern cosmopolitanism's emphasis on global ethics, these ideas have shaped our understanding of what it means to be a global citizen. While challenges and critiques remain, the concept of global citizenship provides a powerful framework for fostering solidarity, compassion, and justice in an increasingly interconnected world. As humanity faces shared challenges, embracing the principles of global citizenship may be essential for building a sustainable and equitable future.

Why Global Citizenship Matters in Today's Interconnected Society

In an era defined by globalization, where economies, cultures, and technologies transcend borders, the concept of global citizenship has gained significant importance. Global citizenship emphasizes the interconnectedness of all people and promotes a sense of shared responsibility for the world's challenges. It compels individuals to think and act beyond their national or cultural identities, embracing a broader perspective that values inclusivity, justice, and sustainability. Let's examine why global citizenship is vital in today's interconnected society, focusing on its role in addressing global challenges, fostering cross-cultural understanding, and promoting social responsibility.

Addressing Global Challenges

One of the most compelling reasons global citizenship matters is its capacity to address pressing global challenges. Issues like climate change, pandemics, poverty, and armed conflicts cannot be solved by nations acting in isolation. These challenges require collective action and a mindset that prioritizes global well-being over narrow national interests.

Climate change, for instance, exemplifies the need for global cooperation. The impacts of rising temperatures, extreme weather events, and biodiversity loss are felt worldwide, regardless of national borders. The 2015 Paris Agreement is a testament to the importance of global citizenship, as countries committed to reducing carbon emissions for the benefit of the planet. Yet, achieving these goals requires more than governmental agreements; it demands active participation from individuals who identify as global citizens to adopt sustainable practices in their daily lives.

Similarly, the COVID-19 pandemic highlighted the interconnected nature of public health. The virus spread rapidly across borders, emphasizing the need for coordinated responses, resource-sharing, and equitable access to vaccines. Global citizens played a critical role by advocating for vaccine distribution to low-income countries and supporting public health measures to protect vulnerable populations.

Global citizenship fosters a sense of collective responsibility, encouraging individuals and nations to collaborate on solutions that benefit humanity as a whole. This mindset is essential for tackling the interconnected challenges of the 21st century.

Fostering Cross-Cultural Understanding

In an increasingly globalized world, cross-cultural understanding is more important than ever. Migration, international trade, and digital communication have brought people from diverse cultural backgrounds into closer contact. While this interconnectedness has the potential to enrich societies, it can also lead to misunderstandings, prejudice, and conflict. Global citizenship promotes empathy and respect for cultural diversity, laying the foundation for peaceful coexistence and mutual learning.

Global citizens recognize that cultural differences are not barriers but opportunities for growth and collaboration. By embracing a global perspective, individuals can appreciate the unique contributions of different cultures to art, science, and philosophy. Programs like international exchange initiatives and global education curricula play a pivotal role in fostering this understanding. They encourage students to engage with diverse perspectives, challenging stereotypes and broadening their worldviews.

Furthermore, global citizenship counters the rise of xenophobia and nationalism by promoting inclusivity and solidarity. In times of crisis, such as the Syrian refugee crisis or the displacement of communities due to natural disasters, global citizens advocate for compassionate responses that uphold human dignity. This commitment to cross-cultural understanding is essential for building harmonious and equitable societies.

Promoting Social Responsibility

Global citizenship instills a sense of social responsibility, encouraging individuals to take action for the greater good. This involves recognizing one's privilege, addressing systemic inequalities, and supporting initiatives that uplift marginalized communities. In today's global society, social responsibility extends beyond local or national boundaries, encompassing global efforts to create a fairer world.

One area where global citizenship and social responsibility intersect is the fight against poverty and inequality. According to the World Bank, nearly 700 million people live in extreme poverty, surviving on less than $2.15 a day. Global citizens advocate for policies that address wealth disparities, such as fair trade practices, debt relief for developing nations, and equitable access to education and healthcare. Organizations like Oxfam and Amnesty International rely on the support of global citizens who are committed to promoting social justice on a global scale.

Another example is corporate social responsibility (CSR), which reflects the principles of global citizenship in the business world. Companies that embrace CSR prioritize ethical practices, environmental sustainability, and community engagement. For instance, Patagonia, a global outdoor clothing brand, has committed to environmental advocacy by donating a percentage of its profits to conservation efforts and encouraging customers to repair rather than replace clothing. Such initiatives demonstrate how global citizenship can inspire socially responsible actions across various sectors.

By fostering a sense of shared responsibility, global citizenship empowers individuals to challenge injustice, advocate for systemic change, and contribute to a more equitable society.

Preparing for the Future

The rapid pace of technological advancement and globalization presents both opportunities and challenges. Global citizenship equips individuals with the skills and mindset needed to navigate this dynamic landscape. Critical thinking, adaptability, and ethical decision-making are essential for addressing emerging issues like artificial intelligence, cybersecurity, and the ethical use of data.

Education plays a crucial role in preparing future generations for the responsibilities of global citizenship. UNESCO's Global Citizenship Education (GCE) framework emphasizes the importance of teaching students to think critically about global issues, engage in meaningful dialogue, and take action to address societal challenges. By fostering global awareness and a commitment to ethical responsibility, GCE prepares young people to become active participants in shaping a sustainable and inclusive future.

Moreover, global citizenship encourages innovation by promoting collaboration across disciplines and borders. For example, the field of medical research relies heavily on international cooperation to develop treatments and vaccines. The Human Genome Project, a landmark initiative that mapped the entire human genome, involved scientists from 20 countries working together toward a common goal. Such achievements highlight the potential of global citizenship to drive progress and innovation.

Overcoming Critiques of Global Citizenship

While the concept of global citizenship is widely celebrated, it is not without critiques. Some argue that it is an idealistic notion, disconnected from the realities of geopolitical power dynamics and economic inequalities. Others contend that global citizenship risks undermining local identities and loyalties, leading to cultural homogenization.

However, these critiques can be addressed through a nuanced approach to global citizenship. Instead of replacing local identities, global citizenship complements them by encouraging individuals to recognize their interconnectedness while preserving cultural diversity. Kwame Anthony Appiah's concept of "rooted cosmopolitanism" emphasizes this balance, advocating for a form of global citizenship that values both local and global affiliations.

Additionally, efforts to make global citizenship more inclusive can address concerns about its elitism. Initiatives that prioritize access to education, digital connectivity, and economic opportunities ensure that global citizenship is not limited to privileged groups but accessible to all.

By addressing these critiques, global citizenship can continue to serve as a powerful framework for fostering solidarity and collective action in today's interconnected society.

Global citizenship matters in today's interconnected society because it provides a framework for addressing global challenges, fostering cross-cultural understanding, and promoting social responsibility. As humanity faces complex issues like climate change, inequality, and technological advancement, the principles of global citizenship offer a path toward sustainable and equitable solutions. While critiques of global citizenship highlight important challenges, they underscore the need for a balanced and inclusive approach that values both local and global perspectives. Ultimately, embracing global citizenship is not just an ethical choice but a necessity for building a better future for all.

Chapter 2
Identity and Belonging in a Borderless World

The belief that migration and cultural blending are common only in our Era are false. It is part of political propaganda meant to create social divisions to distract the majority of the population from the oppression they are subject of to benefit the oligarchy. On my previous book: *We Are All In This Together- Holistic Ethno-psychology Approach* we have presented an extensive description on the history of immigration from pre-historical times to today's day. The middle ages presented a very dynamic interchange of goods, science, art and technology between the different Asian, African and Arabian countries, with great success on respecting and preserving their own identities, in a harmonious co-existence of different religions, values, cultures and political regimes. The world's current power and economic dynamics are, however, more complex due to an enhanced sense of competitiveness, power thirst and more destructive weapons, creating different challenges.

This chapter delves into the dynamics of cultural and national identity within the framework of global citizenship. How can we maintain a sense of cultural heritage while embracing a broader, global identity? This chapter provides perspectives on balancing these identities, finding common ground, and understanding the power of shared values. The very lessons we once mastered quite effectively as humanity during medieval times, but have forgotten over the years.

<u>Balancing Local and Global Identities</u>

In an increasingly interconnected world, the challenge of balancing local and global identities has become a central theme in discussions about culture, politics, and individual identity. Globalization has brought people from diverse cultural and national backgrounds closer together through trade, communication, and travel. While this connectivity creates opportunities for understanding and collaboration, some seem to struggle with conflicts over preserving local traditions, values, and ways of life. Balancing these dual identities—maintaining a connection to one's local roots while embracing a global perspective—requires navigating complex cultural, social, and personal dynamics. In reality, those cultural, knowledge and values blending have proven to be enriching to all, strengthening everyone. It is, in other words an asset instead of a problem.

The Rise of Globalization and Its Impact

Globalization, a process driven by technological advancements and economic integration, has significantly reshaped cultural landscapes. It has fostered the spread of ideas, products, and practices across borders, creating a shared global culture. A trade that before would take months, with merchants traveling on horses or camels, now happens in seconds, and in much larger proportions. This phenomenon can be seen in the worldwide popularity of brands like Nike and McDonald's, the influence of Hollywood movies, and the global reach of social media platforms.

While globalization brings economic benefits and exposes people to new perspectives, it can also give the illusion of overshadowing local traditions and identities. It is important to distinguish between regular blending of cultures, arts and values through immigration and the effect that massification has on creating cultural homogenization, where local cultures are absorbed or overshadowed by dominant global influences. The first enriches and the later threatens the diversity that enriches human societies. For instance, traditional crafts and cuisines in many regions are being replaced by mass-produced goods and fast food chains. This shift raises questions about the survival of unique cultural heritages in a world increasingly dominated by global norms.

The Importance of Local Identity

Local identity, rooted in shared history, language, and traditions, provides individuals and communities with a sense of belonging. It serves as a foundation for cultural pride and social cohesion. For many, local identity is deeply tied to specific practices, such as religious ceremonies, folk music, and regional dialects, which connect them to their ancestors and surroundings.

Preserving local identity is not merely about maintaining traditions but also about fostering resilience and adaptability. Communities that prioritize their local identity can resist the negative effects of cultural homogenization by celebrating their unique heritage. For example, the Basque region in Spain has actively promoted its language, Euskara, and traditional sports like pelota to maintain its cultural distinctiveness in a globalized Europe.

Moreover, local identity can provide a counterbalance to the alienation that often accompanies globalization. As people move across borders or interact with others from diverse backgrounds, retaining a connection to their roots can help them navigate the complexities of multicultural settings. This connection acts as a cultural anchor, ensuring that individuals do not lose their sense of self amid rapid change.

However, it is equally important to point out that embracing a wiser horizon when comes to cultural identity is a sign of emotional and spiritual maturity. As more individuals and communities become more compassionate toward other cultures, values and beliefs, they all feel more included into this larger global community. In my clinical experience working with immigrants and refugees from different parts of the world, I see clearly their needs to cling to their local cultural values as a response to the rejection they feel in the local cultures where they migrated to. In its essence, human do not need to have local identities but to feel they belong. Through the spread of this more evolved and mature sense of global identity, humans of all races, creeds, religions, cultures and ethnical backgrounds will naturally feel welcomed, having their basic need of belonging satisfied everywhere in the world. Trust is a give and take process. If you give a welcoming hand, others will, with time, feel they can also trust to others, without the need to cling to the crumbs of local cultures.

Embracing a Global Identity

As mentioned at the last section, developing a global identity is crucial for individuals and societies in as we evolve as a species. A global identity is characterized by an openness to diverse cultures, a sense of shared responsibility for global challenges, and an awareness of the interconnectedness of human societies.

This mindset is particularly important in addressing pressing global issues such as climate change, pandemics, and economic inequality. These problems transcend national boundaries and require collaborative solutions that depend on mutual understanding and cooperation. For example, international organizations like the United Nations rely on the participation of individuals and states that view themselves as part of a global community.

Embracing a global identity also fosters empathy, cross-cultural understanding and ultimately less violence and less wars. Exposure to different perspectives through travel, education, and digital communication allows individuals to appreciate the richness of diverse cultures. This appreciation can lead to more inclusive societies where differences are celebrated rather than feared.

Navigating the Tension

Balancing local and global identities involves navigating the tensions between preserving tradition and embracing change; between the past and the future. This process often requires a nuanced approach that neither clings rigidly to the past nor uncritically adopts global trends. Instead, individuals and communities must selectively integrate global influences into their local contexts without losing the wisdom and knowledge acquired by their ancestors, the essence of their cultural heritage.

For example, many communities have adapted global technologies to serve local needs. Indigenous groups in South America have used social media platforms to raise awareness about environmental issues affecting their lands, combining traditional knowledge with modern tools. Similarly, chefs around the world have fused local ingredients with global culinary techniques, creating innovative dishes that honor their roots while appealing to international audiences.

Education also plays a vital role in striking this balance. Schools and universities can encourage students to be knowledgeable about their own as well as other local cultures while equipping them with the skills needed to thrive in a globalized world. Programs that teach both local languages and international "linguas francas" (trade languages), such as English, enable students to communicate effectively across cultures while learning and appreciating different local heritages.

The Role of Governments and Institutions

Governments and cultural institutions have a significant role in supporting the balance between local and global identities. Policies that promote cultural preservation, such as funding for traditional arts and heritage sites, can counteract the homogenizing effects of globalization. At the same time, governments can encourage international collaboration and exchange through cultural diplomacy and educational programs.

For instance, UNESCO's efforts to designate World Heritage Sites highlight the importance of protecting cultural and natural treasures while fostering global awareness. These initiatives remind us that preserving local identities contributes to the richness of the global community.

Balancing local and global identities is a dynamic and ongoing process. As globalization continues to shape the world, individuals and communities must find ways to honor the wisdom contained not only on their own local traditions, but also in others, while engaging with the broader global context. This balance requires a commitment to preserving cultural diversity, fostering empathy and understanding, and adapting to change without feeling threatened but other points of view and ways of living. All this becomes significantly easier as our morality and collective codes of conduct as humanity becomes more mature, more compassionate, empathetic, respectful and welcoming toward the beautiful diversity that granted us the great adaptability in every part of the globe. A mind set of becoming more cooperative and less competitive, as a consequence of a deeper and much wider understanding of the reality of belonging to this complex universe. This mindset is not a hippie, cute or utopic delusion. It is the law of nature, in which we all belong, rather if we are aware or not.

By embracing both the wisdom of our ancestors and global identities, humanity can create a world where traditions are respected, diversity is celebrated, and shared challenges are met with collective strength. This harmonious coexistence of the local and the global holds the key to building a more inclusive, resilient, and sustainable future to all of us, without exception.

<u>Embracing Cultural Diversity</u>

In an era of rapid globalization, embracing cultural diversity has emerged as a cornerstone for fostering peace, mutual understanding, and progress. Cultural diversity refers to the presence of multiple cultural groups within a society, each with unique traditions, languages, beliefs, and customs. It enriches human life by offering a tapestry of perspectives, skills, and ideas that enhance creativity and problem-solving. The challenges that this triggers, such as managing prejudice and ensuring equity in diverse settings diminishes as we evolve into more understanding and respectful attitude toward each other's identities and cultures. By appreciating cultural differences, promoting inclusion, and addressing the barriers that hinder integration, individuals and societies can harness the transformative power of diversity.

The Value of Cultural Diversity

Cultural diversity is a source of strength for individuals and communities. It promotes creativity and innovation by introducing different ways of thinking and solving problems. In workplaces, for instance, diverse teams are more likely to generate innovative ideas because they bring a variety of perspectives to the table. A multinational company like Google thrives by fostering an inclusive environment where employees from diverse backgrounds collaborate and contribute their unique experiences to product development and decision-making.

Moreover, cultural diversity enriches personal and collective growth by broadening individuals' horizons, which creates a ripple effect on their communities. Exposure to different cultures fosters empathy, tolerance, and a deeper understanding of the world. People who travel to or live in multicultural environments often gain new insights about themselves and others, challenging stereotypes and reducing biases. These experiences not only promote personal development but also strengthen social cohesion by fostering respect for differences, while decreasing childish egotistic perspectives of the world and of self.

The Challenges of Embracing Cultural Diversity

While cultural diversity offers numerous benefits, it also presents challenges that must be addressed to fully embrace it. One significant obstacle is prejudice and discrimination, which often stem from fear or misunderstanding of differences as well as competitiveness, power and control. Stereotypes and biases can lead to social divisions, marginalization, and unequal opportunities for minority groups. For instance, immigrants in some countries may face barriers to employment or education due to cultural or linguistic differences, hindering their integration into society. Paradoxically, immigrants and refugees are proven to bring enrichment to the local societies, an above the average work ethic and innovative solutions to the existing problems.

Language barriers and cultural misunderstandings can also create difficulties in communication and collaboration. In multicultural workplaces or classrooms, individuals may struggle to navigate differences in communication styles, norms, or values. These challenges can lead to conflicts or feelings of exclusion if not managed effectively.

Much of the harshest prejudice, biases, rejection and even violence against minorities are social constructs, artificially created by political propagandas, intended to divide the workforce, deviating the overall population's attention from the exploitation they all, locals, minorities and immigrants equally suffer. Again, the development of critical thinks, through education, emotional and moral development are critical tools to prevent being sucked into those dangerous misleading ideas of marginalization, prejudice and hate against others.

Strategies for Embracing Cultural Diversity

To embrace cultural diversity, individuals and societies must actively promote inclusion, equity, and mutual respect. Education plays a pivotal role in this process. By teaching students about the histories and contributions of diverse cultures, schools can foster an appreciation for cultural differences and reduce prejudice. Programs that encourage intercultural exchange, such as study abroad opportunities or multicultural festivals, provide hands-on experiences that deepen understanding and build bridges between communities.

Workplaces and organizations can also take steps to create inclusive environments. Diversity training programs, mentorship initiatives, and policies that ensure fair hiring practices can help break down barriers and foster a sense of belonging for all employees. Celebrating cultural holidays and encouraging dialogue about diversity further strengthens relationships among colleagues.

On a societal level, governments and institutions can support cultural diversity through inclusive policies and initiatives. Laws that protect against discrimination, funding for cultural preservation, and efforts to promote multilingualism demonstrate a commitment to diversity. For example, Canada's policy of multiculturalism recognizes the value of cultural diversity and actively encourages the integration of immigrant communities while respecting their cultural heritage.

The Role of Individuals

While systemic efforts are crucial, individuals also play a significant role in embracing cultural diversity. Open-mindedness and curiosity are key to building relationships across cultural divides. Engaging in meaningful conversations, learning about others' traditions, and questioning one's own biases are essential steps in fostering mutual respect.

Additionally, individuals can serve as advocates for inclusion by challenging discriminatory behaviors or practices. Simple actions, such as supporting businesses owned by underrepresented groups or participating in cultural exchange programs, contribute to creating a more inclusive society. By actively promoting diversity in their personal and professional lives, individuals help build environments where everyone feels valued and respected.

The Global Significance of Cultural Diversity

Embracing cultural diversity is not only beneficial at the individual and community levels but also essential for addressing global challenges. Many of the world's pressing issues, such as climate change, conflict resolution, and public health crises, require collaborative efforts that draw on diverse perspectives and expertise. A global mindset that values cultural diversity can lead to more effective, peaceful and inclusive solutions.

For example, international organizations like the United Nations rely on the input of diverse member states to develop policies and initiatives that reflect the needs and interests of a wide range of populations. By incorporating different cultural perspectives, these organizations ensure that their work is more equitable and impactful.

Furthermore, cultural diversity contributes to the preservation of humanity's shared heritage. Every culture offers unique knowledge, traditions, and artistic expressions that enrich the global community. Efforts to protect endangered languages, traditional crafts, and indigenous knowledge systems help ensure that future generations can benefit from this wealth of cultural diversity.

Embracing cultural diversity is both a moral imperative and a practical necessity in today's interconnected world. By valuing the unique contributions of different cultures, promoting inclusion, and addressing the barriers that hinder integration, individuals and societies can unlock the full potential of diversity. While challenges such as prejudice and cultural misunderstandings persist, they can be overcome through education, systemic support, and individual action.

Cultural diversity is a source of enrichment, strength, and resilience that benefits everyone. In a world facing shared challenges and opportunities, fostering a culture of respect and understanding for differences is essential for building more inclusive, harmonious, and prosperous communities. As humanity continues to evolve, embracing cultural diversity will remain a vital part of shaping a more equitable and interconnected future.

<u>The Role of Shared Values in Bridging Identities</u>

In a world characterized by diversity in culture, religion, politics, and personal identities, finding common ground is essential for fostering understanding and cooperation. Shared values act as powerful tools for bridging these diverse identities, offering a foundation for mutual respect and collaboration. Values such as empathy, justice, freedom, and respect for human dignity transcend cultural and individual differences, creating a sense of unity while preserving diversity. Exploring the role of shared values in bridging identities involves understanding their significance, the challenges to their adoption, and the strategies for promoting them in various contexts.

The Importance of Shared Values

Shared values serve as a connective tissue that binds individuals and groups, enabling them to navigate differences constructively. They provide a moral framework that facilitates trust and cooperation in diverse communities. For instance, the value of equality resonates universally, fostering the idea that all individuals, regardless of their background, deserve equal rights and opportunities. This shared commitment has driven global movements for civil rights, gender equality, and the eradication of discrimination.

Moreover, shared values create a sense of belonging and collective identity. In multicultural societies, values like tolerance and respect for diversity allow individuals from different backgrounds to coexist peacefully. For example, countries like Canada and the Netherlands emphasize multiculturalism and inclusion as core values, promoting a harmonious integration of various cultural identities. These values help bridge the gap between majority and minority groups, ensuring that no one feels alienated or marginalized. As a consequence, the whole community, including both locals and foreigners, enjoy a life with lower crime rates, more creative solutions for collective problems, higher productivity, significant economic growth, a much healthier quality of life, lower mortality rates and an enriched life experience to all.

Entangled   Sandra Ferreira

Bridging Personal and Group Identities

At the individual level, shared values help people navigate the complexities of their personal and group identities. Many individuals identify with multiple communities—cultural, religious, professional, or national—which can sometimes lead to conflicting loyalties or values. Shared principles act as a unifying thread, enabling individuals to reconcile these tensions. For instance, Up to 10 years ago, someone who identified as both a devout religious adherent and a supporter of secular governance could find common ground in values like freedom of belief and mutual respect. Nowadays distortions of those values misled millions of Americans to support candidates and conservative political agendas that denies freedom for the majority of the population, instigate hatred, bigotry, segregation, racism, and violence, just by disguising themselves as religious and utilizing words, such as "freedom" and "patriotism" to gain support from the masses on their individualistic and self-indulging policies. Christian Nationalists nowadays preach and work hard to forcefully implement values, political and social agendas that are radically the opposite of the core of their own religion. Those Nationalist Cristian leaders, intermingled with several countries governments, defend and fight for anti-democratic, socially oppressive and oligarchic social structures, completely denying Jesus teachings of feeding the poor, protecting women, children, detachment from earthly wealth and embracing a life of love and compassion to all, without exception.

Such distortions, although having roots centuries ago, became suddenly prominent in the political scene of the world nowadays, causing confusion, conflicts, political and social chaos in both individuals and communities.

Shared positive values foster solidarity among groups with distinct identities. In global crises such as pandemics or climate change, the shared value of protecting human life transcends national or cultural boundaries. Collaborative efforts to combat these challenges demonstrate how universal principles can unite diverse populations in pursuit of a common goal.

This not a mere pejorative "woke" idea. It reflects an emotionally and spiritually mature way of living, based on the same laws that govern the universe. The same laws we can experience in everyday life. For example, the physics law of action and reaction: what we give is what we get. If we give solidarity, love and compassion to others around us, we will receive the same in return. But if we give hatred, violence, discrimination, racism and oppression, we are planting an unstable, unhealthy, unsafe and self-destructive society, where EVERYONE suffers, one way or another. The oppressors may have a temporary illusion they are winner, but the law of cause and effect inevitably come back to get them, sooner or later. I see this in a daily basis in my psychology clinics. Sociopaths, violent and selfish individuals cause a lot of damages to those around them and initially have their needs of power and control satisfied. But in their intimacy, they suffer excruciating emotional pain, which sometimes lead them to deep depression and suicide attempts. Hitler killed himself in the end. Their cure does not come from more money, power or social recognition. These just bring them a volatile immediate gratification band-aid. After awhile, they fall back into their own internal nightmare, which they have no idea where it comes from or have the power to fix. Their real healing comes when they finally understand that the nature and power of real love and compassion. Sometimes it takes them a lifetime, disability or terminal disease to get there. And some unfortunately never really concur their internal freedom and happiness.

Inclusive and healthy groups, communities and countries start with mature and evolved individuals. As mentioned, political and social leaders have a pivotal contribution on this outcome. However, history shows us that real changes start with individuals becoming more and more aware of their own personal and collective issues and joining together to change them. So, a fair and inclusive society starts with emotionally and spiritually mature individuals, who understands the importance of leading a life based on tolerance for the differences, love and compassion toward one another.

Challenges to Establishing Shared Values

While shared values hold immense potential for bridging identities, their adoption is not without challenges. One significant barrier is cultural relativism, the idea that certain moral values are culture-specific and cannot be universally applied. This perspective can create tensions when values such as gender equality or freedom of expression clash with cultural or religious traditions. For example, debates about women's rights in patriarchal societies often highlight the difficulty of reconciling universal values with deeply rooted local norms. The resistance to the new and letting go of the old, even when the old norms no longer serve those same individuals and communities. It takes time, effort, self-awareness and critical thinking.

Another challenge is the politicization of values, where principles like justice or equality are co-opted to serve particular agendas. This can lead to polarization, as groups with differing interpretations of these values struggle to find common ground. For instance, disagreements over the meaning of freedom—whether it pertains to individual liberties or collective responsibilities—have fueled ideological divides in many countries.

Additionally, historical injustices and power imbalances can undermine efforts to establish shared values. Marginalized communities may view calls for unity or common principles with skepticism, perceiving them as attempts to erase their unique identities or experiences. Addressing these concerns requires acknowledging historical contexts and ensuring that shared values do not become tools for assimilation or domination.

This is especially evident in our work at our nonprofit organization, which provides mental health and social services to homeless communities. The reality they experience is very different from that of those who have never lived on the streets or experienced serious financial hardship. Contrary to popular belief, the homeless are a very diverse community, made up of individuals from many different backgrounds. Some come from two or three generations of homeless families. Others have earned degrees, held prestigious jobs and social status, but lost everything due to some serious psychiatric crisis, drug or alcohol addiction. Those who grew up on the streets do not trust or trust health care providers, law enforcement, or institutions of any kind. A helping hand is met with skepticism and great reluctance. This distrust often stems from real-life experiences of discrimination and abuse they have suffered from these institutions. Both women and men report being raped, beaten, and incarcerated without cause due to abuse of power. Experiencing a life of violence, lack of civil rights and brutality, both from each other and the system, it is quite understandable that they have a total lack of trust in society and any call for community unity. The world for them has indeed been an unsafe, violent, unjust and threatening place, with nothing good to offer.

Practical Steps to Integrate Quantum Thinking into Daily Life

Quantum thinking refers to a way of processing information that is based on the principles of quantum mechanics, the fundamental theory in physics that explains how subatomic particles behave. Unlike classical mechanics, which deals with deterministic and predictable systems, quantum mechanics is inherently probabilistic, interconnected, and non-local. These characteristics—such as superposition, entanglement, and uncertainty— offer a new lens through which to view the world. While quantum mechanics may seem like an abstract or highly technical field, its principles can offer profound insights into how we approach problem-solving, decision-making, and interpersonal relationships in daily life.

Integrating quantum thinking into our daily routines is not about mastering complex physics but about adopting a mindset that embraces uncertainty, interconnectedness, and creative possibilities.

Following is some practical steps for integrating quantum thinking into everyday life, with a focus on fostering adaptability, increasing awareness, and encouraging innovative problem-solving approaches.

I. Embracing Uncertainty: The Power of Flexibility

One of the core tenets of quantum mechanics is the idea of uncertainty. The Heisenberg Uncertainty Principle suggests that we cannot simultaneously know both the position and momentum of a particle with complete precision. In everyday life, this principle can be applied to how we approach decisions and navigate the unknown.

1.   Cultivate an Open-Minded Approach to Uncertainty

Rather than seeking absolute certainty in all situations, embracing uncertainty can lead to more flexible, adaptive thinking. This might involve:

- **Letting go of rigid expectations:** In the same way that quantum particles can exist in multiple states at once (superposition), we can allow ourselves to hold multiple possibilities for the future without needing to lock into a single outcome.

- **Reframing fear of the unknown:** Many decisions in life come with ambiguity. By recognizing that uncertainty is not inherently negative, but a space for creativity, we can become more comfortable in ambiguous situations, such as job changes, relationships, or new projects, as well as dealing with diversity and changes from other people's perspectives.

2. Practice Mindfulness and Presence

Quantum thinking encourages an awareness of the present moment, where the future is not predetermined. By practicing mindfulness—whether through meditation, conscious breathing, or simply paying attention to your surroundings—we can train our minds to focus on the "now," which can help reduce anxiety about future outcomes. Being present allows for more fluid thinking and decision-making, much like the wave-particle duality in quantum physics, where particles are observed as both waves and particles depending on the situation.

II. Interconnectedness: Seeing the Bigger Picture

Quantum mechanics reveals that everything in the universe is interconnected through a phenomenon called entanglement. Entangled particles remain connected, regardless of the distance between them, meaning that a change in one particle can instantly affect the other. This can serve as a way for understanding how our actions and choices have far-reaching consequences, even in ways we may not immediately understand. Quantum physicist David Bohm explains the concept of entanglement as a metaphoric way to describe the universe that is, in fact, an indivisible whole, rather than the sum of individual parts.

1.   Recognize the Interconnectedness of People and Events

Incorporating quantum thinking into daily life requires an acknowledgment that our actions affect others, which has a ripple effect back to us. This can be applied in various ways:
- **Mindful Communication:** Just as particles in quantum entanglement influence each other, our words and actions influence those around us. By practicing active listening, empathy, and constructive feedback, we can foster better relationships.
- **Long-Term Perspective:** Understanding the ripple effect of decisions can help us make choices that align with our values and long-term goals. Whether in business, personal finances, or relationships, acknowledging the interconnectedness of all things encourages more thoughtful and respectful decision-making.

2. Collaborative Problem-Solving

Quantum thinking highlights the idea that systems are rarely isolated. Solutions to problems are often found through collaboration and collective intelligence. We can apply this to our daily interactions by:
- **Seeking Diverse Perspectives:** Whether at work or in personal matters, asking for input from people with different backgrounds, expertise, and viewpoints can reveal solutions that we may not have considered on our own.
- **Engaging in Group Problem-Solving:** Quantum systems are often best understood through collaboration—similar to how collective brainstorming or

teamwork can yield better results than solo efforts. Being opened to working with others and pooling resources can lead to more innovative solutions.

III. Superposition: Navigating Multiple Possibilities

In quantum mechanics, superposition refers to the ability of a quantum system to exist in multiple states simultaneously, only collapsing into one state when observed. This concept can be applied to our daily decision-making processes, where we are often faced with multiple options, each with different outcomes.

1.   Keep Multiple Options Open

Rather than committing to a single course of action, quantum thinking encourages keeping multiple possibilities in mind. For instance:
- **Explore Diverse Pathways:** When faced with a decision, such as choosing a career path or making an investment, consider the potential benefits of keeping multiple options open rather than locking into a single choice. Allow yourself the freedom to explore different possibilities.
- **Avoid Overcommitting:** Superposition teaches us that it's okay to hold space for uncertainty and multiple outcomes. We don't need to decide everything immediately or be certain about every choice, as the future is not predetermined.

2. Embrace Creativity and Innovation

Superposition can also be a powerful tool for creativity. Just as particles can exist in multiple states, we can adopt a mindset that embraces creative thinking by exploring different angles for a solution to a problem. Rather than thinking in binary terms—right or wrong, yes or no—consider multiple perspectives and approaches.
- **Brainstorming with "What If" Scenarios:** When tackling a challenge, ask yourself "what if" questions. What if this situation could play out in several ways? This can help us think outside the box and identify solutions that may not be immediately obvious.

IV. Quantum Mindset in Decision-Making: Embracing Probability

Quantum thinking emphasizes the role of probability in understanding outcomes. In classical physics, outcomes are typically seen as deterministic, whereas in quantum mechanics, the future is probabilistic. This shift can help us better understand the role of chance and likelihood in our decisions.

1.   Reframe Risk as Probability

In many aspects of life, we face situations that involve risk—be it financial investments, career decisions, or personal endeavors. By embracing quantum thinking, we can reframe risk as probability rather than certainty. For instance:

- **Risk as Opportunity:** Understand that life involves probabilities, and while the future is uncertain, we can make educated guesses based on available data. Rather than avoiding risk, look at it as a series of probabilities, and assess the potential outcomes to make informed decisions.
- **Accepting Failures as Part of the Process:** Just as quantum mechanics involves inherent uncertainty and unpredictability, we can approach failure as part of the learning process. A failed attempt is simply one possible outcome in a range of potential results, and it does not negate future successes.

2. Using Intuition as a Guide

Quantum thinking also acknowledges the importance of intuition. Intuition can be seen as a tool that helps us navigate the complex and uncertain terrain of our daily lives. By listening to our inner voice and integrating it with rational analysis, we can make decisions that align with both our logical and intuitive senses.

V. Harnessing Quantum Thinking for Personal Growth

The principles of quantum thinking not only influence our interactions with the world but also our personal development. By applying quantum ideas to our growth, we can expand our potential and cultivate a greater sense of self-awareness.

1.   Self-Reflection and Awareness

Quantum thinking encourages self-awareness and introspection, as it emphasizes the fluidity and interconnectedness of all aspects of life. Taking time to reflect on our behaviors, thoughts, and feelings allows us to better understand how we fit into the broader context of the world.
- **Journaling:** Regular self-reflection through journaling can help individuals track their thoughts and emotions, identifying patterns and areas for growth.
- **Mindful Awareness of Thought Patterns:** By becoming aware of our thoughts, we can better understand how they shape our reality and decide whether to embrace or challenge them.

2. Pursuing Personal Evolution

Quantum thinking suggests that personal growth is not a linear process but one that involves multiple potential pathways. Embrace the idea that you are always evolving and that new possibilities and opportunities are available for exploration.

Integrating quantum thinking into daily life is not about mastering complex scientific theories but about adopting a mindset that embraces uncertainty, interconnectedness, creativity, and flexibility. Whether through reframing our understanding of uncertainty, recognizing the interconnectedness of people and events, or embracing the fluidity of multiple possibilities, quantum thinking can provide valuable insights into how we approach decision-making, problem-solving, and personal growth. By weaving these principles into our everyday experiences, we can foster greater resilience, creativity, and innovation in our lives.

Exercises for Fostering Global Awareness and Empathy

In a world that is increasingly interconnected, fostering global awareness and empathy has never been more crucial. Global awareness involves understanding the issues, cultures, and perspectives of people from around the world, while empathy refers to the ability to understand and share the feelings of others. These two qualities are essential in navigating the challenges of a diverse and complex world. Cultivating them can lead to more harmonious relationships, greater social responsibility, and a more peaceful global community.

Here we will explore various exercises that can be used to develop global awareness and empathy. These activities can be applied in educational settings, workplaces, communities, and personal development practices. They range from experiential learning activities to reflective exercises that help individuals see the world through the eyes of others. The goal of these exercises is to create a more inclusive, understanding, and compassionate world by nurturing empathy and awareness on a global scale.

I. Engaging with Diverse Cultures

One of the most effective ways to foster global awareness and empathy is by immersing oneself in different cultures. This can be done through direct experiences or by engaging in activities that allow individuals to learn about the customs, values, and perspectives of others.

1.   Cultural Exchange Programs

Participating in cultural exchange programs, whether physical or virtual, is a powerful way to experience the customs, languages, and daily lives of people from different countries. These exchanges can take place through travel, work-study programs, or even online platforms. Direct interaction with people from different cultures fosters mutual understanding and helps to break down stereotypes.

- **Example Exercise:** Students or employees from different countries can engage in virtual exchange sessions where they share their cultural practices, challenges they face, and their views on global issues. Participants can also swap daily life routines, meals, and language lessons to further connect on a personal level.

2. Hosting or Attending Cultural Events

Local cultural festivals, international food fairs, and language meet-ups provide an excellent opportunity to experience global cultures without leaving home. By attending these events, individuals can learn about the art, food, music, and history of different cultures, which cultivates a deeper understanding and appreciation of global diversity.

• **Example Exercise:** Organize a global awareness day where participants learn about and celebrate a different country or culture through food, music, fashion, and storytelling. The event can include guest speakers from the represented culture to provide firsthand insights.

II. Reading and Storytelling from Different Perspectives

Reading books, watching films, and consuming other media from various parts of the world is an excellent way to foster empathy and global awareness. This allows individuals to see the world through different lenses, understand the struggles faced by others, and appreciate the diversity of human experiences.

1. Reading Global Literature

Literature offers a window into the emotional lives and experiences of people from different cultures. Novels, short stories, and poetry written by authors from various countries can help readers understand the complexities of global issues, such as poverty, migration, gender equality, and environmental concerns. This exercise can open the mind to different perspectives, giving voice to those who are often marginalized.

• **Example Exercise:** Organize a book club focused on global literature. Each month, participants can read a book written by an author from a different country or region. Afterward, they can discuss the themes of the book, how it relates to global issues, and what personal insights they gained from the experience.

2. Sharing Personal Stories

Storytelling is an ancient practice that allows people to connect on an emotional level. When people share personal stories of hardship, resilience, or hope, it fosters a deeper understanding of others' experiences and builds empathy. Whether through writing, art, or spoken word, storytelling helps bridge the gap between cultures and histories.

• **Example Exercise:** Create a platform or safe space for individuals to share their personal experiences related to global issues. This could take the form of an open-mic night, a storytelling workshop, or an online forum where people from different backgrounds share their stories of overcoming challenges and fostering change in their communities.

III. Volunteering and Service Learning

Volunteering in communities that face different challenges—whether locally or internationally—provides hands-on experience in understanding the needs and struggles of others. Service-learning programs, in which individuals engage in volunteer work while reflecting on the cultural and social implications of their work, are a particularly effective tool for building empathy and global awareness.

1.   Volunteering Abroad or at Local Organizations

Traveling abroad to volunteer offers direct exposure to global issues, such as poverty, healthcare, and education. Similarly, volunteering with local immigrant communities or refugees helps individuals develop an understanding of the challenges faced by newcomers, including language barriers, cultural adjustment, and discrimination.
- **Example Exercise:** Volunteer with a local organization that supports refugees or immigrants. Through this experience, volunteers can learn about the cultural, social, and economic factors that influence the lives of refugees, while offering support through language tutoring, community building, or advocacy efforts.

2. Participating in Global Service Projects

Organizations such as Habitat for Humanity, the Peace Corps, and Global Vision International offer opportunities for individuals to participate in service projects worldwide. These projects are an opportunity to contribute to local communities while learning about the broader socio-political and economic issues that shape those communities.
- **Example Exercise:** Plan a group service project that focuses on addressing a global issue, such as climate change, hunger, or education. Participants can work together to raise awareness, fundraise, and physically contribute to the cause. This exercise fosters a sense of global responsibility and the desire to make a difference in the world.

IV. Engaging in Discussions and Debates on Global Issues

Open discussions and debates about global issues, such as climate change, inequality, or human rights, can deepen understanding and encourage individuals to see the world from multiple perspectives. By engaging in thoughtful, respectful conversations, participants can challenge assumptions, broaden their views, and cultivate empathy for others who may be directly affected by these issues.

1.   Global Issue Debates

Participating in debates on global topics encourages critical thinking and the exploration of different viewpoints. Whether discussing international politics, environmental policies, or humanitarian efforts, debates allow individuals to articulate their beliefs while considering the experiences and needs of others.
- **Example Exercise:** Host a debate or discussion on a pressing global issue. Assign participants different roles—representing different countries, perspectives, or stakeholders—to help them understand the complexity of the issue. This exercise will

encourage participants to think beyond their personal beliefs and develop a more comprehensive understanding of global challenges.

2. Global Awareness Workshops

Workshops focused on specific global issues can serve as educational platforms for raising awareness. These workshops can cover topics such as human trafficking, environmental sustainability, or social justice. Facilitators can invite experts to share their knowledge, followed by group discussions and interactive activities that allow participants to explore these issues on a deeper level.

- **Example Exercise:** Organize a series of workshops that focus on different global issues. After each session, participants can reflect on how these issues are interconnected and what actions they can take to contribute to a solution, either locally or globally.

V. Practicing Reflection and Mindfulness

Empathy and global awareness are not only cultivated through active engagement but also through quiet reflection. By practicing mindfulness and reflecting on one's own biases, assumptions, and privileges, individuals can develop a deeper understanding of their place in the world and how they relate to others.

1. Journaling on Global Issues

Journaling offers a private space for reflection on global issues and personal growth. Individuals can use journaling to explore their thoughts on cultural differences, international conflicts, or their personal role in addressing global challenges. This exercise helps individuals connect their internal thoughts and beliefs with the broader global context.

- **Example Exercise:** Encourage individuals to keep a global awareness journal where they reflect on their experiences with diversity, current events, and interactions with people from different cultures. Writing about these experiences helps individuals gain clarity on their attitudes and how they might need to change in order to become more empathetic.

2. Practicing Empathy Meditation

Empathy meditation is a practice that helps individuals develop compassion for others by imagining themselves in another person's shoes. This practice involves sitting in a quiet space, focusing on the breath, and visualizing someone from a different background or culture. By contemplating their struggles and experiences, individuals can deepen their empathy.

- **Example Exercise:** Lead a guided empathy meditation in which participants are asked to envision the life of a person living in a different country, experiencing a different set of challenges. This practice cultivates a sense of connectedness and emotional resonance with people from diverse backgrounds.

Fostering global awareness and empathy is an ongoing journey that involves active participation, reflection, and engagement with people and cultures beyond our own. By engaging in exercises such as cultural exchanges, volunteering, reading diverse literature, and participating in global discussions, we can begin to break down the barriers that divide us and build a more compassionate, understanding world. These exercises not only help us understand the global community but also cultivate the empathy necessary to navigate our interconnected world with kindness and respect. Through these practices, we can develop a deeper appreciation for the richness of the human experience and contribute to a more inclusive, peaceful global society.

Strategies for Staying Engaged in Global Issues While Cultivating Personal Wellbeing and Mental Health

The modern world is filled with interconnected global challenges—climate change, poverty, inequality, political instability, and human rights violations. With the rise of social media and constant access to news, it has become increasingly difficult to avoid exposure to these issues. While remaining engaged with global concerns is essential for fostering positive change, it can also take a toll on personal wellbeing and mental health. The emotional burden of constantly absorbing information about crises, suffering, and injustice can lead to feelings of helplessness, burnout, and anxiety.

Finding a balance between staying informed about global issues and preserving mental and emotional health is critical. It is possible to contribute to meaningful causes and maintain a sense of purpose without compromising personal wellbeing. This essay will explore various strategies that individuals can use to stay engaged with global issues while cultivating mental resilience and emotional health. These strategies will focus on emotional regulation, establishing boundaries, seeking support, engaging in positive action, and practicing mindfulness.

I. Emotional Regulation: Managing Emotional Responses to Global Events

One of the greatest challenges when engaging with global issues is managing the emotional responses they can provoke. Constant exposure to negative news can lead to emotional overwhelm, frustration, sadness, or anger. Developing emotional regulation skills is crucial in maintaining a healthy balance between being informed and caring for one's mental health.

1.   Acknowledging Emotions Without Becoming Overwhelmed

It is natural to feel emotions such as sadness or anger when learning about global injustices or crises. However, acknowledging these emotions without allowing them to consume us is important for maintaining mental health. Emotional regulation involves recognizing feelings, allowing oneself to process them, and then finding ways to cope constructively.

- **Strategy:** Whenever you feel overwhelmed, practice naming the emotion you're experiencing (e.g., "I feel sad about the situation in X country") and take a step back to reflect on the bigger picture. Recognize that your feelings are valid, but they do not define your entire reality.

2. Developing Healthy Coping Mechanisms

In moments of emotional distress, it is important to have healthy coping strategies that help calm the mind. This could include physical activities such as exercise, creative outlets like painting or writing, or practicing relaxation techniques like deep breathing and progressive muscle relaxation. Coping mechanisms can help process difficult emotions without suppressing them or allowing them to escalate.

- **Strategy:** Develop a personal toolkit for emotional regulation. When overwhelmed by global news, take a break and engage in activities that ground you, such as taking a walk, journaling, or spending time in nature. These practices help reset your emotional state.

II. Establishing Boundaries: Managing Media Consumption

Constant exposure to global news can lead to information fatigue and a sense of helplessness. Setting clear boundaries around media consumption is one of the most effective strategies for staying engaged without compromising mental health.

1.   Limiting News Intake

While it is important to stay informed, overconsumption of distressing news can contribute to anxiety and burnout. Establishing a healthy routine for consuming news, such as limiting time spent reading or watching global news, can help reduce the emotional impact.

- **Strategy:** Set specific times during the day for consuming news, and commit to not checking the news outside of those hours. Use tools such as news apps with "quiet hours" or set alarms to remind yourself when to stop consuming news for the day.

2. Curating Sources and Media

It is also essential to curate the sources of information to avoid sensationalist or overwhelming content. Consuming news from reliable, balanced sources can ensure that information is accurate and does not contribute to unnecessary fear or panic.

- **Strategy:** Subscribe to newsletters, websites, or social media channels that provide balanced and informative perspectives. Avoid constantly refreshing your social media feed or scrolling through news outlets that sensationalize or focus on the most traumatic aspects of global events.

III. Seeking Support: Connecting with Like-Minded Individuals

Caring about global issues can sometimes feel isolating, especially when it seems that others are not as engaged or aware. Building a supportive community with like-minded individuals can help combat feelings of loneliness and provide a space for mutual understanding and shared action.

1.   Joining Activist Groups and Communities

Finding groups or organizations dedicated to global causes can provide a sense of camaraderie and collective purpose. Being part of a community working towards positive change can reduce feelings of helplessness, as it shifts focus from individual problems to collective efforts.

- **Strategy:** Participate in local or online activist groups that align with your values and passions. Whether through environmental organizations, human rights initiatives, or social justice movements, working alongside others provides emotional support and shared motivation.

2. Talking to Friends or Professionals

Sharing your thoughts, emotions, and concerns with friends, family, or mental health professionals is an important way to alleviate the burden of global issues. Having open conversations allows for the expression of complex emotions and can offer new perspectives or coping strategies.

- **Strategy:** Schedule regular check-ins with friends or loved ones where you can discuss global issues in a safe, supportive space. Additionally, if news-related anxiety becomes overwhelming, consider speaking to a mental health professional who can help you develop strategies to manage distress.

IV. Engaging in Positive Action: Contributing to Change

Engaging in meaningful action toward solving global problems can help individuals feel more empowered, reduce feelings of helplessness, and create a sense of purpose. Taking proactive steps, whether through volunteering, advocacy, or charitable contributions, can give individuals a tangible way to address the global challenges they care about.

1.   Volunteering Locally or Globally

Volunteering offers a direct way to contribute to global or local causes. Whether helping in one's own community or participating in international volunteer efforts, this form of engagement fosters a sense of connection to a broader purpose while simultaneously benefiting others.

- **Strategy:** Commit to regular volunteer work that aligns with your values, whether it's working with a local nonprofit, organizing community events, or supporting causes related to global issues such as climate change or human rights.

2. Advocacy and Awareness Campaigns

Raising awareness about critical global issues, such as climate change, poverty, or gender inequality, is another way to make an impact. Advocacy can be done through social media, writing to lawmakers, participating in protests, or supporting petitions.

- **Strategy:** Dedicate a specific amount of time each week to advocacy work, whether it's sharing educational posts on social media, signing petitions, or participating in letter-writing campaigns. Small acts of advocacy contribute to larger systemic change.

V. Practicing Mindfulness and Self-Care: Nurturing Inner Peace

Practicing mindfulness and self-care is essential in maintaining mental and emotional health while staying engaged with global issues. Mindfulness allows individuals to stay grounded in the present moment, reducing anxiety and fostering emotional resilience. Self-care practices are also important for replenishing emotional energy and preventing burnout.

1.   Mindfulness Meditation

Mindfulness meditation is a powerful tool for cultivating awareness and emotional regulation. It involves focusing on the present moment, observing thoughts and feelings without judgment, and cultivating compassion for oneself and others. Regular mindfulness practice can help individuals detach from overwhelming emotions tied to global issues.

- **Strategy:** Set aside time each day for mindfulness meditation. Apps like Headspace, Calm, or Insight Timer offer guided sessions that focus on reducing stress and increasing emotional resilience. Even just a few minutes of mindful breathing can help reset emotional balance.

2. Physical Self-Care

Engaging in regular physical activities—such as exercise, yoga, or outdoor activities—supports mental and emotional health by releasing endorphins, reducing stress, and promoting overall well-being. Physical self-care nurtures the body and mind, helping individuals recharge so they can remain engaged in global issues without burning out.

- **Strategy:** Incorporate physical self-care practices into your routine, whether it's a morning yoga session, regular walks in nature, or hitting the gym. Ensure that physical activity is something you enjoy, as this will make it easier to maintain consistency.

Entangled   Sandra Ferreira

Staying engaged in global issues while cultivating personal wellbeing and mental health requires a delicate balance and accomplishing it successfully, requires emotional maturity, wisdom and a strong mind to scape division creating political propagandas. By practicing emotional regulation, self-awareness, psychological development, setting boundaries around media consumption, seeking support from others, engaging in positive action, and prioritizing mindfulness and self-care, individuals can contribute meaningfully to global change without sacrificing their emotional and mental health. These strategies help maintain a sense of empowerment and purpose while ensuring that personal resilience is nurtured in the process. In a world that can often feel overwhelming, it is possible to stay connected to global causes while also fostering inner peace and well-being. In my personal experience, along with millions of others all over the world who dedicates their lives to serving collective causes, there is nothing more rewarding then contributing to find equality, justice, and the well-being of others.

Strategies for Promoting Shared Values

Promoting shared values in diverse societies requires deliberate efforts at the individual, institutional, and societal levels. As we have mentioned, education plays a crucial role in this process. Schools and universities can teach students about universal human rights, ethical principles, and the importance of empathy and mutual respect. Programs that encourage intercultural exchange and dialogue also help individuals appreciate the commonalities that exist across differences.

Media and art are powerful tools for promoting shared values. Films, literature, and music that celebrate universal themes like love, resilience, and justice can inspire people to see beyond their differences. For example, Malala Yousafzai's advocacy for girls' education resonates globally because it taps into the shared value of equal opportunity. Similarly, international campaigns like the United Nations' *HeForShe* movement leverage storytelling and activism to unite people around gender equality.

Governments and organizations also have a critical role in fostering shared values. Policies that promote inclusivity, protect minority rights, and encourage civic engagement can create environments where diverse identities coexist harmoniously. For instance, truth and reconciliation commissions, such as those in South Africa, aim to address historical grievances and establish shared commitments to justice and healing.

Shared Values in a Globalized World

In today's world, shared values are essential for addressing global challenges and fostering international cooperation. Issues like climate change, terrorism, and economic inequality require collective action that transcends national and cultural boundaries. Shared principles, such as the commitment to sustainability or the protection of human rights, provide a basis for collaboration among nations and organizations.

The United Nations' Sustainable Development Goals (SDGs) exemplify the power of shared values in bridging global identities. Goals like eradicating poverty, ensuring gender equality, and promoting peace and justice reflect principles that resonate universally. By rallying governments, businesses, and civil society around these objectives, the SDGs demonstrate how shared values can drive collective progress.

The Interplay Between Diversity and Unity

One of the most remarkable aspects of shared values is their ability to foster unity while respecting diversity. They do not require individuals to abandon their unique identities or traditions; instead, they provide a common ground where differences are acknowledged and celebrated. For example, the value of freedom of expression allows people to voice their perspectives while respecting the rights of others to do the same. It's important here to highlight the definition of freedom of expression. By definition it implies respect for different points of view. However when those "expressions" infringe the rules of a civilized coexistence by instigating hatred, promoting violence or discriminating lies or fake news, it is no longer freedom of expression but transgression of the law and boundaries of any civilized society. Groups like KKK, Neo-Nazis, and many other extremist civil, religious or political organizations complain about having their manifestations contained or suppressed, but don't see that their very violent, intolerant, racist and cultist actions and attacks represent a threat to millions of human's lives, which are considered criminal, terroristic and barbarian. As humanity, we are far beyond barbarism. All the development of science, technology and the numerous lessons we learned throughout history, placed us far from those primitive ways of thinking, feeling and living. Humanity have achieved enough experience and growth to let go the besties we once have being back on pre-historical times. It's up to us to succumb back to the dark ages and be extinct by destroying each other and our planet, or to keep moving forward through rationally and maturity dealing with our differences, solving our problems with constructive cooperation, using critical thinking, knowledge, mutual respect and respect to our environment, to which we irrefutably belong and depend on.

This interplay between diversity and unity is particularly evident in democratic societies, where shared values like justice, equality, and individual rights underpin the political system. These principles allow for pluralism, enabling diverse groups to coexist and participate in decision-making processes. By emphasizing common values, democracies create spaces where different identities can thrive without compromising collective harmony. Every time a sector of the society tries to forcefully impose a set of values to be accepted by everyone, this balance is compromised and the whole structure is threatened. Denying access to learning, prohibition of books, imposition or prohibition of any religious practices, denial of people's human's rights (women, minorities, LGBTQs, etc) are threats to democracy and to a harmonious, healthy, sustainable and just society.

Shared values play a pivotal role in bridging identities in a world marked by diversity and complexity. They provide a foundation for trust, understanding, and collaboration, enabling individuals and groups to navigate differences constructively. While challenges such as cultural relativism, historical grievances, radicalisms and divisive political propaganda can hinder the adoption of shared values, education, unbiased media, and inclusive policies offer pathways for promoting them.

By embracing shared principles like empathy, justice, and respect for human dignity, societies can foster unity, progress and sustainability, while celebrating diversity. These values serve as a reminder that, despite our differences, we are united by our common humanity. As the world becomes increasingly interconnected, the role of shared values in bridging identities will remain essential for building inclusive, peaceful, and prosperous communities.

Chapter 3
The Responsibility of a Global Citizen

What responsibilities do global citizens hold? From environmental stewardship to advocating for human rights, this chapter explores the moral, ethical, and practical duties of a global citizen. It includes stories of ordinary individuals who have taken extraordinary steps toward change and offers practical guidance on how each of us can make a positive impact.

In this chapter we will reflect briefly on the issues related to climate change, its impact on people's lives and the dangers of its denial or neglect. It is one of the most obvious examples of how interconnected we are as humanity and as a planet. The more complex our world has become over the centuries, the more we lost sense of our interdependence of nature; that we are part of nature and without it, we and our whole planet cannot survive. It's about time for us as individuals and society to face this pressing problem with urgency, responsibility and maturity, without letting ourselves be fooled by political manipulations that has only one goal: to save money to the large corporations on following environmental regulations to save money at the cost our our planet existence. It is not only irresponsible, but inhumane and childish, as they too are humans and depend on the planet. Their naive and immediate view of life, thinking that they can still continue to irresponsibly take advantage of nature, as if they were exempt from the destructive consequences that this causes to humanity and ecosystems, is indescribably barbaric. So, let us take a brief look at some scientific data related to the environmental crisis we are facing and its impact on people's and communities' lives.

Environmental Responsibility and Climate Change Action: A Call to Collective Change

Environmental responsibility has become a crucial topic in the 21st century as humanity faces the intensifying consequences of climate change. The global rise in temperatures, more frequent extreme weather events, and loss of biodiversity underscore the urgency of taking action. Here we will explore the significance of environmental responsibility, the role of individuals and institutions in mitigating climate change, and actionable strategies for a sustainable future.

Climate change is no longer a distant threat; it is a present reality with wide-ranging consequences:

- **Global Temperature Rise**

Scientific consensus attributes global warming to the accumulation of greenhouse gases, such as carbon dioxide and methane, primarily from human activities like industrial processes and deforestation. Since the pre-industrial era, global temperatures have risen by approximately 1.1°C, with catastrophic projections if emissions remain unchecked.

- **Extreme Weather Events**

The intensification of hurricanes, prolonged droughts, and devastating wildfires exemplify climate change's impact. For instance, Hurricane Katrina and the Australian wildfires of 2019–2020 underscore the human and ecological toll of these events.

- **Biodiversity Loss**

The disruption of ecosystems due to rising temperatures and habitat destruction has led to unprecedented species extinction rates. Coral reef bleaching and deforestation of Europe, United States by the first generations of settlers and lately the Amazon rainforest serve as critical warnings of the biodiversity crisis.

- **Socioeconomic Effects**

Climate change disproportionately affects vulnerable populations, particularly in developing nations. Rising sea levels displace communities, while agriculture-dependent economies suffer from erratic weather patterns. These challenges exacerbate poverty and inequality, underscoring the intersection of climate justice and social equity. However, the raise of diseases and unexplainable deaths, affecting humans of all levels and ages as a consequence of our unhealthy way of living, from air pollutants, agro-toxics, to processed industrialized food and other factors, are understated.

2. The Concept of Environmental Responsibility

Environmental responsibility emphasizes the need for individuals and societies to act in ways that protect the planet.

- **Definition and Importance**

Environmental responsibility involves minimizing ecological footprints and adopting sustainable practices to mitigate climate change. It acknowledges the interconnectedness of human actions and environmental health.

- **Historical Perspective**

Milestones such as the Paris Agreement of 2015, which seeks to limit global warming to below 2°C, and the UN's Sustainable Development Goals (SDGs) highlight collective efforts to address environmental crises. These initiatives demonstrate the potential for international cooperation in driving meaningful change. Extreme right wing, environmental denier governments in the USA, Russia and others, represent a threat to the small progresses we have mad in the last decades to address those urgent issues.

- **Moral and Ethical Dimensions**

Humanity holds a moral duty to safeguard Earth's resources for future generations. Ethical stewardship emphasizes the intrinsic value of nature, advocating for its preservation beyond economic or utilitarian considerations.

3. The Role of Institutions in Climate Action

Institutions are pivotal in driving systemic change to combat climate change.
- **Governments**

Policy-making plays a crucial role in climate action. Initiatives such as carbon pricing, renewable energy subsidies, and international agreements foster accountability and incentivize sustainable development.
- **Corporations**

Businesses must prioritize sustainability by integrating eco-friendly practices into their operations. Corporate social responsibility (CSR) and innovation in green technologies can reduce emissions and influence global supply chains.
- **Non-Governmental Organizations (NGOs)**

NGOs are instrumental in raising awareness, advocating for policy reforms, and implementing grassroots projects. Organizations like Greenpeace and the World Wildlife Fund amplify public engagement and mobilize resources for local and global initiatives.

4. Individual Responsibility and Grassroots Movements

Individual actions and community-driven efforts are essential complements to institutional strategies.
- **Lifestyle Changes**

Simple shifts, such as conserving energy, reducing single-use plastics, and embracing plant-based diets, significantly reduce individual carbon footprints. Collective adoption of these habits can amplify their impact.
- **Community Initiatives**

Grassroots movements, like tree-planting drives and waste management projects, empower communities to take localized climate action. These efforts foster environmental awareness and collaboration.
- **Youth Advocacy**

Movements such as *Fridays for Future*, led by Greta Thunberg, demonstrate the power of youth activism. Younger generations are increasingly vocal about climate change, holding leaders accountable and inspiring global solidarity.

5. Strategies for Future Action

Addressing climate change requires multifaceted approaches that combine technological, political, and educational solutions.
- **Investment in Renewable Energy**

Scaling up renewable energy sources, such as solar and wind power, is critical to reducing reliance on fossil fuels. It is crucial to invest in developing better technologies on solar power, as the current ones are, in fact, not really eco-friendly. The solar panels production require charcoal mining and they are not biodegradable. Both factors create more destructive environmental consequences than the conventional electricity. Advances in energy storage and smart grid technologies further enhance their feasibility.

- **Technological Innovation**

Emerging technologies, such as carbon capture and storage (CCS) and regenerative agriculture techniques, offer promising recommendations.

Governments must enforce stricter emissions standards and promote international collaboration. Policies like reforestation programs and incentives for green businesses create pathways for large-scale transformation.

- **Education and Awareness**

Environmental literacy empowers individuals to make informed decisions. Integrating climate education into school curricula and public campaigns raises awareness and fosters a culture of sustainability.

Climate change is a defining challenge of our time, necessitating a collective response that bridges individual, institutional, and global efforts. By embracing environmental responsibility, humanity can mitigate its impacts, promote social equity, and redefine its relationship with nature. This is not merely an obligation but an opportunity to shape a sustainable and harmonious future for all.

Social Justice and Human Rights Advocacy: A Psychotherapist's Perspective

Social justice and human rights are fundamental principles that underpin equitable societies. For marginalized communities, access to mental health services often remains a challenge due to systemic inequalities. As a psychotherapist, my clinical experience has highlighted the critical role mental health plays in human rights advocacy. I invite you to explore with me the intersection of social justice and mental health, my contributions as a psychotherapist, and the broader implications for advancing human rights through mental health advocacy.

1. Understanding Social Justice and Human Rights in Mental Health
Defining Social Justice and Human Rights

Social justice refers to the pursuit of a society where resources, opportunities, and privileges are distributed equitably. In mental health, this means ensuring every individual has access to quality care, regardless of their socioeconomic status, race, gender, or identity. But also stands to understand how social injustices and inequality affects the mental and physical health of individuals and communities. Core principles include:

- **Equity:** Tailoring care to meet the unique needs of individuals.
- **Access:** Removing barriers to mental health services, such as financial constraints or geographic limitations.
- **Participation:** Involving clients and communities in decisions about their care.
- **Rights:** Recognizing mental health as integral to human rights.

Mental Health as a Human Right

The Universal Declaration of Human Rights (Article 25) underscores the right to an adequate standard of living, including healthcare. Similarly, the **Convention on the Rights of Persons with Disabilities (CRPD)** highlights mental health as a fundamental right, advocating for:
- Freedom from discrimination.
- Community-based care over institutionalization.
- Respect for autonomy in treatment decisions.

Systemic Inequalities in Mental Health Access

Systemic barriers disproportionately affect marginalized populations:
- **Racial minorities**: Experience higher rates of mental illness yet face stigma and cultural insensitivity within care systems.
- **LGBTQ+ individuals**: Encounter unique stressors, such as rejection or discrimination, often resulting in higher rates of depression and suicidality.
- **Economically disadvantaged groups**: Struggle with limited access to affordable mental health services.

One of my patients, from a low-income background had undiagnosed anxiety for years due to lack of access to mental health care ended up on emergency care during a panic attack at the workplace, with intense chest pain, difficulties breathing, diseases and nauseas. At the hospital, after ruling out cardiac arrest, they were diagnosed with generalized anxiety disorder, prescribed anti-anxiety psychotropic medications and referred to me by the hospital upon discharge for outpatient treatment.

In therapy, they disclosed having those symptoms for decades, which progressively increased. Their 80 hrs/ week work load, with 2 full time jobs to manage providing for themselves, their 3 children and disabled parents, a life long of emotional, financial and social hardships, facing discrimination, racist assaults and violence, left them with no time or resources to look for help. Addressing their challenges required connecting them to subsidized services and advocating for workplace accommodations.

2. My Clinical Experience: Psychotherapy as a Tool for Advocacy
Providing Culturally Competent Care

Cultural competence involves understanding clients' unique sociocultural contexts and addressing implicit biases in therapy. For example:
- Creating a safe space for LGBTQ+ clients to discuss their identities without fear of judgment.
- Using trauma-informed approaches with clients who have faced systemic oppression.

Working with a transgender client who experienced workplace discrimination, part of therapy focused on affirming their identity while also strategizing advocacy within their workplace.

Empowering Clients
Therapy helps clients navigate systemic barriers by:
- Recognizing societal contributors to their distress.
- Building self-advocacy skills.
- Connecting them to community resources and support networks.

Another clinical case refers to a racial minority client navigating workplace microaggressions. Part of therapy included helping the client process emotions, develop assertive communication strategies, and connect with workplace diversity initiatives.

3. The Role of Psychotherapy in Advancing Social Justice
Addressing the Trauma of Oppression

Systemic injustice often manifests as trauma:
- **PTSD**: Linked to experiences of violence or discrimination.
- **Anxiety and depression**: Heightened in individuals facing social inequities.
- **Cultural trauma**: Intergenerational impacts of systemic racism or colonization.

Trauma-informed care involves understanding these systemic factors and ensuring therapy avoids re-traumatization.

Psychotherapists as Advocates
Beyond individual sessions, therapists can:
- Educate clients about their rights.
- Empower clients to challenge oppressive systems.
- Advocate for systemic change, such as equitable healthcare policies.

Collaboration with Communities
Mental health professionals can partner with community organizations to provide outreach and culturally relevant services. For example, I once collaborated with a local LGBTQ+ center to offer group therapy sessions addressing minority stress.

4. Contributions Beyond the Therapy Room

Educational Workshops and Advocacy
Facilitating workshops on mental health literacy and stigma reduction, particularly in underserved communities, can bridge knowledge gaps.

I have led multiple community seminar on recognizing signs of trauma in immigrant families.

Policy Advocacy
Engaging in systemic change involves:

• Advocating for increased funding for community mental health clinics.
• Supporting legislation that addresses mental health disparities, such as Medicaid expansion.
Collaborating with policymakers to highlight the mental health needs of rural communities in policy proposals.

Supporting Marginalized Groups
Participating in initiatives that address the needs of specific populations, such as:
• Creating support groups for LGBTQ+ youth.
• Partnering with racial justice organizations to provide trauma counseling after community incidents.

5. Bridging Mental Health and Social Justice for the Future
Advancing Equity in Mental Health Access

Strategies include:
• **Telehealth**: Expanding access to rural or underserved populations.
• **Community-based interventions**: Embedding mental health resources in schools, churches, and community centers.
Building Awareness
Therapists can raise awareness by:
• Speaking at public events.
• Publishing articles on the intersection of mental health and human rights.
• Training other professionals in culturally competent care.
I encourage my fellow mental health professionals to:
• Advocate for clients beyond therapy.
• Address their own biases and privilege.
• Commit to ongoing education about systemic inequities.
A Holistic psychotherapy approach such as mine is inherently intertwined with social justice and human rights. One cannot properly provide effective mental health care, by ignoring the socio-political-economic and historical contexts the patient is inserted. By addressing the mental health needs of marginalized communities, therapists amplify the voices of the underserved and foster resilience. Through culturally competent care, advocacy, and collaboration, mental health professionals have the power to create lasting change. By embedding social justice into every aspect of practice, we pave the way for a more equitable and compassionate future.

The Importance of Ethical Consumption and Business Practices for Health and Well-being

Ethical consumption and business practices have become increasingly critical in an interconnected global economy. The choices consumers make and the values businesses uphold significantly influence individual and community health. From the production of goods to their distribution and consumption, the ethical and environmental implications of these processes affect physical, mental, and social well-being. This essay explores how ethical consumption and business practices directly impact health, emphasizing the role of sustainable and socially responsible actions in creating healthier communities.

1. Defining Ethical Consumption and Business Practices

- **Ethical Consumption**: Refers to the mindful purchasing of products and services that are socially responsible, environmentally sustainable, and promote fairness.
- Examples include buying fair-trade goods, reducing waste, and supporting companies with transparent supply chains.
- **Ethical Business Practices**: Encompasses corporate behaviors that prioritize people, planet, and profit in equal measure.
- Includes fair wages, sustainable sourcing, and reducing environmental harm.

Both concepts are interconnected, with consumer demand often driving businesses to adopt more ethical practices.

2. The Impact of Unethical Practices on Health

- **Environmental Degradation**: Pollution from industries harms air and water quality, leading to respiratory diseases, cancers, and other health issues. For example, Communities near industrial waste sites often experience higher rates of chronic illnesses.
- **Labor Exploitation**: Poor working conditions, low wages, and lack of worker protections lead to physical and mental health problems for laborers. Sweatshops and child labor, for instance, deprive individuals of a healthy and safe environment.
- **Food and Product Safety**: Companies that prioritize profit over safety may produce goods with harmful chemicals or low nutritional value. Fast fashion and low-cost goods often contain toxins that harm both users and workers during production.

3. Positive Impacts of Ethical Consumption and Practices on Health

- **Improved Community Health**: Ethical businesses reduce pollution and promote sustainable resource use, creating cleaner and healthier living environments.
  Case studies shows that Organic farming reduces pesticide exposure, improving both farmer and consumer health.
- **Economic Empowerment**: Fair-trade practices ensure workers earn livable wages, improving access to healthcare, education, and nutritious food. Coffee and cocoa farmers in fair-trade cooperatives report better community health outcomes.

- **Mental Well-being**: Ethical consumption fosters a sense of purpose and alignment with personal values, reducing feelings of guilt or helplessness about global issues.

4. The Role of Consumers in Driving Change

- **Supporting Ethical Brands**: Consumers can influence corporate behavior by prioritizing companies with strong ethical commitments. Increased demand for cruelty-free cosmetics has led to legislative bans on animal testing in many countries.
- **Advocating for Transparency**: Consumers can push businesses to disclose sourcing, labor conditions, and environmental impacts.
- **Education and Awareness**: Making informed choices requires awareness of the health and social consequences of consumption.

5. The Role of Businesses in Promoting Healthier Communities

- **Corporate Social Responsibility (CSR)**: Ethical companies prioritize the well-being of stakeholders, including employees, consumers, and surrounding communities. Patagonia's commitment to sustainable manufacturing and environmental activism inspires similar practices across industries.
- **Investment in Sustainable Practices**: Businesses that adopt renewable energy, waste reduction, and circular economy models contribute to global health improvements.
- **Partnerships with Communities**: Companies that collaborate with local communities often achieve more sustainable and impactful health outcomes.

6. Challenges and Opportunities

- **Challenges**:
- High Costs: Ethical practices may increase production costs, leading to higher consumer prices.
- Greenwashing: Some businesses falsely market themselves as ethical, misleading consumers.
- Systemic Barriers: Global supply chains often obscure unethical practices.
- **Opportunities**:
- Technology: Blockchain and AI can increase supply chain transparency.
- Policy Support: Governments can incentivize ethical practices through subsidies, regulations, and trade agreements.
- Consumer Power: The growing demand for sustainable and fair products demonstrates that collective consumer action can drive meaningful change.

7. A Vision for the Future: Building Ethical Economies

- **Collaboration Between Stakeholders**: Governments, businesses, and consumers must work together to prioritize ethical consumption and production.
- **Education and Accessibility**: Making ethical products affordable and widely available can encourage broader adoption.
- **Sustainable Development Goals (SDGs)**: Ethical practices align with global goals to eradicate poverty, improve health, and ensure sustainable consumption and production.

The importance of ethical consumption and business practices cannot be overstated. They directly influence the health of individuals and communities, shaping the social and environmental conditions in which people live. By choosing ethically and advocating for responsible business practices, consumers and corporations can drive systemic changes that promote health, equity, and sustainability. In a world grappling with climate change, inequality, and health crises, embracing ethical principles is not just a moral imperative—it is essential for the well-being of current and future generations.

Chapter 4
Global Citizenship in the Digital Age

The internet has fundamentally changed how we communicate, connect, and engage with the world. This chapter explores the digital dimensions of global citizenship. From social media to online activism, it examines both the benefits and the challenges of a digital world. How can we use technology responsibly to bridge gaps, advocate for change, and connect across borders?

The Power and Pitfalls of Social Media for Social Change and Mental Health

Social media has transformed communication, revolutionizing the way people connect, share information, and mobilize for causes. Platforms like Facebook, Instagram, Twitter, and TikTok have become critical tools for advancing social change, spreading awareness, and amplifying marginalized voices. Simultaneously, however, the impact of social media on mental health has raised concerns. While social media can empower individuals and foster positive community connections, its overuse or misuse can lead to anxiety, depression, and misinformation. In this chapter we will explore the dual-edged nature of social media in promoting social change and influencing mental health, weighing its transformative potential against its inherent risks.

The Power of Social Media for Social Change

Social media has become a potent force for activism, enabling grassroots movements to gain visibility and influence global conversations. Historically, organizing for social change required significant resources and centralized leadership, but social media democratizes activism. For example, movements like #BlackLivesMatter, #MeToo, and #ClimateStrike gained traction online, uniting millions of people worldwide to advocate for racial justice, gender equality, and environmental sustainability. These campaigns illustrate how social media serves as a catalyst for systemic change, empowering ordinary individuals to challenge oppressive systems, to have access and to join international movements and resources.

The immediacy of social media allows rapid dissemination of information, making it possible to mobilize protests, fundraise, and pressure policymakers in real-time. During the Arab Spring of the early 2010s, platforms like Twitter and Facebook played an instrumental role in organizing demonstrations, spreading awareness of human rights violations, and connecting activists across borders. Similarly, the #MeToo movement exposed widespread sexual harassment and abuse, holding powerful individuals accountable and sparking reforms in workplace policies.

Moreover, social media creates spaces for marginalized groups to share their stories and advocate for their rights. It facilitates dialogues that were previously inaccessible or taboo. Indigenous activists, LGBTQ+ advocates, and people with disabilities, for instance, have utilized platforms to challenge stereotypes, educate the public, and build supportive communities.

The Pitfalls of Social Media for Social Change

Despite its power, social media poses challenges for sustained activism and social change. The decentralized nature of online platforms often leads to fragmented movements, with competing narratives diluting collective efforts. While hashtags and viral posts can spark awareness, they may fail to translate into meaningful, long-term action. Critics argue that "slacktivism"—performing minimal effort actions, such as sharing posts or signing petitions—can give users a false sense of accomplishment without addressing systemic issues.

Additionally, misinformation spreads rapidly on social media, undermining trust in legitimate movements. Algorithms that prioritize sensational content over factual information exacerbate this issue. For instance, during the COVID-19 pandemic, false narratives about vaccines and public health policies proliferated, complicating efforts to manage the crisis. Similarly, manipulated videos, doctored images, and fake news articles can discredit social movements or incite division among supporters.

Online activism can also expose individuals to harassment and doxxing, particularly those from marginalized communities. The same platforms that amplify voices can be weaponized against them, discouraging participation and perpetuating systemic oppression.

The Impact of Social Media on Mental Health

Social media's influence on mental health is profound and multifaceted. On the positive side, it fosters connectivity, especially for individuals who might otherwise feel isolated. Support groups on platforms like Reddit and Facebook provide safe spaces for people with mental health conditions to share experiences and access resources. For many, these connections can alleviate feelings of loneliness, providing a sense of belonging and validation.

Social media also raises awareness about mental health issues, reducing stigma and encouraging people to seek help. Campaigns like #BellLetsTalk and #MentalHealthAwarenessMonth leverage platforms to disseminate information, fundraise for mental health services, and promote open conversations about emotional well-being, depression, suicide prevention and the benefits of psychotherapy.

However, the negative effects of social media on mental health cannot be overlooked. Studies show that excessive social media use is linked to increased rates of anxiety, depression, and low self-esteem, particularly among adolescents. Platforms designed to maximize user engagement often promote unhealthy comparisons, as users are exposed to curated, idealized versions of others' lives. This "highlight reel" effect can lead to feelings of inadequacy and dissatisfaction.

Moreover, social media's addictive nature can disrupt sleep, productivity, and real-world relationships. The constant notifications and algorithm-driven content cycles encourage compulsive use, making it difficult for individuals to disconnect. Cyberbullying and online harassment further exacerbate mental health challenges, with victims experiencing heightened stress, anxiety, and trauma.

Balancing the Benefits and Risks

The dual impact of social media necessitates a balanced approach to its use. For social change, activists must complement online campaigns with offline actions to achieve sustainable progress. Educating users about media literacy can mitigate the spread of misinformation and foster critical engagement with content. Platforms themselves bear responsibility for implementing policies that protect users from harassment and misinformation, while promoting authentic and diverse voices.

In terms of mental health, individuals should adopt mindful social media practices. Limiting screen time, curating positive content, and prioritizing in-person interactions can reduce the adverse effects of social media use. Parents, educators, and policymakers must also advocate for age-appropriate guidelines and digital wellness education to equip young users with the tools to navigate social media responsibly.

Social media's power to effect social change and impact mental health is undeniable. It provides unprecedented opportunities for connectivity, advocacy, and self-expression, empowering individuals and communities to drive meaningful progress. At the same time, its potential for harm—from spreading misinformation to exacerbating mental health issues—underscores the need for vigilance and intentional use. As society continues to grapple with the complexities of social media, fostering a balanced and ethical digital environment is essential to harness its transformative potential while mitigating its pitfalls.

Digital Literacy and Responsible Online Engagement: Its Impact on Mental Health

In the 21st century, digital technology has become ubiquitous in daily life, transforming how we interact with the world, consume information, and engage with others. The internet, social media, and online platforms have revolutionized communication, education, and entertainment, but they have also introduced new challenges, particularly in the realm of mental health. With the rapid expansion of digital spaces, digital literacy—the ability to effectively and critically navigate online environments—has become a crucial skill for individuals to possess.

Digital literacy is not only about technical proficiency but also about responsible online engagement, which encompasses understanding the impact of digital content on well-being and practicing ethical behavior online. Let us reflect on187 the importance of digital literacy, the role of responsible online engagement in promoting mental health, and the consequences of neglecting these aspects in the context of the digital age.

Entangled   Sandra Ferreira

Understanding Digital Literacy

Digital literacy goes beyond the ability to operate digital devices; it involves a comprehensive understanding of how to access, evaluate, and create information in an online environment. This encompasses a range of skills, including information literacy (evaluating the reliability and credibility of online content), media literacy (understanding how media shapes our perceptions), and digital citizenship (engaging in online communities ethically and responsibly). Digital literacy is critical for navigating the vast amount of information available on the internet and making informed decisions about what to consume, share, and create.

In a rapidly evolving digital landscape, digital literacy also involves understanding the tools and platforms used for communication and content creation. This includes social media platforms, online forums, blogs, and news websites. Being digitally literate means not only using these platforms for personal and professional purposes but also recognizing the power these platforms have in shaping public opinion, societal norms, and personal identities.

Furthermore, digital literacy is vital in protecting one's mental health in a digital world. As social media and online interactions become increasingly central to daily life, understanding how to engage with these platforms in a balanced, informed way is key to mitigating the potential negative effects on mental health. Digital literacy empowers individuals to make conscious decisions about their online activities and interactions, avoiding the pitfalls of misinformation, cyberbullying, and harmful content.

The Role of Responsible Online Engagement

Responsible online engagement refers to the conscious and ethical use of digital platforms, characterized by actions such as critical consumption of information, respectful communication, and mindful participation in online communities. In an era where online interactions often define personal and professional relationships, understanding the nuances of responsible engagement is essential to maintaining a positive digital experience.

One critical aspect of responsible online engagement is managing one's digital footprint. This includes being aware of the information shared online, from personal details to opinions and behaviors, and considering how these might affect one's reputation and relationships. Engaging responsibly also involves understanding the potential harm that can result from online actions, such as spreading misinformation, engaging in online harassment, or promoting unrealistic body standards and lifestyles.

Social media platforms, in particular, are where responsible online engagement is most crucial. The culture of instant gratification, constant comparison, and engagement-driven algorithms can lead individuals to feel pressured to present a curated version of themselves. This can result in feelings of inadequacy, low self-esteem, and mental distress. Being digitally literate and engaging responsibly means recognizing the distorted nature of online portrayals and not allowing them to influence one's self-worth or mental health.

Another important element of responsible online engagement is understanding the psychological effects of social media and digital content. Platforms that encourage likes, shares, and comments can create addictive cycles, leading to a constant desire for validation. This quest for online approval can undermine an individual's sense of self and contribute to negative mental health outcomes such as anxiety, depression, and loneliness. Responsible online engagement involves creating boundaries, being aware of how digital consumption impacts emotional well-being, and limiting time spent on platforms that cause distress.

Digital Literacy and Mental Health

The relationship between digital literacy and mental health is increasingly complex. While the internet offers immense opportunities for education, entertainment, and social connection, it also presents risks that can adversely affect mental health. Digital literacy plays a critical role in mitigating these risks by helping individuals navigate the digital world in ways that promote well-being.

One of the primary mental health concerns related to digital engagement is the phenomenon of social comparison. Social media platforms often present idealized versions of people's lives, which can create unrealistic standards and lead to feelings of inadequacy. Digital literacy can help individuals recognize that these portrayals are frequently curated and edited, providing a buffer against harmful comparisons. A digitally literate person is more likely to understand the distinction between online personas and real-life experiences, reducing the negative impact of social media on their self-esteem.

Additionally, exposure to cyberbullying and harassment can have a severe impact on mental health, particularly for vulnerable populations such as teenagers and marginalized communities. The anonymity of the internet and the reach of social media can amplify instances of bullying, leading to increased stress, anxiety, and even suicidal ideation. By fostering digital literacy, individuals can be better equipped to recognize when they are being harassed or manipulated online and take steps to protect themselves. This may include blocking or reporting harmful accounts, engaging in positive online behaviors, or seeking help from trusted individuals or mental health professionals.

Another critical mental health issue in the digital age is the overuse of digital devices and social media. Studies have shown that excessive screen time, particularly before bed, can interfere with sleep patterns, leading to increased levels of anxiety and depression. Digital literacy includes not only the ability to use technology effectively but also the self-regulation to limit its negative impact on mental health. By understanding the effects of technology on well-being, individuals can make informed choices about how much time to spend online and when to disconnect.

The Importance of Digital Literacy Education

To reap the benefits of digital technology while safeguarding mental health, it is essential to integrate digital literacy education into both formal and informal learning environments. Schools, universities, and community organizations should prioritize teaching digital literacy skills to equip individuals with the knowledge and tools needed to engage responsibly online.

Digital literacy education should focus on critical thinking and media literacy, helping individuals discern between credible and unreliable sources of information. As misinformation and conspiracy theories proliferate online, teaching individuals how to verify facts and evaluate sources is crucial in preventing the spread of harmful content. Additionally, education should include lessons on digital etiquette, online communication, and ethical behavior, ensuring that individuals understand the importance of treating others with respect in virtual spaces.

Equally important is fostering a culture of digital well-being, where individuals are encouraged to take breaks from screens, practice mindfulness, and engage in activities that promote mental health, such as physical exercise or face-to-face interactions. By embedding these practices into digital literacy curricula, individuals can learn to balance their online and offline lives in ways that support mental health.

Digital literacy and responsible online engagement are indispensable in today's digital world, with significant implications for mental health. As individuals increasingly turn to online platforms for communication, information, and entertainment, understanding how to navigate these spaces ethically and critically is vital for well-being. Digital literacy empowers individuals to evaluate digital content critically, engage with online communities responsibly, and protect themselves from the negative psychological impacts of excessive or harmful digital interactions.

In a world where technology is ever-evolving, fostering digital literacy is not just a matter of teaching technical skills but of promoting emotional intelligence and self-regulation in the digital sphere. By equipping individuals with the knowledge to engage responsibly online, society can mitigate the mental health risks associated with digital spaces and harness the positive potential of the internet to enrich lives, foster connections, and drive social progress.

Using Technology to Promote Inclusivity and Understanding

In an increasingly globalizing world, technology has the potential to be a transformative force for inclusivity and understanding. The rapid advancement of digital tools has revolutionized the way people communicate, access information, and interact with one another. Technology, when used effectively, can foster inclusivity by breaking down barriers related to geography, ability, culture, and language. It can also facilitate a deeper understanding of diverse perspectives, encouraging empathy and collaboration across various social, political, and cultural divides.

However, as with any tool, the way technology is implemented plays a crucial role in its effectiveness. Let us explore how technology can be harnessed to promote inclusivity and understanding, highlighting its positive impacts in areas such as education, communication, and social advocacy, while also addressing the challenges that must be overcome for technology to fulfill its potential.

Technology in Education: Bridging Gaps and Promoting Access

One of the most significant ways that technology promotes inclusivity is in the field of education. Technology provides innovative ways to bridge gaps in access to quality education, particularly for marginalized groups or those facing geographical, physical, or socio-economic barriers. Digital platforms and educational tools, such as online learning modules, video conferencing, and interactive content, can offer equal learning opportunities to individuals who may otherwise have limited access to educational resources.

For students with disabilities, assistive technologies such as screen readers, voice recognition software, and adaptive devices can make learning more accessible. For example, students with visual impairments can use text-to-speech software to access reading materials, while students with hearing impairments can rely on captioning and sign language interpretation for audiovisual content. This kind of technological integration ensures that all students, regardless of their abilities, have access to the same educational opportunities, fostering a more inclusive environment.

Moreover, digital learning tools provide opportunities for individuals from diverse backgrounds to engage with educational content tailored to their needs. Massive Open Online Courses (MOOCs), for example, have democratized access to high-quality education by making courses from prestigious universities available for free or at a low cost. These platforms offer learners from low-income communities or remote areas the chance to gain knowledge and skills that would have otherwise been out of reach. By breaking down barriers to education, technology fosters greater inclusivity and empowers individuals to achieve their potential.

Social Media and Communication: Facilitating Cross-Cultural Understanding

Social media platforms like Facebook, Twitter (now X), Instagram, and TikTok have become essential tools for communication and community-building, enabling individuals to connect with others from around the world. One of the most profound impacts of social media is its ability to facilitate cross-cultural understanding by giving people from different backgrounds a platform to share their experiences and perspectives. This exposure can lead to increased empathy and awareness of global issues.

For example, campaigns like #BlackLivesMatter and #MeToo have used social media to highlight issues of racial and gender inequality. By sharing personal stories and organizing online movements, these campaigns have raised awareness about systemic oppression and called for social and policy changes. The widespread dissemination of these movements, particularly through visual content, has allowed people from various parts of the world to understand the struggles faced by marginalized communities, prompting conversations about race, gender, and justice on a global scale.

Additionally, social media can create spaces for individuals from different cultural or religious backgrounds to engage in dialogue, breaking down stereotypes and fostering mutual respect. In a world where misunderstandings and prejudices often stem from a lack of knowledge about others, social media offers a way for people to see the humanity in one another. For example, users can share cultural traditions, personal experiences, and histories that promote greater understanding and reduce misconceptions about different cultures and beliefs.

While social media has the potential to foster inclusivity, it also poses challenges, such as the spread of hate speech, misinformation, and polarization. The key to promoting inclusivity on these platforms is encouraging responsible engagement and fostering digital literacy. When used thoughtfully and ethically, social media can be a powerful tool for increasing understanding and promoting inclusivity.

Technology for Accessibility: Breaking Down Barriers for Disabled Individuals

In the realm of accessibility, technology plays a pivotal role in ensuring that individuals with disabilities can participate fully in society. Advances in assistive technology have made it possible for people with disabilities to engage in activities that were once inaccessible to them, whether it's reading, communicating, or navigating physical spaces. These technologies not only promote inclusivity but also empower individuals to lead more independent lives.

For instance, voice-activated virtual assistants like Siri, Alexa, and Google Assistant allow individuals with mobility impairments to control smart home devices, make phone calls, and access information without needing to physically interact with a device. Similarly, screen magnification software and Braille displays have made it easier for individuals with visual impairments to access digital content. These innovations have transformed the way disabled individuals experience technology, allowing them to interact with digital environments and services in ways that were previously impossible.

Furthermore, accessible websites and mobile applications that adhere to Web Content Accessibility Guidelines (WCAG) ensure that digital spaces are navigable by individuals with disabilities. These tools have transformed online shopping, banking, education, and entertainment, allowing individuals to access services with greater ease and confidence. When designed with accessibility in mind, technology can help dismantle barriers to social, economic, and cultural participation, promoting inclusivity and creating opportunities for people with disabilities to fully engage with the world.

Virtual Reality (VR) and Empathy: Experiencing Other Perspectives

One of the most innovative uses of technology in promoting understanding and inclusivity is through virtual reality (VR). VR allows users to immerse themselves in environments that simulate the experiences of others, offering a unique opportunity to foster empathy and a deeper understanding of different social and cultural realities. By stepping into someone else's shoes, VR can break down prejudices and promote compassion.

For example, VR has been used in educational settings to help students experience life from the perspective of individuals facing social challenges, such as homelessness, poverty, or racial discrimination. VR simulations can also offer experiences related to global issues like climate change, refugee crises, or civil rights struggles, helping users understand the human impact of these crises. These immersive experiences can make the realities of others more tangible, fostering empathy and encouraging individuals to take action in their communities.

In the context of corporate training or diversity education, VR has been used to raise awareness of unconscious bias, providing employees with scenarios that challenge their assumptions about race, gender, and other aspects of identity. These types of VR applications promote a greater understanding of inclusivity and create more empathetic and socially aware individuals.

Challenges and Ethical Considerations

While technology has immense potential to promote inclusivity and understanding, it is not without its challenges and ethical considerations. One of the primary concerns is the digital divide—the gap between those who have access to technology and those who do not. In many parts of the world, especially in rural or low-income areas, access to the internet and digital devices is limited. Without access to the tools and resources necessary to engage with technology, individuals in these communities are excluded from the benefits of digital inclusivity.

Additionally, technology can reinforce existing inequalities if not implemented carefully. For example, algorithmic biases in artificial intelligence (AI) and machine learning systems can perpetuate discrimination, particularly against marginalized groups. Ensuring that technology is designed with inclusivity in mind requires addressing these biases and ensuring that all voices are represented in the creation of digital tools. In other words, humanity has to evolve to the level of eradicating those malicious intents of create and spreading hate, racism, discrimination, division, along with misinformation to manipulate the masses in supporting devious political, social and economic agendas. It is also up to each one of us, users and regular citizens, to educate ourselves and understand the responsibility we all have on utilizing this tools responsibly and ethically to promote inclusivity, empathy and understanding, instead of hate, violence, racism, discrimination, chaos and misinformation.

Moreover, the ethical use of technology is a critical consideration in fostering inclusivity. Platforms must prioritize privacy, security, and respect for users' rights while also combating the spread of harmful content, misinformation, and hate speech. Fostering a safe and supportive digital environment is essential to creating spaces where inclusivity and understanding can thrive.

Technology has the potential to be a powerful force for promoting inclusivity and understanding across the globe. From education to communication, accessibility to empathy-building, digital tools are helping break down barriers, foster cross-cultural dialogue, and empower marginalized communities. However, the full potential of technology can only be realized when it is implemented thoughtfully, ethically, and with a focus on accessibility for all.

Entangled   Sandra Ferreira

By addressing the challenges associated with the digital divide, algorithmic bias, and the ethical implications of technology, society can ensure that digital spaces remain inclusive, diverse, and supportive of understanding. As technology continues to evolve, it offers an unprecedented opportunity to create a more inclusive world—one where people from all backgrounds can engage with one another, learn from each other, and work together for a more equitable and understanding future.

Chapter 5
Education for Global Citizenship

Education plays a central role in fostering global citizenship. This chapter examines the role of schools, universities, and informal learning spaces in cultivating a global mindset. It introduces readers to inspiring programs that have successfully taught empathy, cultural awareness, and environmental stewardship and offers practical ways for educators to integrate global perspectives into their curricula.

Developing Empathy and Intercultural Understanding

In today's international scene, the ability to understand and empathize with people from different cultural backgrounds has never been more essential. As globalization brings people together from diverse corners of the world, fostering empathy and intercultural understanding becomes a critical component of personal and societal development. Developing empathy—the ability to recognize and share the feelings of others—along with a deeper understanding of different cultures, plays a crucial role in building harmonious relationships, combating prejudice, and ensuring more effective communication across cultural boundaries. It is important to reflect on the significance of empathy and intercultural understanding, the challenges faced in cultivating these qualities, and strategies for their development.

The Importance of Empathy and Intercultural Understanding

Empathy is an essential element of human connection. It allows individuals to step into the shoes of others, perceive their feelings and experiences, and respond with sensitivity and support. When it comes to intercultural understanding, empathy is a cornerstone. Without it, misunderstanding and conflict are more likely to arise between individuals of differing cultural backgrounds.

Cultural differences affect not only communication styles but also values, behaviors, and perspectives. Misinterpretations and stereotypes often emerge when people fail to see beyond their own cultural lens. In contrast, intercultural understanding—defined as the ability to recognize and respect cultural differences—can pave the way for greater mutual respect and smoother interactions. This is particularly important in the context of global business, education, and diplomatic relations, where cultural awareness can influence decision-making, collaboration, and conflict resolution.

Empathy fosters tolerance, inclusivity and decreases violence and social conflicts. It promotes acceptance of diversity, which is crucial in multicultural societies where people from different racial, ethnic, and religious backgrounds coexist. Intercultural understanding encourages curiosity and learning, helping individuals embrace the richness of cultural diversity. It allows people to bridge gaps, dispel stereotypes, and find common ground despite differences.

Challenges in Developing Empathy and Intercultural Understanding

Despite the importance of empathy and intercultural understanding, several challenges hinder their development. One of the primary barriers is ethnocentrism—the tendency to evaluate other cultures based on the standards of one's own. Ethnocentric individuals often view their culture as superior, making it difficult for them to accept or understand cultural practices and norms that differ from their own. This mindset can lead to a lack of interest in other cultures and a failure to recognize their value.

Another obstacle is the presence of biases and stereotypes. People often hold preconceived notions about certain groups based on their race, nationality, religion, or other cultural markers. These stereotypes can shape how individuals perceive and interact with others, reinforcing negative attitudes and fostering division. Stereotyping undermines empathy, as it reduces people to a set of oversimplified characteristics rather than seeing them as complex individuals.

Additionally, language differences present challenges to effective intercultural communication. Language barriers can make it difficult for individuals to express themselves fully and understand others' experiences, which can impede empathy. Non-verbal cues, such as body language and facial expressions, also vary across cultures. A gesture that may be perceived as friendly in one culture could be considered offensive in another, leading to misunderstandings and hurt feelings.

A lack of exposure to diverse cultures can also limit one's ability to develop empathy and intercultural understanding. People who live in homogenous communities or have limited international experience may struggle to relate to individuals from other cultural backgrounds. This lack of exposure can perpetuate ignorance and lead to insular thinking.

Strategies for Developing Empathy

1.   **Active Listening**: One of the most effective ways to develop empathy is through active listening. Active listening involves not only hearing the words being spoken but also paying attention to the emotions and non-verbal cues that accompany them. It requires individuals to be present in the moment, refrain from interrupting, and refrain from passing judgment. When interacting with someone from a different cultural background, it is essential to listen attentively to their perspective and ask open-ended questions to encourage deeper dialogue.

2.   **Perspective-Taking**: Empathy involves understanding the emotions and experiences of others, which requires perspective-taking—the ability to put oneself in another person's shoes. To develop intercultural empathy, individuals must seek to understand how others perceive the world based on their cultural backgrounds. This can involve asking questions about cultural norms, values, and traditions to gain insight into the motivations and beliefs of others.

3.   **Exposure to Diverse Perspectives**: Engaging with diverse cultures through travel, reading, or participating in intercultural events can broaden one's worldview and enhance empathy. Traveling to foreign countries exposes individuals to

new ways of life, while reading books or watching documentaries about different cultures can provide valuable insights into the experiences of others. Additionally, interacting with people from different backgrounds in everyday life, such as in the workplace or community, provides opportunities to practice empathy and learn about other perspectives.

4.   **Cultivating Emotional Intelligence**: Emotional intelligence (EI) refers to the ability to recognize and manage one's own emotions while understanding and influencing the emotions of others. Developing EI is key to building empathy, as it allows individuals to better attune themselves to the emotional states of others. EI involves self-awareness, self-regulation, motivation, empathy, and social skills, all of which are essential for fostering understanding in intercultural interactions.

5.   **Challenging Stereotypes**: One of the first steps in developing empathy is recognizing and challenging stereotypes. By consciously examining preconceived notions about other cultures, individuals can begin to dismantle the barriers that prevent them from fully understanding and connecting with others. Engaging with people from diverse backgrounds and questioning assumptions can help break down stereotypes and promote a more inclusive mindset.

6.   **Engaging in Cross-Cultural Dialogue**: Dialogue is an essential tool for fostering intercultural understanding. When individuals engage in meaningful conversations with people from different cultures, they have the opportunity to learn about their beliefs, values, and experiences. Cross-cultural dialogue provides a platform for individuals to share their perspectives while also listening to others with respect and curiosity. This exchange of ideas fosters greater understanding and helps build bridges across cultural divides.

The Role of Education in Promoting Empathy and Intercultural Understanding

Education plays a pivotal role in shaping individuals' attitudes toward other cultures. Schools and universities are key environments for promoting intercultural understanding, as they bring together students from diverse cultural backgrounds. Through classroom discussions, collaborative projects, and extracurricular activities, educational institutions can provide opportunities for students to develop empathy and learn about different cultures.

Cultural exchange programs, study abroad opportunities, and virtual exchange platforms are also effective ways to foster intercultural understanding. These initiatives allow students to immerse themselves in different cultural contexts, learn firsthand about foreign societies, and form lasting connections with people from around the world.

Moreover, educators can integrate global perspectives into the curriculum, ensuring that students are exposed to a variety of cultural viewpoints. By teaching students about the histories, values, and contributions of different cultures, educators can help them develop a broader understanding of the world and its diverse peoples.

In conclusion, developing empathy and intercultural understanding is essential for building a more harmonious, inclusive, and collaborative world. Empathy allows individuals to connect with others on an emotional level, while intercultural understanding fosters respect for diversity and reduces prejudice. Although challenges such as ethnocentrism, biases, and language barriers can hinder the development of these qualities, there are numerous strategies to overcome them, including active listening, perspective-taking, and exposure to diverse cultures. Education plays a critical role in promoting empathy and intercultural understanding, providing opportunities for individuals to broaden their horizons and engage with others in meaningful ways. As we continue to navigate a globalized world, cultivating these qualities will help bridge cultural divides and create stronger, more empathetic communities.

The Role of Educational Institutions and Health Systems in Fostering Global Awareness and Its Impact on Mental Health

In our historical moment, fostering global awareness is a crucial aspect of preparing individuals to engage with the complexities of global challenges. Educational institutions and health systems play vital roles in promoting global awareness, offering opportunities for individuals to gain insights into the interconnectedness of cultures, societies, and global issues. This awareness can influence various facets of life, including mental health. By promoting understanding, empathy, and collective responsibility, both educational and healthcare institutions help individuals become more resilient in the face of global crises, improving their mental health and well-being. Bellow, we will explore the role of educational institutions and health systems in fostering global awareness and discuss the significant impact that this awareness has on mental health.

The Role of Educational Institutions in Fostering Global Awareness

Educational institutions are fundamental in shaping the perspectives and attitudes of individuals toward global issues. They are key spaces where students first learn about the interconnected nature of the world and the shared challenges that humanity faces. By promoting global awareness, educational institutions help cultivate a sense of empathy, tolerance, and social responsibility among young people.

1. **Curriculum and Pedagogy**

One of the primary ways in which educational institutions foster global awareness is through the design and implementation of curricula that incorporate global issues, such as climate change, poverty, human rights, migration, and conflict. Global education programs teach students to think critically about global challenges and their implications, encouraging them to become active, informed global citizens. The inclusion of topics such as international relations, global health, environmental sustainability, and social justice helps students understand the complexities of the world, promoting a deeper appreciation for the diversity of cultures and experiences.

Moreover, global awareness programs encourage interdisciplinary learning, which can foster a more holistic understanding of global issues. For example, subjects like geography, history, economics, and political science all offer perspectives on global challenges, helping students recognize how these issues transcend national borders and affect people worldwide. By integrating diverse cultural viewpoints into lessons and discussions, educators can help students develop a more open and inclusive mindset.

2.   **Global Citizenship Education (GCE)**

Global Citizenship Education (GCE) is a framework that seeks to promote understanding, respect, and a sense of responsibility among individuals toward global issues. GCE focuses on cultivating a mindset of global solidarity, where students recognize that their actions can have far-reaching effects beyond their own communities. By engaging with concepts like social justice, environmental sustainability, and human rights, students become more aware of the global systems that shape the world around them.

Educational institutions that prioritize GCE encourage students to actively participate in global causes, such as climate change mitigation or social equity initiatives. These initiatives help students develop a sense of agency and responsibility, as they understand that they can contribute to solving global problems. Furthermore, GCE fosters critical thinking, allowing students to analyze the complexities of global challenges and consider their ethical responsibilities as global citizens.

3.   **International Exposure and Exchange Programs**

One of the most effective ways to promote global awareness is through international exchange programs and study abroad opportunities. By immersing students in different cultural contexts, these programs provide firsthand experience of global diversity. Students can engage with peers from different countries, learn new languages, and experience different educational systems, helping them gain a more nuanced understanding of global issues.

Study abroad programs also allow students to experience the challenges faced by other societies, whether through exposure to economic disparities, political struggles, or environmental crises. These experiences can deepen students' empathy and understanding, fostering global citizenship and a broader perspective on life. As students return to their home countries, they are often more aware of the interconnectedness of global issues and better equipped to contribute to addressing these challenges.

4.   **Social Media and Technology as Tools for Global Awareness**

In the digital age, social media and technology play a pivotal role in fostering global awareness. Educational institutions are increasingly incorporating technology into learning environments, allowing students to access information from around the world. Social media platforms, online courses, and virtual exchange programs enable students to interact with peers across the globe and learn about different cultural perspectives.

While there are challenges associated with the use of technology, such as the spread of misinformation, it can also be a powerful tool for raising awareness about global issues. By using social media to connect students with international organizations, activists, and experts, educational institutions can expose students to global movements, debates, and causes. This not only enhances global awareness but also encourages students to think critically about the world around them.

The Role of Health Systems in Fostering Global Awareness

Health systems, particularly those with a global health focus, are crucial in raising awareness about health disparities and global health challenges. By addressing the mental and physical health needs of populations, health systems promote global well-being and create opportunities for individuals to understand the interconnectedness of health issues across borders.

1.   Public Health Education and Advocacy

Health systems play an essential role in educating the public about global health issues, such as the spread of infectious diseases, malnutrition, and the impact of climate change on health. Through public health campaigns, healthcare providers raise awareness about the importance of hygiene, vaccination, and disease prevention, which have global implications. These efforts not only contribute to improving health outcomes but also foster a greater understanding of the global interconnectedness of health.

For example, the response to the COVID-19 pandemic highlighted the need for global cooperation in addressing health crises. Health systems worldwide worked together to share information, resources, and best practices. By emphasizing the importance of global health solidarity, healthcare systems helped individuals recognize that their health is tied to the health of others, encouraging a collective response to the crisis.

2.   Promoting Mental Health Awareness

Global awareness also extends to mental health, as many mental health challenges, such as depression, anxiety, and trauma, have global dimensions. Health systems can promote mental health awareness by providing education on the mental health impacts of global crises, including conflict, migration, and climate change. Mental health services can be integrated into public health campaigns to address the psychological effects of such challenges.

Health professionals also help foster global awareness by advocating for the inclusion of mental health in global health agendas. Mental health is often underrepresented in international health discussions, but the recognition of its importance has grown in recent years. By addressing the mental health needs of populations affected by global crises, healthcare systems can promote greater global solidarity and understanding of the mental health implications of global events.

3. **Cultural Competency in Healthcare**

As the world relations expand, healthcare providers must be culturally competent in order to meet the needs of diverse populations. Health systems that prioritize cultural competence help providers understand the social, cultural, and economic factors that influence health behaviors and outcomes. This awareness improves the quality of care and fosters better relationships between healthcare providers and patients from different cultural backgrounds.

Cultural competency also extends to the recognition of how mental health is perceived and treated across different cultures. In some societies, mental health issues may carry stigma or be approached differently. Health professionals trained in cultural competence can better understand these differences and provide more effective care, ensuring that mental health issues are addressed with sensitivity and respect for cultural beliefs.

4. **Global Health Initiatives and Advocacy**

Healthcare systems contribute to global awareness by engaging in global health initiatives and advocating for policies that address health disparities. Organizations such as the World Health Organization (WHO) work with national health systems to improve global health outcomes and promote health equity. Healthcare providers who participate in global health initiatives, such as humanitarian missions or research collaborations, help raise awareness about global health challenges and the need for international cooperation in addressing them.

These initiatives also provide opportunities for healthcare professionals to witness firsthand the health disparities that exist between countries and regions. This experience can foster a greater sense of global responsibility and awareness, encouraging healthcare providers to contribute to addressing health inequities through policy, advocacy, and direct care.

The Impact of Global Awareness on Mental Health

Fostering global awareness has profound implications for mental health, both at the individual and societal levels. Understanding the global context of mental health helps individuals develop greater empathy and resilience, which can improve their psychological well-being.

1. **Increased Empathy and Emotional Resilience**

When individuals develop an understanding of the global challenges faced by others, they are more likely to develop empathy for those affected. This empathy helps foster emotional resilience, as individuals are able to relate to others' struggles and find common ground despite differences. This sense of shared humanity can buffer against feelings of isolation and helplessness, which can otherwise lead to mental health issues.

Moreover, global awareness helps individuals understand that mental health challenges are not confined to any one culture or society. The recognition that people everywhere face similar struggles, despite different contexts, can help reduce stigma and promote a more compassionate approach to mental health.

2.   Improved Mental Health through Collective Action

Global awareness encourages individuals to participate in collective action, such as activism, volunteering, or supporting global causes. Engaging in these activities can provide individuals with a sense of purpose and belonging, both of which are essential for good mental health. Collective action also fosters a sense of solidarity and shared responsibility, which can alleviate feelings of anxiety and stress about global issues.

3.   Addressing Global Mental Health Challenges

As global awareness of mental health increases, it becomes possible to address widespread mental health challenges that are exacerbated by global crises. For example, the mental health impact of displacement due to war, natural disasters, or economic instability is a growing concern. By fostering awareness of these challenges, healthcare systems and educational institutions can work together to provide support and resources for those affected, improving overall mental health outcomes.

In conclusion, educational institutions and health systems play vital roles in fostering global awareness, which has significant implications for mental health. Through curriculum development, global citizenship education, and international exposure, educational institutions help students develop a broader understanding of global issues. Health systems contribute by raising awareness of global health challenges, promoting mental health education, and advocating for policies that address health inequities. By fostering global awareness, both educational and healthcare systems help individuals become more empathetic, resilient, and engaged with.

Practical Approaches to Teaching Global Citizenship at Any Age

The concept of global citizenship is more important than ever. Global citizenship involves recognizing and embracing the interdependence of all people and nations, understanding shared global challenges, and developing the skills to work collaboratively to address them. Teaching global citizenship is not only about providing information but also about fostering a mindset of empathy, respect, and responsibility. Following, we will present practical approaches to teaching global citizenship across different age groups, from young children to adults, highlighting strategies that educators, parents, and community leaders can use to nurture these values.

Defining Global Citizenship

Global citizenship refers to the awareness that one's identity extends beyond national and local boundaries to encompass a broader, more inclusive sense of belonging to humanity as a whole. It is based on the recognition that global problems, such as climate change, inequality, and conflict, require cooperative and collective solutions. A global citizen is someone who actively engages with and contributes to the well-being of the world, respecting cultural diversity, human rights, and sustainability. Global citizenship education (GCE) focuses on equipping individuals with the knowledge, skills, and values necessary to be active, responsible participants in a global society.

Approaches to Teaching Global Citizenship at Different Ages

Teaching global citizenship can be adapted to suit the developmental stages of different age groups. Whether working with young children, adolescents, or adults, there are numerous approaches that educators can employ to foster global awareness and responsibility.

1. Teaching Global Citizenship to Young Children (Ages 3-8)

At a young age, children begin to develop an understanding of the world around them. Though their grasp of complex global issues is limited, they are highly receptive to ideas of fairness, empathy, and respect for others. Teaching global citizenship to young children focuses on building the foundational values of respect, cooperation, and responsibility.

a. Storytelling and Literature

One of the most effective ways to introduce young children to the concept of global citizenship is through storytelling. Books and stories featuring characters from diverse backgrounds or addressing issues such as friendship, helping others, and environmental stewardship can provide children with an early understanding of global interconnectedness. Picture books, for example, can introduce children to different cultures and ways of life, showing them that people around the world share many common experiences.

Books like "The Sneetches" by Dr. Seuss, which addresses themes of inclusion and tolerance, or "Last Stop on Market Street" by Matt de la Peña, which highlights community and social responsibility, can help foster empathy for others. Stories that explore global issues in an age-appropriate way, such as climate change or migration, can also be effective in broadening children's understanding of the world.

b. Interactive Activities

Children learn best when they are actively engaged. Interactive activities, such as role-playing, arts and crafts, or games, can be used to teach global citizenship in a fun and meaningful way. For instance, children can participate in games where they take on roles from different countries, exploring the challenges faced by people in various parts of the world.

Teachers can also organize activities like "International Days," where children learn about different countries, try international foods, and participate in cultural exchanges. This helps children appreciate cultural diversity while reinforcing the value of inclusivity and respect for differences.

c. Teaching Empathy and Compassion

Teaching empathy at a young age is crucial for fostering global citizenship. Simple practices like teaching children to share, take turns, and help others can develop their sense of empathy. In the classroom, teachers can use strategies like "circle time," where children are encouraged to share their feelings and listen to others, helping them develop emotional intelligence and understanding. These skills form the basis for becoming a compassionate global citizen in later years.

2. Teaching Global Citizenship to Adolescents (Ages 9-18)

As children mature, they begin to understand more complex ideas and can engage with global issues in a more critical way. At this stage, adolescents can begin to explore topics like human rights, environmental sustainability, and social justice in greater depth. The key to teaching global citizenship to adolescents is to encourage critical thinking, active engagement, and social responsibility.

a. Project-Based Learning

One effective way to teach global citizenship to adolescents is through project-based learning (PBL). PBL involves students working on real-world problems and projects, often with a focus on issues like sustainability, human rights, or community development. These projects can take many forms, such as creating awareness campaigns, organizing charity events, or collaborating with local organizations to address global issues.

For example, students could work on projects related to climate change, such as researching the impacts of deforestation or promoting renewable energy. They could also explore global human rights issues, such as child labor or access to education, and work on advocacy campaigns to raise awareness. Through these projects, students not only gain knowledge about global issues but also develop the skills to take action and make a difference in the world.

b. Debates and Discussions

Adolescents benefit from engaging in debates and discussions about current events and global issues. These activities encourage critical thinking and the ability to consider multiple perspectives. Teachers can organize debates on topics like climate change, immigration, or global inequality, helping students understand the complexity of these issues while encouraging them to formulate their own opinions.

In addition, teachers can guide discussions that explore the ethical dimensions of global citizenship, such as the responsibility of wealthy nations to address poverty in developing countries or the role of individuals in protecting the environment. These discussions promote not only intellectual engagement but also moral reasoning, empathy, and social awareness.

c. Service Learning and Volunteering

Service learning, which combines community service with academic learning, is another powerful approach to teaching global citizenship to adolescents. By participating in service projects—whether local, national, or international—students can directly contribute to solving real-world problems. This hands-on approach helps students see the tangible impact of their actions and understand how they can make a difference in the world.

Students could volunteer, for instance, with organizations that address global issues, such as refugee support services, environmental advocacy, or public health initiatives. These experiences can deepen their understanding of global challenges and help them develop a sense of personal responsibility toward addressing those challenges.

3. Teaching Global Citizenship to Adults

Adults, particularly those who may not have been exposed to global citizenship education during their school years, can also benefit from opportunities to engage with global issues. Adult education programs, workplace initiatives, and community-based activities can all provide adults with the tools to become more informed, engaged global citizens.

a. Continuing Education and Workshops

Workshops and courses focused on global citizenship can help adults deepen their understanding of global issues and the importance of social responsibility. These educational programs can cover topics such as sustainable development, global health, and international relations. Offering these programs in community centers, libraries, or online can make them accessible to a wide audience.

One example can be found on community organizations hosting workshops on the United Nations Sustainable Development Goals (SDGs), exploring how individuals and communities can contribute to achieving these goals. Similarly, programs that focus on the impact of global challenges, such as the refugee crisis or climate change, can help adults become more informed about the world and their role in creating positive change.

b. Promoting Active Citizenship and Advocacy

Adults can engage with global citizenship through active participation in advocacy and social justice initiatives. Encouraging adults to join or create advocacy groups focused on global issues can empower them to take action and make a difference. These groups can work on issues such as climate change, human rights, and global poverty, organizing campaigns, petitions, and awareness-raising activities.

Through participation in advocacy, adults not only contribute to global causes but also develop a sense of agency and responsibility. This sense of empowerment can lead to greater involvement in community activities, helping to create a ripple effect of positive change.

c. Global Travel and Cultural Exchange

For adults, one of the most effective ways to understand global citizenship is through travel and cultural exchange. Experiencing different cultures firsthand can be a transformative experience that fosters empathy, appreciation, and respect for diversity. Organizations that facilitate cultural exchange programs or volunteer travel opportunities can provide adults with the chance to live and work in different cultural contexts, broadening their understanding of global challenges.

Teaching global citizenship is a crucial endeavor that can be adapted to suit individuals of all ages. Whether through storytelling for young children, project-based learning for adolescents, or community engagement for adults, the goal is to foster an understanding of the interconnectedness of all people and the shared responsibility to address global challenges. By teaching values of empathy, social responsibility, and active engagement, educators can empower individuals to become active global citizens who contribute to creating a more just, equitable, and sustainable world. The practical approaches outlined here demonstrate that global citizenship education is not only possible at any age but is essential for building a more compassionate and responsible global society.

Chapter 6
Building a Global Community

A global community doesn't require a physical location; it's a community built on shared values, empathy, and mutual support. This chapter looks at examples of how communities around the world are transcending borders and building connections. Through stories of grassroots initiatives, nonprofit organizations, and cross-cultural partnerships, readers will gain insight into how global communities are formed and sustained.

Cross-cultural partnerships and collaborations.
Nonprofit and grassroots initiatives making a global impact

In a globalized world, cross-cultural partnerships and collaborations have become central to various sectors, including business, education, politics, and social initiatives. These partnerships involve the collaboration of individuals or groups from diverse cultural backgrounds, bringing together different values, beliefs, and practices. Cross-cultural psychology, a field that explores the impact of culture on human behavior, plays a crucial role in understanding how these partnerships function and how individuals can work together effectively across cultural boundaries.

In this chapter we will delve into the concept of cross-cultural partnerships, examining the challenges and opportunities they present, the importance of cultural understanding, and how cross-cultural psychology contributes to improving such collaborations. Through this exploration, we aim to understand how cultural dynamics influence human interactions and provide insights into fostering successful cross-cultural relationships.

Cross-Cultural Partnerships and Collaborations

Cross-cultural partnerships are collaborative relationships between individuals or organizations from different cultural backgrounds. In today's globalized world, businesses, governments, educational institutions, and non-governmental organizations (NGOs) are increasingly working across borders to tackle complex global issues, such as climate change, poverty, and health crises. The ability to form successful partnerships across cultures is essential for achieving shared goals.

1.   **The Importance of Cross-Cultural Partnerships**

Cross-cultural partnerships are essential for fostering innovation, expanding markets, and addressing global challenges. When individuals from different cultures come together, they bring unique perspectives and solutions to the table, which can lead to more creative outcomes. This diversity of thought is especially valuable in business environments where global expansion is often a key goal.

Just as an example, a multinational corporation that partners with local businesses in various countries can gain deeper insights into regional consumer preferences, local customs, and market conditions. This understanding is crucial for developing products that meet local needs while respecting cultural sensitivities. Similarly, international academic collaborations help broaden research perspectives by incorporating diverse methods and viewpoints.

2.   Challenges in Cross-Cultural Collaborations

Despite the many advantages, cross-cultural collaborations come with inherent challenges. One of the primary challenges is the potential for cultural misunderstandings. Cultural norms regarding communication styles, decision-making processes, and hierarchy can differ greatly. In some cultures, direct communication is valued, while in others, indirect communication is preferred. Similarly, attitudes toward authority can vary, with some cultures favoring a more hierarchical structure, while others embrace egalitarian approaches.

A Western organization accustomed to quick decision-making might face challenges when collaborating with a partner from a culture that emphasizes consensus-building and takes a longer time to reach decisions. These differences can lead to frustration, miscommunication, and delays. Overcoming such challenges requires an awareness of cultural differences and the willingness to adapt to alternative ways of working.

3.   The Role of Technology in Cross-Cultural Collaborations

The rise of digital communication tools has facilitated cross-cultural partnerships by overcoming geographical barriers. Platforms such as video conferencing, collaborative document sharing, and instant messaging allow individuals from different cultural backgrounds to collaborate in real-time, despite being located in different parts of the world. These tools help bridge gaps in time zones, reduce the impact of physical distance, and support faster decision-making.

However, reliance on technology can also exacerbate cultural differences. For example, virtual communication often lacks the non-verbal cues present in face-to-face interactions, which can make understanding emotions, tone, and intent more difficult. Additionally, not all cultures are equally comfortable with technology, and this can create a digital divide in terms of accessibility and engagement.

Cross-Cultural Psychology: Understanding Human Behavior Across Cultures

Cross-cultural psychology is the scientific study of human behavior and mental processes in different cultural contexts. It seeks to understand how culture shapes the way individuals think, feel, and behave. This branch of psychology provides valuable insights into how individuals from different cultures interact with one another, both within their own cultural group and in cross-cultural situations.

1.   **Theories and Frameworks in Cross-Cultural Psychology**

Several key theories and frameworks in cross-cultural psychology help explain how culture influences human behavior. One prominent theory is *cultural relativism*, which posits that beliefs, values, and behaviors must be understood within the context of the culture from which they originate. This theory challenges the notion of cultural superiority and emphasizes the need to respect and understand diverse cultural practices.

Another important concept is *cultural dimensions theory* by Geert Hofstede, which identifies six dimensions of cultural differences: power distance, individualism vs. collectivism, masculinity vs. femininity, uncertainty avoidance, long-term vs. short-term orientation, and indulgence vs. restraint. These dimensions help categorize cultures along various continuums and provide insights into how cultural values shape behavior in a variety of settings, including work, communication, and conflict resolution.

Understanding these cultural dimensions allows individuals and organizations to develop strategies for effective cross-cultural communication and collaboration. For example, cultures with high power distance may place a greater emphasis on respect for authority and hierarchy, while those with low power distance may favor more egalitarian structures.

2.   **Cultural Influence on Communication Styles**

Communication is one of the most crucial aspects of cross-cultural interactions, and cross-cultural psychology emphasizes how culture shapes communication behaviors. Cultures differ significantly in their use of verbal and non-verbal communication, as well as in their attitudes toward conflict, negotiation, and decision-making.

In high-context cultures, such as those in Japan and many Middle Eastern countries, communication relies heavily on implicit messages, body language, and context. In contrast, low-context cultures like the United States and many European countries place greater emphasis on explicit, direct communication. These differences can lead to misunderstandings if individuals are not attuned to the subtleties of each other's communication styles.

Non-verbal cues, such as eye contact, facial expressions, and gestures, also vary across cultures. Direct eye contact may be perceived as a sign of confidence in some cultures but as a challenge to authority in others. Similarly, hand gestures that are common in one culture may be offensive in another. Understanding these cultural differences in non-verbal communication is crucial for successful cross-cultural partnerships.

3.   Cultural Influences on Leadership and Decision-Making

Cross-cultural psychology also examines how cultural values shape leadership styles and decision-making processes. In individualistic cultures, leaders are often expected to make decisions independently and take personal responsibility for outcomes. In contrast, in collectivist cultures, decision-making is often more collaborative, with a focus on group consensus and harmony.

In business partnerships, understanding these differences can help bridge gaps in leadership expectations. A Western leader accustomed to making quick, individual decisions might need to adjust when working with a team from a culture that values group consensus and long deliberations. By recognizing these cultural preferences, leaders can adapt their approach to enhance cooperation and minimize friction.

4.   Cultural Adaptation and Cultural Intelligence

The concept of *cultural intelligence* (CQ) refers to an individual's ability to adapt to, understand, and work effectively across cultures. This ability is crucial for successful cross-cultural partnerships, as it enables individuals to navigate cultural differences with sensitivity and respect. High CQ involves cognitive, emotional, and behavioral components: knowledge about different cultures, the ability to relate to people from diverse backgrounds, and the capacity to adjust one's behavior in different cultural contexts.

Cultural adaptation is a dynamic process that involves learning about the host culture, adjusting one's behaviors, and seeking to understand and integrate cultural differences. People with high CQ are more likely to develop positive relationships with people from different cultures and succeed in cross-cultural collaborations.

Cross-cultural partnerships and collaborations are increasingly vital in today's world. They offer opportunities for innovation, growth, and tackling global challenges but also present significant challenges related to cultural differences. By applying the insights from cross-cultural psychology, individuals and organizations can better navigate these differences, enhance communication, and foster more effective collaborations.

Cross-cultural psychology provides a framework for understanding how culture shapes behavior, communication, leadership, and decision-making. Through cultural intelligence and an awareness of cultural dimensions, individuals can build more successful cross-cultural partnerships that respect and leverage cultural diversity. As the world becomes more interconnected, the ability to collaborate effectively across cultures will continue to be a key determinant of success in many areas of life.

Non-Profit and Grassroots Initiatives Making a Global Impact

In the last decades, non-profit and grassroots initiatives have emerged as critical actors in addressing some of the most pressing challenges faced by communities across the globe. These initiatives, often led by individuals or small organizations, have proven to be powerful tools for social change, enabling marginalized communities to advocate for their rights, address local issues, and create sustainable solutions. From tackling poverty and health crises to addressing environmental degradation and advocating for human rights, non-profit and grassroots movements are making a profound global impact.

Here, we will explore the role of non-profit and grassroots initiatives in addressing global issues, examining the key characteristics that enable them to make an impact, and providing examples of successful movements that have had significant global influence. Additionally, the challenges these initiatives face and the potential for future growth will be discussed.

The Role of Non-Profit and Grassroots Initiatives in Global Change

Non-profit and grassroots initiatives are often born out of the recognition that traditional systems and structures may not be adequately addressing the needs of marginalized communities. Unlike large-scale international organizations, which may struggle to connect with local communities, grassroots initiatives focus on the specific needs of people on the ground, drawing on local knowledge and fostering community participation. These initiatives aim to create sustainable and inclusive solutions through direct action, collaboration, and advocacy.

1.   Characteristics of Effective Non-Profit and Grassroots Initiatives

Successful non-profit and grassroots movements are typically characterized by their bottom-up approach, community empowerment, and adaptability. These initiatives are driven by the people they aim to serve, often starting with small-scale actions that gradually grow and gain momentum. They focus on building local capacity, promoting leadership within the community, and encouraging individuals to take ownership of their own development.

Another key characteristic of these initiatives is their ability to adapt to changing circumstances. Grassroots organizations, in particular, are able to respond quickly to emerging issues, whether they are political, social, or environmental. This flexibility allows them to be responsive to immediate needs, such as providing disaster relief or advocating for policy changes, while simultaneously working on long-term goals like systemic change.

Furthermore, non-profit and grassroots initiatives emphasize collaboration and networking, both locally and globally. These organizations often form partnerships with other organizations, governments, and international bodies to amplify their efforts and bring attention to critical issues. By combining local expertise with global networks, they can maximize their reach and impact.

Examples of Non-Profit and Grassroots Initiatives with Global Impact

Several non-profit and grassroots initiatives have achieved significant global impact by addressing diverse issues, from health and education to environmental sustainability and social justice. These movements demonstrate the power of collective action and the importance of grassroots leadership in creating lasting change.

1.   The Grameen Bank and Microfinance

Founded by Nobel Peace Prize laureate Muhammad Yunus, the Grameen Bank revolutionized the concept of microfinance and demonstrated how small loans could empower individuals, particularly women, in impoverished communities. The Grameen Bank's approach to lending, which focuses on providing small, low-interest loans to people who do not have access to traditional banking services, has had a profound impact on poverty alleviation.

Through its work, the Grameen Bank has lifted millions of people out of poverty by enabling them to start small businesses, improve their homes, and send their children to school. The success of microfinance as a model for poverty reduction has been adopted worldwide, with similar initiatives now operating in countries across Africa, Asia, and Latin America. The Grameen Bank's success exemplifies the power of grassroots financial empowerment and its ability to transform communities on a global scale.

2.   The Fair-Trade Movement

The Fair-Trade movement is a grassroots initiative aimed at ensuring that producers in developing countries receive fair wages and work under safe, ethical conditions. Fair Trade organizations work directly with farmers, artisans, and producers, providing them with access to international markets while ensuring they receive fair compensation for their work.

Fair Trade products—ranging from coffee and chocolate to clothing and handicrafts—are sold in countries around the world, with consumers increasingly aware of the ethical implications of their purchasing decisions. This movement has not only improved the livelihoods of millions of producers but has also raised awareness about the global inequalities in trade and commerce. By emphasizing direct trade relationships and sustainable practices, the Fair-Trade movement has made a lasting impact on global supply chains.

3.   Global Health Initiatives: Partners In Health

Partners In Health (PIH) is a non-profit organization that has made a significant global impact by providing healthcare to impoverished communities in countries like Haiti, Rwanda, and Liberia. Founded by Dr. Paul Farmer, PIH focuses on delivering high-quality healthcare to underserved populations, regardless of their ability to pay. The organization works with local governments and communities to strengthen healthcare infrastructure, improve health outcomes, and address the social determinants of health.

One of PIH's most notable achievements is its work in combatting infectious diseases like tuberculosis and HIV/AIDS. In addition to providing direct medical care,

PIH emphasizes the importance of community-based approaches, training local healthcare workers, and promoting long-term health education. Through its work, PIH has demonstrated the importance of global solidarity in tackling health inequities and has set a powerful example of how grassroots organizations can have a global impact.

4.   Environmental Advocacy: Greenpeace

Greenpeace, an international environmental organization, has had a profound impact on global environmental issues by raising awareness, conducting direct action campaigns, and lobbying for policy change. Known for its bold and often controversial campaigns, Greenpeace focuses on issues such as climate change, deforestation, overfishing, and pollution.

Greenpeace's grassroots approach has enabled it to mobilize millions of individuals worldwide to take action on environmental issues. By organizing protests, conducting investigations, and using media to highlight environmental crises, Greenpeace has forced governments and corporations to confront pressing environmental issues. The organization's advocacy has contributed to significant global policy changes, including international agreements on climate change and the protection of endangered species.

5.   Social Justice Movements: Black Lives Matter

The Black Lives Matter (BLM) movement is an example of a grassroots initiative that has sparked a global conversation about racial injustice and inequality. Founded in 2013, the movement has grown into a global network advocating for the end of police brutality, racial profiling, and systemic racism. Through protests, social media campaigns, and grassroots organizing, BLM has mobilized millions of people worldwide to demand justice for Black communities.

While BLM started in the United States, it quickly became a global movement, with protests and advocacy taking place in countries across Europe, Africa, and Latin America. The movement has played a key role in raising awareness about racial discrimination and has pushed for policy changes in law enforcement, education, and criminal justice systems. Its global impact is a testament to the power of grassroots organizing and the ability of individuals to spark widespread social and political change.

Challenges Faced by Non-Profit and Grassroots Initiatives

While non-profit and grassroots initiatives have had a significant global impact, they also face several challenges that can hinder their effectiveness and sustainability. One of the most common challenges is limited funding. Many grassroots organizations operate with limited resources, relying on donations, volunteer labor, and small-scale grants. This can restrict their ability to scale their efforts, reach more people, and invest in long-term projects.

Another challenge is the difficulty of navigating political and social barriers. Grassroots initiatives, especially those advocating for human rights or environmental justice, may face opposition from governments, corporations, or other powerful stakeholders. In some cases, activists and organizers have faced threats, harassment, or even imprisonment.

Despite these challenges, many non-profit and grassroots organizations have found ways to overcome these obstacles by building strong networks, collaborating with other organizations, and engaging in advocacy and public awareness campaigns. The resilience and determination of these initiatives continue to drive meaningful change across the globe.

Non-profit and grassroots initiatives are crucial drivers of global change, addressing complex social, economic, and environmental issues through localized, community-driven solutions. From microfinance and fair trade to environmental advocacy and social justice, these initiatives have made a significant impact by empowering communities, raising awareness, and advocating for systemic change. Despite facing challenges related to funding, political opposition, and resource limitations, non-profit and grassroots organizations continue to play a vital role in creating a more equitable and sustainable world.

As global challenges continue to evolve, the role of grassroots movements and non-profit organizations will remain essential. Their ability to connect with local communities, build global networks, and create innovative solutions positions them as key actors in shaping a more just and sustainable future for all.

How Individuals Can Connect and Build Their Own Global Communities

In today's hyper-connected world, individuals have unprecedented opportunities to connect with others across geographical, cultural, and social boundaries. The rapid advancement of technology, particularly through the internet, has revolutionized the way people interact, collaborate, and build relationships. Whether driven by professional goals, personal interests, or shared values, the desire to form global communities has become a hallmark of the modern era.

Building a global community is not solely the domain of large organizations or nation-states; individuals now play an essential role in creating networks that transcend borders. How can individuals connect with others across the world and build their own global communities? We will examine the importance of digital platforms, shared interests and goals, cultural exchange, and collaborative efforts in building meaningful, inclusive, and sustainable global communities.

The Role of Technology in Facilitating Global Connections

The internet has fundamentally changed how individuals can connect and build relationships. Social media platforms, messaging apps, online forums, and collaborative tools offer individuals the ability to interact in real time, regardless of their location. Technology removes the barriers of time and space, enabling individuals to engage in conversations, share ideas, and participate in communities without needing to be physically present.

1.   **Social Media and Networking Platforms**

Platforms like Facebook, X (former Twitter), Instagram, LinkedIn, and more recently, specialized forums like Reddit or Discord, have allowed individuals to connect based on common interests, professions, and ideologies. These platforms facilitate the creation of online communities where people can interact with like-minded individuals, share knowledge, and form friendships. A user can join a global network based on their personal interests, whether it is related to fitness, travel, literature, activism, or professional development.

For instance, platforms like LinkedIn enable professionals to connect, share career insights, collaborate on projects, and even find job opportunities around the world. Similarly, Facebook groups and subreddits allow individuals to interact with others who share common hobbies, concerns, or goals. These spaces foster a sense of belonging and allow individuals to build relationships that extend beyond their local environments.

2.   **Digital Collaboration Tools**

Another critical factor in building global communities is the ability to collaborate digitally. Platforms such as Google Docs, Slack, Zoom, and Trello have made it easier for individuals to work together, share ideas, and organize projects in a collaborative environment. Whether it is a group of entrepreneurs building a global business or a group of activists organizing for a cause, these tools facilitate seamless communication and coordination.

Open-source projects, where people from around the world contribute to the development of software or online content, are prime examples of how digital collaboration can foster a global sense of community. Many open-source software platforms, such as Linux, WordPress, or Mozilla Firefox, rely on global contributions to innovate and develop technologies that have widespread impact.

Shared Interests and Common Goals: The Foundation of Global Communities

While technology is an essential tool for connecting individuals, the foundation of any lasting global community lies in shared interests, values, or goals. Building a global community requires individuals to come together around a common purpose or mission, whether it is social, environmental, cultural, or political. This shared vision helps create bonds and a sense of collective identity, driving collaboration and engagement.

1.   **Passion for Causes: Social Activism and Advocacy**

One of the most significant ways individuals build global communities is through social activism. With the rise of social media and the internet, individuals passionate about causes such as climate change, human rights, racial justice, or gender equality can find others who share their vision and collaborate on campaigns, raise awareness, and drive change. Movements like #MeToo, Black Lives Matter, or Fridays for Future have demonstrated the power of individuals coming together through digital networks to advocate for social justice and create global movements.

Social media allows individuals to share personal stories, mobilize supporters, and influence global public opinion. These platforms have given rise to a new form of global activism, where individuals can advocate for change without the need for physical proximity. By using hashtags, organizing online petitions, and engaging in virtual protests, individuals can raise awareness and make a significant impact on a global scale.

2.   Cultural Exchange and Learning

Building global communities is also about sharing and learning from different cultures. As people from diverse backgrounds come together, they create a space for cultural exchange that enriches individuals' lives and deepens their understanding of the world. Platforms like YouTube, TikTok, and Instagram allow individuals to share their cultures, experiences, and traditions with others across the globe, offering opportunities for cross-cultural learning.

Language learning apps, such as Duolingo, Babbel, or HelloTalk, also facilitate connections between individuals from different parts of the world who want to learn new languages and explore different cultures. Such platforms enable individuals to form relationships that transcend borders, while simultaneously broadening their own worldview and cultural understanding.

Cultural exchange initiatives, such as travel blogs, cooking classes, and virtual events, enable individuals to create cross-cultural communities that foster respect, empathy, and mutual understanding. This engagement allows people to break down stereotypes, challenge misconceptions, and appreciate the richness of human diversity.

The Power of Collaboration: Working Together to Achieve Global Goals

To build a truly impactful global community, individuals need to focus on collaboration. Global communities are not only about connecting for social or cultural reasons but also about coming together to address common challenges and solve problems. Collaboration allows people from different backgrounds and areas of expertise to pool their resources, skills, and knowledge to work toward a common goal.

1.   Crowdsourcing and Crowdfunding Initiatives

Crowdsourcing and crowdfunding have become powerful tools for individuals to come together and fund projects that can make a difference on a global scale. Platforms like Kickstarter, GoFundMe, and Indiegogo allow sandividuals to raise funds for entrepreneurial ventures, community projects, and humanitarian efforts. These platforms make it possible for a small group of people to turn their ideas into reality by tapping into a global pool of financial and intellectual resources.

For example, crowdfunding campaigns have supported humanitarian efforts in disaster-stricken areas, the development of new technologies to address global issues like clean energy, and social initiatives that support marginalized communities. By leveraging a global community of donors, creators, and supporters, individuals can launch initiatives that have the potential to reach and positively impact large populations.

2.   **Global Volunteer Networks**

Individuals can also build global communities through volunteerism. Numerous organizations connect volunteers with projects and causes that need assistance, allowing people to contribute their time and expertise to initiatives that benefit others. Websites like VolunteerMatch, Idealist, and Workaway facilitate global volunteerism, providing individuals with the opportunity to give back to communities around the world.

Additionally, organizations like the United Nations Volunteers program and Habitat for Humanity organize global volunteer opportunities, where individuals can engage in meaningful work that addresses global challenges, such as poverty, education, health, and environmental sustainability. These volunteer initiatives not only help individuals make a tangible impact but also foster a sense of global solidarity and connection.

Building Sustainable and Inclusive Global Communities

While connecting and collaborating on a global scale is exciting, it is essential that individuals focus on creating communities that are sustainable, inclusive, and respectful of diverse voices and perspectives. Successful global communities prioritize equity and ensure that all members, regardless of their background or identity, have the opportunity to contribute and benefit.

1.   **Inclusivity and Representation**

For a global community to thrive, it must be inclusive and represent the interests of people from different cultural, socioeconomic, and geographic backgrounds. This inclusivity ensures that global communities are not dominated by one perspective but rather reflect the diversity of experiences and voices around the world. By making space for marginalized groups, a more balanced and empathetic community can be created, where everyone's contributions are valued.

In practice, this means ensuring that online platforms and initiatives are accessible to people from different parts of the world, and that communities prioritize representation in leadership positions and decision-making processes. By fostering an environment of inclusivity, individuals can ensure that global communities are truly global and not limited by a particular demographic, or even worse, not controlled by malicious-narcissistic oligarchs, who's only interest is to accumulate more and more power and wealth at the expense of the oppression of individuals, communities and countries.

Although global platforms are now equally accessible to people of different backgrounds, statuses and cultures around the world, we must never lose sight of the social, political and economic agendas of their owners. Yes, all these platforms are private properties, owned by their creators or someone with enough money to buy them like any other business. Therefore, we must keep our eyes wide open and know who they are, observe their values, history, origins, political and social positions, behaviors towards their employees, minorities, women and those who oppose their views. This will give us a clear picture of what they can do with our information, posts and personal identity, as well as the "ethics" that govern these digital spaces, any fake news to manipulate the masses for their personal and political-economic interests. With the proliferation of extreme authoritarian political regimes around the world, freedom and accessibility become scarcer and human rights can easily be violated using channels like these, in a subtle and unnoticed way to the less attentive and unsuspecting. Having lived through the 20 years of military dictatorship in Brazil, from the mid-1960s to the 1980s, I saw up close the immeasurable abuses, horrors, corruption, arbitrariness, immorality, brutality and injustices imposed by authoritarian regimes on individuals, families, communities and countries. Considering that, at that time, there was no social media, internet and computers were the privilege of institutions and very few scientists, which required much more effort to spy, control and violently oppress the population, imagine how much easier this control and abuse would be in today's world.

2.   **Sustainability in Community Building**

Building sustainable communities requires individuals to think long-term. It's important to consider the impact of global community efforts on the environment, economies, and societies. Whether it's advocating for sustainable practices, supporting ethical businesses, or ensuring that initiatives are resilient in the face of challenges, sustainability should be a guiding principle in global community building.

By promoting eco-friendly practices, ethical consumption, and sustainable development goals, individuals can build global communities that contribute to the well-being of people and the planet for generations to come.

The ability for individuals to connect and build their own global communities has never been more accessible or important. Through the use of technology, shared interests, and collaborative efforts, individuals can engage with others around the world and create communities that transcend geographic boundaries. Whether through social media, volunteerism, or crowdfunding, individuals can leverage global networks to bring about change, address challenges, and create meaningful connections.

As individuals continue to build global communities, it is essential to focus on inclusivity, sustainability, and respect for diversity. By working together toward shared goals and supporting each other, individuals can foster a more interconnected and compassionate world.

Chapter 7
The Challenges of Global Citizenship

The path of global citizenship isn't always easy. In this chapter, we address the common challenges: cultural misunderstandings, political tensions, economic disparities, and more. By understanding these obstacles, readers can better prepare themselves to approach global citizenship with resilience, patience, and a commitment to progress.

<u>Overcoming Cultural and Political Tensions: A Path to Global Unity</u>

In today's interconnected world, cultural and political tensions are increasingly prevalent, often manifesting in conflicts that threaten global stability and social harmony. From international disputes to local social divisions, these tensions can stem from a variety of factors including historical legacies, ethnic differences, ideological divides, and economic disparities. However, overcoming these tensions is not only possible but essential for fostering peace, progress, and mutual understanding. We may ask ourselves, how to find ways in which can cultural and political tensions be addressed and resolved through dialogue, education, empathy, and systemic change? By examining historical examples, current strategies, and potential future solutions, we can envision a world in which cultural and political conflicts no longer stand in the way of collective progress.

Understanding Cultural and Political Tensions

Cultural tensions often arise from differences in values, beliefs, and traditions among various groups of people. These differences can be based on ethnicity, religion, language, historical experiences or political-economic differences. Cultural tensions are not inherently negative; in fact, diversity can be a source of strength. However, when people from different cultures or economic status fail to understand or respect each other's differences, misunderstandings and prejudice can ensue. In the worst cases, these tensions can lead to discrimination, marginalization, and violence.

Political tensions, on the other hand, are typically linked to disagreements over governance, resources, and power. Political ideologies and systems of governance vary widely across the world, and when these differences are not reconciled through peaceful means, they can escalate into conflict. Political tensions can also arise from inequalities within a nation, such as economic disparities, lack of political fanrepresentation, or authoritarian governance, leading to social unrest and calls for reform.

Both cultural and political tensions are interconnected, as cultural differences often play a role in shaping political ideologies, and political decisions can exacerbate or mitigate cultural conflicts. In order to address these tensions, it is essential to first understand their origins and the ways in which they affect individuals and societies.

Finding consensus and common grounds in both cases require knowledge of each other's points of view as well as moral and emotional maturity to compromise in pro of the common good. History shows us numerous examples of elites and oligarchies holding on to power and wealth at the cost of oppression and abuse of the rest of the community. This can work for a while but inevitably ends up in conflicts and war. Understanding our history across eras and cultures, detecting the patterns and the agendas behind actions from government and economic elites, we can avoid being manipulated into supporting those who does not have the interest of the common good in mind. Let us not to be fooled by their rhetoric but observe them on their actions and behaviors.

Doing the right thing with regard to the environment requires effort and money invested in green energy, technology, training and the application of environmentally safe practices. Irresponsible corporations refuse to spend money on anything that does not generate immediate profits. However, they spare no expense in lobbying against environmental protection laws and regulations and in creating campaigns with false anti-scientific ideas to convince voters and communities to support their illicit ways of doing business. This is not only irresponsible, but also criminal, as they know and ignore the implications of such conduct, causing illness and death to millions of people. The destruction of ecosystems leads to an increase in global temperatures, which generates climate disasters, water, air and food pollution, and causes global pandemics of all kinds. Their vision is so short-sighted and selfish that they ignore the fact that they are killing themselves and their descendants in the process: a true epiphany of emotional immaturity.

The Role of Dialogue and Communication

One of the most effective tools in overcoming cultural and political tensions is dialogue. Open, honest, and respectful communication fosters mutual understanding and allows people to express their concerns and grievances in a constructive manner. Through dialogue, individuals can move beyond stereotypes and misconceptions, realizing that many of their differences are not as insurmountable as they may seem at first.

At the international level, diplomacy plays a crucial role in managing political tensions between countries. Diplomatic negotiations allow for the peaceful resolution of disputes and provide a platform for countries to find common ground. Similarly, at the local level, community dialogue can bridge divides between different cultural or ethnic groups. It is important for these conversations to be inclusive, allowing all voices to be heard, especially those who have been historically marginalized or oppressed.

In many cases, dialogue can be facilitated by third parties, such as mediators or peacekeeping organizations. These intermediaries can help to create a safe space for difficult conversations and ensure that discussions remain productive rather than degenerating into conflict. Additionally, international organizations like the United Nations (UN) and regional bodies such as the European Union (EU) play a vital role in promoting dialogue and conflict resolution on a global scale.

Education as a Tool for Tolerance and Empathy

Education is another powerful tool for overcoming cultural and political tensions. By teaching individuals about different cultures, histories, and political systems, education can help dispel myths and stereotypes, fostering greater empathy and understanding. In many cases, cultural tensions arise from ignorance—people simply do not understand the experiences or worldviews of others. Through educational programs that promote cross-cultural understanding and respect, societies can begin to break down these barriers.

Education should also focus on developing critical thinking skills, allowing individuals to question political ideologies that instigate divisions, and recognize the complexities of cultural differences. This can help prevent the rise of extremist views that often stem from oversimplified and polarized narratives. In the last decades, United States have seen a radicalization of extreme right wind political sectors with supporters who are adopting the racist, chauvinistic, discriminatory and violent narratives of those leaders. Not by coincidence, educational standards are declining at exponential levels, with the great majority of American citizens reading at or bellow 6th grade level. Furthermore, education can play a key role in teaching individuals about their rights and responsibilities within a society, empowering them to participate in the political process and advocate for change in a peaceful and constructive manner.

In post-conflict societies, education can also serve as a tool for reconciliation. In places like Rwanda, where ethnic tensions and violence left deep scars, educational programs aimed at fostering unity and healing have been instrumental in rebuilding relationships between different communities. By focusing on shared values and common goals, education can help individuals move beyond past grievances and work together for a better future.

The Power of Empathy and Understanding

Empathy is crucial in overcoming cultural and political tensions. It allows individuals to put themselves in the shoes of others, understanding their struggles and perspectives. Empathy can bridge divides by highlighting the common humanity that exists despite cultural or political differences. When people are able to empathize with others, they are more likely to engage in peaceful dialogue and seek compromise rather than confrontation.

One of the most powerful examples of empathy in action is seen in the efforts to heal after major conflicts. In post-apartheid South Africa, for instance, the Truth and Reconciliation Commission (TRC) was established to allow individuals to share their experiences of suffering and injustice. Through this process, victims and perpetrators alike were able to engage in a collective process of healing and understanding. The TRC's focus on restorative justice, rather than punitive measures, allowed South Africa to move forward as a nation, despite the deep scars left by apartheid.

Empathy also plays a key role in overcoming political tensions. In polarized political environments, it is easy for individuals to demonize those who hold opposing views. However, by fostering empathy and recognizing the humanity of political adversaries, it is possible to find common ground and work toward solutions that benefit everyone. Political leaders, in particular, have a responsibility to model empathy and encourage constructive dialogue, rather than exacerbating divisions for personal or partisan gain.

Structural Change and Policy Reforms

While dialogue, education, and empathy are important tools in overcoming cultural and political tensions, they must be accompanied by structural changes and policy reforms to address the root causes of these tensions. Inequality, injustice, and lack of representation are often at the heart of political conflicts, and without addressing these issues, tensions are likely to persist.

In many cases, political reforms are necessary to ensure that all individuals have equal access to power and resources. This might involve implementing democratic reforms to ensure free and fair elections, strengthening human rights protections, or creating policies that promote economic equality. In regions where ethnic or religious groups are marginalized, policies that promote inclusivity and representation can help to reduce cultural tensions and foster greater unity.

At the international level, efforts to resolve political tensions often involve diplomatic negotiations aimed at creating fair and just agreements. Treaties, peace accords, and trade agreements can serve as frameworks for resolving political disputes and ensuring that all parties are treated equitably. For example, the Paris Agreement on climate change represents a global effort to address a common problem, with countries from diverse political and cultural backgrounds working together toward a shared goal.

Overcoming cultural and political tensions is a complex and ongoing process that requires a multifaceted approach. Through dialogue, education, empathy, and systemic reforms, it is possible to bridge divides and build a more peaceful and unified world. While challenges remain, historical examples show that it is possible to move past conflict and create societies where individuals from diverse cultural and political backgrounds can live together in harmony. By fostering mutual understanding, promoting inclusivity, and addressing the underlying causes of tension, we can build a future in which cultural and political conflicts no longer stand in the way of global progress.

<u>Navigating Economic Disparities and Addressing Inequality: A Path to Sustainable Development</u>

Economic inequality has been a persistent challenge for societies across the globe. It refers to the unequal distribution of wealth, income, and resources within and between countries, and it manifests in a wide range of disparities, from disparities in education and healthcare to differences in employment opportunities and access to capital. As the world becomes increasingly interconnected, the consequences of these disparities are more pronounced, affecting individuals, communities, and nations. While some argue that economic inequality is a natural consequence of a market-driven economy, others assert that it is an issue that requires urgent attention and systemic change. Following, we will explore the root causes of economic disparities, examine their impacts, and suggests practical strategies for addressing inequality. By analyzing policies and approaches from across the world, we aim to demonstrate that navigating economic disparities is not only an economic and political challenge but a moral imperative that must be addressed for sustainable and inclusive development.

Understanding Economic Disparities

Economic disparities arise from multiple factors, including historical legacies, geographic location, education, race, gender, and policy decisions. These disparities are often compounded by systems of power and privilege that perpetuate unequal access to resources and opportunities. Understanding the causes of economic inequality is essential to crafting effective solutions.

At the global level, historical events such as colonialism, imperialism, and slavery have left deep economic scars. Colonized countries often had their resources exploited and their economic systems distorted, leading to long-term poverty and underdevelopment. Even after the end of formal colonial rule, many of these countries continue to face significant economic challenges due to the persistence of exploitative trade practices, debt burdens, and lack of access to international markets.

Within countries, economic disparities can be exacerbated by unequal educational opportunities, discriminatory labor markets, and inadequate healthcare systems. For example, in many societies, people from marginalized racial and ethnic groups face systemic barriers to employment, wealth accumulation, and access to quality education. Gender inequality also plays a significant role, as women and girls often face discrimination in the workplace, earning lower wages and encountering limited career advancement opportunities compared to men. These disparities lead to a vicious cycle in which disadvantaged groups have fewer opportunities to break out of poverty or achieve upward mobility.

Furthermore, globalization has brought about increased wealth and opportunities for some, but it has also intensified inequality. While multinational corporations and global financial markets have facilitated economic growth in certain sectors, they have also contributed to the concentration of wealth in the hands of a few, often exacerbating income inequality. In many developed nations, the gap between the wealthy elite and the middle and lower classes continues to grow, with economic policies that favor the rich and allow for tax avoidance and wealth accumulation at the top.

The Impacts of Economic Inequality

Economic inequality has far-reaching consequences that go beyond income disparities. One of the most significant impacts is social mobility. In societies with high levels of inequality, the opportunity for individuals to improve their economic status is often limited by their starting point. Children born into poverty are more likely to remain in poverty, and those born into wealth enjoy greater opportunities for success. This lack of social mobility creates a cycle of inequality that is difficult to break, perpetuating intergenerational poverty and disenfranchisement.

Moreover, economic inequality undermines social cohesion and stability. When large segments of the population feel excluded from economic opportunities, they are more likely to experience frustration and alienation. This can lead to social unrest, political instability, and the erosion of trust in institutions. High levels of inequality are also linked to worse health outcomes, as people in lower income brackets have less access to quality healthcare, proper nutrition, and safe living conditions. This disparity contributes to higher rates of chronic diseases, mental health issues, and shorter life expectancies in disadvantaged populations.

Economic inequality also affects economic growth. While some argue that inequality is a natural byproduct of a capitalist economy, others contend that extreme inequality can hinder overall economic progress. Joseph Stiglitz, a renowned business and economics scholar, presents this very well on his book "The Price of Inequality": When wealth is concentrated in the hands of a few, the majority of the population lacks the purchasing power to drive demand for goods and services. This limits economic opportunities for businesses and stifles growth. In addition, when large portions of the population are excluded from economic participation, they are not able to contribute their skills and talents to the economy, thus preventing societies from fully utilizing their human capital.

Approaches to Addressing Economic Inequality

Addressing economic inequality requires a multi-faceted approach, as no single solution can tackle such a complex and systemic issue. Both policy interventions and social movements play critical roles in reducing disparities and promoting inclusive development. The following sections outline some of the most promising approaches to addressing inequality.

1.   **Progressive Taxation and Wealth Redistribution**

One of the most direct ways to address economic inequality is through progressive taxation. In a progressive tax system, higher earners pay a larger percentage of their income in taxes, which can be used to fund social services, infrastructure, and public goods that benefit society as a whole. Revenue from progressive taxes can help reduce income inequality by redistributing wealth and providing opportunities for those at the bottom of the income ladder.

Countries like the Scandinavian nations—Sweden, Norway, and Denmark—have adopted progressive tax systems and have seen remarkable success in reducing income inequality. In these countries, taxes fund universal healthcare, free or affordable education, and comprehensive social safety nets, which contribute to a more equitable distribution of resources and opportunities.

2.   **Investing in Education and Workforce Development**

Education is a critical tool in breaking the cycle of poverty and addressing economic disparities. By investing in education, particularly in underprivileged areas, governments can provide individuals with the knowledge and skills needed to access higher-paying jobs and improve their socio-economic status. However, it is essential that education systems are not only accessible but also equitable, providing quality education regardless of a student's background.

Additionally, workforce development programs that focus on skill-building and vocational training can help individuals transition into well-paying jobs, particularly in sectors like technology and renewable energy. These programs can also offer support for workers displaced by automation or economic shifts, ensuring that all members of society have opportunities for growth and advancement.

3. Universal Basic Income (UBI) and Social Safety Nets

Another innovative approach to addressing economic inequality is the implementation of Universal Basic Income (UBI). UBI is a policy in which all citizens receive a regular, unconditional payment from the government to cover basic living expenses. Proponents argue that UBI can reduce poverty and income inequality by providing a financial safety net for all individuals, ensuring that no one falls below a certain standard of living.

While UBI has been tested in several countries and regions, its effectiveness remains a subject of debate. However, variations of this idea, such as expanded unemployment benefits, child allowances, and direct cash transfers, have been successful in alleviating poverty in some places. For example, during the COVID-19 pandemic, many countries implemented temporary cash assistance programs, which helped to reduce the economic hardship faced by vulnerable populations.

4. Promoting Gender Equality and Racial Justice

Economic disparities are often intertwined with issues of gender and racial inequality. To address these inequalities, it is crucial to implement policies that promote gender equality in the workplace, such as equal pay for equal work, paid family leave, and affordable childcare. Empowering women economically not only improves the lives of individuals but also contributes to overall economic growth, as women tend to reinvest their income into their families and communities.

Similarly, policies that promote racial justice, such as affirmative action, anti-discrimination laws, and targeted economic programs for marginalized communities, can help to reduce racial disparities in income and wealth. In countries like South Africa, post-apartheid economic reforms have aimed to address racial inequalities in the labor market, although challenges remain.

Economic disparities and inequality are global issues that require urgent and sustained attention. While the causes of inequality are complex and varied, the consequences are clear: economic inequality undermines social cohesion, stifles economic growth, and perpetuates cycles of poverty. To address these disparities, governments, businesses, and individuals must work together to implement policies that promote wealth redistribution, invest in education and workforce development, and ensure that all individuals, regardless of race, gender, or socio-economic status, have access to opportunities for success. Addressing economic inequality is not just an economic or political challenge—it is a moral imperative that requires collective action and a commitment to creating a fairer, more just world for all.

<u>Strategies for Effective Global Engagement Despite Challenges</u>

Global engagement—be it in terms of diplomacy, trade, cultural exchange, or environmental cooperation—is both an opportunity and a challenge. The need for international collaboration has never been greater, as the world faces issues such as climate change, pandemics, economic inequality, and geopolitical tensions. However, despite these shared global challenges, navigating the complexities of international relations can be daunting. Differences in political systems, cultural values, economic structures, and even national priorities often complicate efforts to forge meaningful partnerships. Following we will explore the strategies for effective global engagement, emphasizing the importance of communication, cooperation, and adaptability in addressing global issues, overcoming challenges, and fostering long-term partnerships.

Understanding the Challenges to Global Engagement

Before delving into strategies for effective engagement, it is essential to first identify the challenges that hinder successful international cooperation. These challenges vary, depending on the region, issue at hand, and stakeholders involved, but some of the most prominent obstacles include:

1.   **Political and Ideological Divides**: Nations are often driven by differing political ideologies, which can lead to conflict over policies, governance systems, and alliances. For instance, democratic and authoritarian regimes may find it difficult to cooperate due to fundamental differences in political freedoms, human rights, and governance structures. Similarly, ideological differences, such as those seen in the ongoing tensions between Western liberal democracies and non-Western powers, complicate consensus-building on global issues.

2.   **Cultural Differences and Misunderstandings**: The diversity of cultural norms, values, and practices across the world can lead to misinterpretations and misunderstandings. What is considered acceptable or efficient in one country may be seen as offensive or ineffective in another. These cultural differences can hinder collaboration, particularly when dealing with delicate issues like human rights, social justice, and religion.

3.   **Economic Disparities**: Uneven economic development and inequality between nations also pose significant barriers to global cooperation. Wealthier nations often hold more power in international decision-making, leading to frustrations among developing countries that feel their needs and interests are sidelined. Additionally, economic disparities complicate efforts to address issues such as climate change, as richer

nations are seen as having a larger responsibility for emissions, while poorer countries argue that they require economic development to improve living standards.

4.   **Global Conflicts and Security Issues**: Ongoing wars, territorial disputes, and regional conflicts can make it difficult for nations to collaborate. In some cases, security concerns take precedence over other forms of global engagement, and in others, competing military interests undermine cooperative efforts.

5.   **Environmental Challenges**: Climate change, resource depletion, and biodiversity loss are global problems that require coordinated action. However, addressing these issues is often challenging due to the complex interactions between nations' economic activities, energy policies, and environmental goals. Moreover, environmental issues like deforestation or pollution are frequently entangled with questions of economic development, industrial growth, and political sovereignty.

6. **Emotional and Moral Immaturity:** Immaturity and underdeveloped morality creates substantial obstacles to overcome the challenges of global engagement. People tend to prioritize their personal interests over collective ones, which reflects lower levels of emotional and moral development. Those with higher levels of morality and consciousness react with indignation to the injustices and suffering of others and feel naturally compelled to help them.

The development of consciousness is the most effective motivator for solving both social and environmental problems. To illustrate this correlation, we can mention the consciousness of a civilized adult with a good education, who understands the importance of personal hygiene in preventing diseases and promoting the well-being of individuals. A child, naturally with little knowledge of life, refuses and feels unmotivated to take a bath or brush his/her teeth daily, because he/she only does it to comply with external rules from his parents or caregivers. But as they grow up and become more knowledgeable about science and anatomy, they understand that bacteria, viruses and fungi can be annihilated through good personal hygiene and thus prevent the individual from contracting diseases.

This awareness leads them to naturally want to incorporate good hygiene habits into their daily lives and to feel uncomfortable if for some reason they cannot do so. The collective context and social practices also influence individuals in their habits, but consciousness is fundamental in the choices of behavior and worldview.

Likewise, awareness of the collective reality, on which we undoubtedly depend on each other in this complex and diverse universe, leads individuals and communities to strive to give up their privileges or use them to create a positive impact in the construction of more egalitarian and fair societies.

Fighting against inequalities and bringing justice to the underprivileged are mature actions and being altruistic reflects a higher level of consciousness, since, whether we like it or not, we are part of an indivisible whole, as we will develop better in the following chapters.

Strategies for Effective Global Engagement

Despite these numerous challenges, there are a range of strategies that can foster effective global engagement. These strategies are not one-size-fits-all solutions but rather principles that can be adapted to suit various circumstances and objectives. The following strategies are essential for navigating the complexities of global collaboration:

1.   Building Strong Diplomatic Relationships

Diplomacy remains one of the most critical tools for fostering international cooperation. Effective diplomacy relies on building trust, respect, and mutual understanding between nations. This is achieved through sustained dialogue, active listening, and respect for differing viewpoints.

Diplomatic engagement involves not only government-to-government interactions but also involving non-state actors, such as NGOs, multinational corporations, and local community groups, in discussions.

One key element of successful diplomacy is the ability to manage and resolve conflicts. This requires diplomats to be skilled in negotiation, conflict resolution, and mediation. In some cases, third-party mediators or international organizations like the United Nations (UN) can facilitate dialogue and ensure that agreements are balanced and sustainable. By engaging in constructive diplomacy, countries can find common ground on a wide range of issues, from peacekeeping and trade to climate change and health.

2.   Promoting Multilateralism and Inclusive Partnerships

One of the most effective strategies for overcoming global challenges is multilateralism, or the pursuit of solutions through international cooperation involving multiple parties. Multilateral institutions like the UN, the World Trade Organization (WTO), and the World Health Organization (WHO) provide platforms for countries to engage in dialogue and negotiation on issues that affect the global community.

Multilateralism is particularly essential in addressing issues that transcend national borders, such as climate change, global health crises, and the refugee crisis. By working together in coalitions, countries can pool their resources and expertise, share responsibility, and ensure that decisions are made collectively. Multilateral approaches are often more inclusive, as they allow smaller or less powerful nations to participate in decision-making processes alongside larger states.

To make multilateralism more effective, inclusivity is crucial. It is important to ensure that all stakeholders—particularly those from marginalized communities or developing countries—are represented in global forums. Without inclusive participation, the resulting agreements may fail to address the needs of those most affected by global challenges, leading to frustration and distrust.

3.   **Leveraging Technology and Innovation for Global Solutions**

Technology and innovation have the potential to transform global engagement by offering new solutions to persistent problems. In areas such as healthcare, energy, agriculture, and education, technological advancements can help address critical challenges, while also facilitating global cooperation. For example, the rapid development of COVID-19 vaccines was a result of international collaboration in research and development, with the global scientific community sharing data and resources to create effective vaccines.

Similarly, renewable energy technologies, such as solar power and wind energy, offer opportunities for collaboration between countries to combat climate change. Wealthier nations can share green technologies with developing countries, enabling them to leapfrog traditional fossil fuel-based energy systems and develop sustainable economies.

Technology also facilitates communication and coordination across borders. In a digitally connected world, countries can more easily share information, conduct virtual meetings, and collaborate on research. Additionally, digital diplomacy—using social media and online platforms for foreign policy engagement—has become an increasingly important tool for governments and NGOs seeking to engage with global audiences.

4.   **Fostering Economic Cooperation and Development**

Economic cooperation and development are central to effective global engagement, particularly in addressing issues of inequality and poverty. To reduce economic disparities, countries must engage in mutually beneficial trade agreements, investment partnerships, and financial assistance programs. For instance, trade deals can create win-win scenarios where countries gain access to new markets and technologies while also supporting sustainable development and poverty reduction in less-developed regions.

A key strategy for fostering economic cooperation is the promotion of fair trade and sustainable development practices. Ensuring that trade agreements prioritize labor rights, environmental protection, and social equity is essential for building a more equitable global economy. International financial institutions like the World Bank and the International Monetary Fund (IMF) can play a role in facilitating investment in infrastructure, education, and healthcare in developing countries.

At the same time, economic development must be accompanied by efforts to promote social justice. Addressing issues such as corruption, lack of political representation, and access to education and healthcare is critical for creating stable, prosperous societies. By working together on both economic and social issues, countries can ensure that growth benefits everyone, not just a privileged few, avoiding chaos, criminality, violence and wars.

5. **Adapting to Changing Geopolitical and Environmental Realities**

In a rapidly changing world, global engagement requires flexibility and adaptability. Geopolitical tensions, economic crises, and environmental challenges can alter the landscape of international relations. To navigate these uncertainties, countries must be willing to adapt their strategies and engage in contingency planning.

Environmental changes, in particular, are having a profound impact on global engagement. Climate change is creating new geopolitical tensions, as countries seek to secure access to resources like water and arable land. Coastal nations face the threat of rising sea levels, while others are experiencing extreme weather patterns, including droughts and floods. In such an environment, international cooperation on climate adaptation and mitigation strategies is essential. Countries must be willing to compromise, share technology, and support each other in facing these challenges.

Global engagement is essential for addressing the pressing challenges of our time, from economic inequality to climate change, to international security. Despite the obstacles posed by political divides, cultural differences, economic disparities, and environmental threats, effective global engagement is possible through the strategic use of diplomacy, multilateralism, technology, economic cooperation, and adaptability.

By fostering collaboration, promoting inclusivity, and staying open to new approaches, countries can navigate the complexities of international relations and work together toward a more stable, sustainable, and prosperous world. As the global landscape continues to evolve, the need for effective engagement will only grow more urgent, requiring collective efforts that transcend borders and address the interconnected issues facing humanity.

Chapter 8
Steps to Becoming a Global Citizen

How can you begin the journey of becoming a global citizen? This chapter provides readers with a step-by-step guide to engaging in the world as a global citizen. From practical advice on volunteerism, advocacy, and travel to tips on building intercultural relationships and staying informed about global issues, readers will come away with actionable steps to start making a difference.

Practicing Empathy and Open-Mindedness in Everyday Life

Empathy and open-mindedness are foundational qualities for creating meaningful relationships and fostering understanding in our increasingly interconnected world. These traits not only enhance individual growth but also contribute to a more harmonious society. Practicing empathy means actively seeking to understand and share the feelings of others, while open-mindedness involves being receptive to diverse perspectives without bias or judgment. Together, these attributes cultivate compassion, mutual respect, and personal enrichment. What is the significance of empathy and open-mindedness, their impact on everyday life, and practical strategies for integrating them into daily interactions?

Understanding Empathy

Empathy is the ability to emotionally connect with others by recognizing their emotions and experiences. It encompasses both cognitive and emotional components. Cognitive empathy involves understanding another person's perspective, while emotional empathy involves sharing in their emotional state. For example, when a friend is grieving, cognitive empathy allows you to grasp the depth of their pain, and emotional empathy enables you to feel sorrow alongside them. This dual approach fosters meaningful connections that transcend superficial exchanges.

In everyday life, practicing empathy helps bridge the gap between differing experiences. For instance, understanding the struggles of someone from a different cultural or socioeconomic background requires stepping into their shoes and acknowledging their reality without judgment. This practice not only deepens interpersonal connections but also challenges preconceived notions, leading to a more compassionate and inclusive worldview.

The Importance of Open-Mindedness

Open-mindedness is the willingness to consider ideas, beliefs, and perspectives that differ from one's own. It requires humility and a recognition of one's limitations in knowledge and understanding. Being open-minded does not mean abandoning one's values; rather, it involves a readiness to explore and appreciate alternative viewpoints.

In everyday interactions, open-mindedness is crucial for resolving conflicts and fostering dialogue. Consider a workplace scenario where colleagues disagree on how to approach a project. Instead of dismissing opposing views outright, an open-minded approach entails listening actively, asking questions, and seeking common ground. This mindset not only enhances collaboration but also promotes innovative solutions by combining diverse perspectives.

The Intersection of Empathy and Open-Mindedness

Empathy and open-mindedness are complementary qualities that amplify each other. Empathy provides the emotional connection needed to understand others, while open-mindedness ensures that this understanding is not clouded by biases or preconceived judgments. Together, they enable individuals to approach differences with curiosity and compassion rather than fear or hostility.

In a practical sense, these traits can be transformative. For example, in addressing social issues such as inequality or climate change; empathy motivates individuals to care about the experiences of those affected, while open-mindedness encourages exploration of diverse solutions. This combination is vital for driving collective action and creating inclusive spaces where all voices are valued.

Challenges to Practicing Empathy and Open-Mindedness

Despite their benefits, empathy and open-mindedness can be challenging to practice consistently. One common obstacle is implicit bias, which often influences how we perceive and interact with others. These biases, shaped by cultural and personal experiences, can hinder our ability to empathize with or remain open to those who differ from us.

Another challenge is emotional fatigue. Constantly empathizing with others, especially in emotionally charged situations, can lead to burnout. Similarly, open-mindedness may be tested when encountering ideas that fundamentally conflict with deeply held beliefs. These challenges highlight the need for balance and self-awareness in cultivating these traits.

Strategies for Practicing Empathy

1.   **Active Listening:** Focus on understanding rather than responding when others speak. Ask clarifying questions and reflect on their emotions to demonstrate genuine interest.

2.   **Perspective-Taking:** Regularly challenge yourself to view situations from another person's perspective. This exercise can help dismantle stereotypes and foster compassion.

3.   **Mindfulness:** Practice being present in conversations and interactions. Mindfulness enhances emotional awareness, making it easier to connect with others on a deeper level.

4.   **Reading and Storytelling:** Engaging with diverse narratives—whether through books, films, or conversations—broadens your understanding of different experiences and fosters empathy.

Strategies for Practicing Open-Mindedness

1.   **Seek Diverse Experiences:** Surround yourself with people, ideas, and cultures different from your own. Attend community events, try new activities, or engage in discussions with individuals who hold contrasting views.

2.   **Ask Questions:** Approach unfamiliar perspectives with curiosity rather than judgment. Questions like "What led you to this belief?" or "How do you see this issue?" encourage dialogue and understanding.

3.   **Reflect on Biases:** Regularly examine your assumptions and beliefs. Identifying areas of bias allows you to approach situations with greater openness.

4.   **Stay Informed:** Educate yourself on global and local issues from reputable sources. A well-rounded understanding of the world helps combat narrow thinking and fosters inclusivity.

The Ripple Effect of Empathy and Open-Mindedness

When individuals practice empathy and open-mindedness, their actions often inspire others to do the same. For example, a manager who listens empathetically to their team's concerns creates a workplace culture of trust and mutual respect. Similarly, a teacher who encourages open-minded discussions in the classroom instills these values in future generations.

At a societal level, these qualities have the power to reduce polarization and build stronger communities. By fostering understanding and cooperation, empathy and open-mindedness help address pressing global challenges, from racial and social justice to climate change.

Empathy and open-mindedness are essential for navigating the complexities of human relationships and societal dynamics. By embracing these qualities, individuals can foster meaningful connections, challenge biases, and create environments where diverse perspectives are celebrated. While practicing empathy and open-mindedness requires intentional effort, the rewards—both personal and collective—are immeasurable. As we strive to understand and appreciate one another, we contribute to a more compassionate and inclusive world, one interaction at a time.

Engaging with Global Issues Through Media, Volunteering, and Traveling

In a world deeply interconnected by shared challenges ferred opportunities, global engagement has become a critical responsibility for individuals. Issues such as climate change, poverty, human rights violations, and public health crises transcend borders, affecting communities worldwide.

Entangled   Sandra Ferreira

While governments and international organizations play significant roles in addressing these challenges, individuals also have the power to contribute meaningfully. Media consumption, volunteering, and traveling are three pathways through which people can engage with global issues. By staying informed, taking direct action, and experiencing other cultures firsthand, individuals can foster greater understanding, empathy, and meaningful change.

Understanding Global Issues Through Media

Media serves as the primary conduit through which individuals learn about global issues. News outlets, social media, documentaries, and books provide information on topics such as conflict, environmental degradation, and inequality. It is pivotal to be aware of potential manipulation of media by unscrupulous agendas. Authoritarian regimes, economic oligarchies and rigid religious ideologies have historically distorted, suppressed and fabricated facts to manipulate the communities and countries into supporting or be blind signed with corruption, injustice and abuses against them. More and more we see facts being distorted into political propaganda that benefits the 1% against the interests of the working class. For example, "news" that instigate division, hatred, discrimination and racism in communities are a notorious trick utilized by fascist authoritarian regimes. Those data are usually fabricated and has no connection with reality.

Consuming media with a critical and informed perspective, consulting and comparing local and international sources, reflecting on it with historical data, allows individuals to grasp the complexity of these issues and make educated decisions about how to contribute to solutions.

Good examples of reliable media are the coverage of climate change that has raised global awareness of its causes and consequences. Documentaries such as *An Inconvenient Truth* and platforms like National Geographic have highlighted the urgency of reducing carbon emissions and preserving biodiversity. Similarly, investigative journalism on human rights violations, such as the refugee crisis, informs the public about the struggles faced by marginalized populations.

Therefore, engaging with media requires discernment. In the digital age, misinformation and bias can distort perceptions of global issues. To navigate this challenge, individuals should seek out reputable sources and diversify their media consumption to include perspectives from different countries and cultures. By doing so, they can build a more nuanced understanding of the world and identify ways to contribute positively.

Volunteering as a Means of Action

Volunteering provides individuals with the opportunity to move beyond passive awareness and take direct action. By dedicating time and skills to causes they care about, volunteers can address global issues at both local and international levels. Volunteering not only benefits the communities being served but also empowers individuals to develop new skills, gain perspective, and create lasting change.

Programs such as Habitat for Humanity, Doctors Without Borders, and the United Nations Volunteers (UNV) offer platforms for people to contribute to global causes, from building homes for displaced families to providing medical care in underserved regions. On a smaller scale, local volunteer opportunities can also have a global impact. For instance, teaching English to immigrants, organizing food drives, or supporting sustainability initiatives in one's community can address global challenges such as poverty and education inequality.

Volunteering also fosters a sense of shared humanity and interconnectedness. When individuals work alongside people from different cultural backgrounds, they gain a deeper appreciation for diverse experiences and perspectives. This cultural exchange helps combat stereotypes and promotes mutual understanding, which is essential for addressing global issues collaboratively.

Traveling to Experience Global Issues Firsthand

Traveling, particularly when done with purpose and mindfulness, offers an unparalleled opportunity to engage with global issues on a personal level. Unlike media consumption or volunteering, which may provide indirect insights, traveling immerses individuals in the realities of other cultures and communities. This immersion allows travelers to witness global issues firsthand, fostering empathy and a deeper sense of responsibility.

Visiting regions affected by environmental degradation, such as the melting glaciers in the Arctic or deforested areas in the Amazon, for instance, brings the abstract concept of climate change into stark reality. Similarly, traveling to areas impacted by poverty or conflict can humanize statistics and headlines, turning them into tangible experiences that inspire action.

Responsible travel, such as participating in eco-tourism or cultural exchange programs, also supports local economies and communities. Organizations like World Expeditions and Global Vision International (GVI) provide opportunities for travelers to contribute to conservation projects, educational initiatives, and disaster relief efforts. These experiences not only enrich the traveler but also leave a positive impact on the communities visited.

However, it is crucial to approach global travel with sensitivity and respect. Travelers must be mindful of their environmental footprint, cultural differences, and the potential for unintentional harm. Ethical travel involves prioritizing the well-being of local communities and avoiding exploitative practices.

The Interplay Between Media, Volunteering, and Traveling

Media, volunteering, and traveling are interconnected pathways that complement and reinforce one another in addressing global issues. Media raises awareness and inspires individuals to take action, whether through volunteering or traveling. Volunteering provides a platform for direct involvement, while traveling deepens understanding and personal connection to global challenges. Together, these experiences create a holistic approach to global engagement.

For example, an individual might learn about the devastating effects of plastic pollution through a documentary, volunteer for a beach cleanup initiative, and later travel to coastal communities impacted by waste accumulation. Each step reinforces the others, transforming abstract knowledge into meaningful action and lasting commitment.

The interplay of these pathways also highlights the importance of lifelong learning and adaptation. As global challenges evolve, individuals must remain open to new information, experiences, and strategies for engagement. By combining the power of media, volunteering, and traveling, individuals can become more effective advocates for change.

Challenges and Ethical Considerations

Engaging with global issues through media, volunteering, and traveling is not without challenges. One major concern is the risk of "voluntourism," where short-term volunteering projects prioritize the traveler's experience over the community's needs. Similarly, consuming media without critical analysis can perpetuate stereotypes or oversimplify complex issues.

To address these challenges, individuals must prioritize ethical practices. This involves selecting reputable volunteer programs that prioritize community needs, seeking diverse and credible media sources, and traveling with an emphasis on sustainability and cultural respect. By approaching these pathways with intentionality and humility, individuals can ensure that their efforts contribute positively to global issues.

Engaging with global issues through media, volunteering, and traveling offers individuals powerful tools to understand and address the challenges facing humanity. Media provides access to information and diverse perspectives, volunteering offers direct opportunities to create change, and traveling fosters empathy and cultural appreciation. Together, these pathways empower individuals to move from awareness to action, bridging the gap between knowledge and impact.

As the world continues to face global challenges, the importance of individual engagement cannot be overstated. By consuming media critically, volunteering ethically, and traveling responsibly, individuals can contribute to a more just, sustainable, and compassionate world. Through these efforts, they not only enrich their own lives but also leave a lasting positive impact on the global community.

Advocating for a Fair and Inclusive World Through Informed Actions

In a world marked by diversity and interconnectedness, the pursuit of fairness and inclusion remains a vital yet complex endeavor. Advocating for a fair and inclusive society involves addressing inequities, dismantling systemic barriers, and ensuring that every individual is valued and empowered. While good intentions often drive advocacy, effective efforts require informed actions that are guided by knowledge, empathy, and collaboration. By staying educated, engaging in meaningful initiatives, and amplifying marginalized voices, individuals can contribute to a more equitable world. This essay explores the importance of informed actions in promoting fairness and inclusion, strategies for advocacy, and the transformative impact of these efforts.

Understanding Fairness and Inclusion

Fairness and inclusion are interrelated principles that emphasize equity, justice, and respect for diversity. Fairness involves creating opportunities and systems that enable individuals to thrive regardless of their background, while inclusion ensures that all people feel welcomed, valued, and empowered to participate fully in society.

Achieving fairness and inclusion requires addressing systemic inequities that disproportionately affect marginalized groups. These inequities manifest in various forms, such as income disparities, racial discrimination, gender bias, and limited access to education or healthcare. For instance, studies show that women and minorities are often underrepresented in leadership positions due to institutional barriers and unconscious biases. Similarly, individuals with disabilities frequently face challenges in accessing employment and public spaces, reflecting the need for systemic change.

Advocating for a fair and inclusive world involves not only recognizing these injustices but also taking informed actions to address them. Understanding the root causes of inequality and listening to the lived experiences of those affected are crucial steps in driving meaningful change.

The Role of Informed Actions in Advocacy

Informed actions are intentional efforts guided by knowledge, research, and critical thinking. Unlike reactive or uninformed responses, informed actions consider the complexity of issues and prioritize sustainable solutions. They are rooted in empathy, cultural competence, and a commitment to continuous learning.

1. **Education and Awareness:**

Advocacy begins with understanding the issues. This involves staying informed about historical and contemporary injustices, as well as the policies and structures that perpetuate them. Reading books, attending workshops, and following credible news sources are effective ways to deepen one's understanding of fairness and inclusion.

For example, understanding the history of systemic racism provides context for present-day disparities in housing, education, and criminal justice. Similarly, learning about intersectionality—the overlapping and interconnected nature of social categorizations such as race, gender, and class—can help advocates address multiple dimensions of inequality.

2. **Listening to Marginalized Voices:**

True advocacy centers the voices of those directly affected by injustice. Listening to marginalized communities allows advocates to understand their needs, priorities, and solutions. This approach shifts the focus from imposing external solutions to amplifying the agency of those most impacted.

Platforms like community forums, social media, and grassroots organizations offer opportunities to hear diverse perspectives. For instance, Indigenous activists have long advocated for environmental justice, emphasizing the importance of traditional knowledge in combating climate change. Supporting their efforts requires recognizing and respecting their expertise.

3.   **Evidence-Based Solutions:**

Informed advocacy relies on data and research to identify effective strategies for promoting fairness and inclusion. For example, addressing the gender pay gap involves understanding statistical disparities, analyzing contributing factors, and implementing policies such as pay transparency and parental leave. Similarly, addressing educational inequities requires data on resource allocation, student outcomes, and the impacts of systemic bias.

Strategies for Advocating for Fairness and Inclusion

Advocacy takes many forms, from individual actions to collective movements. The following strategies highlight ways individuals can promote fairness and inclusion through informed actions:

1.   **Community Engagement:**

Engaging with local communities is a powerful way to advocate for change. Volunteering with organizations that support marginalized groups, attending town hall meetings, or participating in neighborhood initiatives allows individuals to address issues at a grassroots level. For example, mentoring programs can help bridge educational gaps for underprivileged youth, while food banks address immediate needs for those facing economic hardship.

2.   **Policy Advocacy:**

Advocating for systemic change often involves engaging with policymakers to influence legislation and public policy. Writing letters, signing petitions, and participating in advocacy campaigns are effective ways to amplify concerns and demand action. Organizations like the American Civil Liberties Union (ACLU) and Amnesty International provide tools and resources for individuals to support initiatives promoting human rights and social justice.

3.   **Allyship and Solidarity:**

Being an ally involves using one's privilege to support marginalized communities. This includes speaking out against discrimination, challenging biases, and standing in solidarity during protests or campaigns. Allyship also involves ongoing education and accountability, ensuring that advocacy efforts are respectful and inclusive.

4.   **Promoting Diversity and Inclusion in Organizations:**

Advocating within workplaces, schools, and institutions can lead to meaningful change. Encouraging diverse hiring practices, supporting employee resource groups, and implementing anti-bias training are examples of actions that promote inclusion at an organizational level. These efforts not only benefit marginalized individuals but also enhance innovation and collaboration within teams.

The Transformative Impact of Advocacy

Advocating for fairness and inclusion has a ripple effect that extends beyond individual actions. At the societal level, these efforts challenge oppressive systems and create opportunities for marginalized groups to thrive. For example, civil rights movements have historically led to landmark achievements, such as the desegregation of schools and the legalization of same-sex marriage.

On a personal level, advocacy fosters empathy, resilience, and a sense of purpose. By engaging with diverse perspectives and challenging biases, individuals develop greater cultural competence and emotional intelligence. These qualities not only enhance personal relationships but also contribute to a more cohesive, compassionate, more just and safer society to everyone.

The impact of advocacy is further amplified when individuals collaborate across communities and borders. Global initiatives, such as the United Nations Sustainable Development Goals (SDGs), demonstrate the power of collective action in addressing issues such as poverty, inequality, and climate change. By aligning personal efforts with broader movements, individuals can contribute to systemic change on a global scale.

Challenges and Ethical Considerations

While advocating for fairness and inclusion is essential, it is not without challenges. One common issue is performative allyship, where individuals or organizations adopt the appearance of support without meaningful action. Avoiding this requires genuine commitment, accountability, and transparency.

Another challenge is navigating complex and sensitive topics. Advocates must approach these issues with humility, recognizing their own biases and limitations.

Chapter 9
The Quantum Foundations of Reality

To understand global citizenship through the lens of quantum physics, we must first understand the basics of quantum mechanics. This chapter introduces key quantum principles, including entanglement, superposition, and wave-particle duality. These concepts defy conventional thinking but open our minds to possibilities beyond fixed boundaries. With these principles in mind, readers can begin to see parallels with the dynamics of global society.

The Fundamentals of Quantum Physics and Its Paradoxes

Quantum physics, the branch of science that explores the behavior of matter and energy at the smallest scales, stands as one of the most revolutionary yet perplexing fields in modern science. Developed in the early 20th century, quantum mechanics diverges from classical physics by revealing a counterintuitive and probabilistic nature of the universe. Despite its profound successes in explaining phenomena such as atomic structure, chemical bonding, and semiconductor behavior, quantum physics is riddled with paradoxes that challenge our understanding of reality.

The Origins and Fundamentals of Quantum Mechanics

Quantum mechanics emerged as scientists encountered phenomena that classical physics could not explain. One of the pivotal experiments was the double-slit experiment. When light passes through two closely spaced slits, it produces an interference pattern, demonstrating its wave-like nature. However, when the same experiment is performed with individual particles, such as electrons, an interference pattern still forms—suggesting particles also behave like waves. This discovery, known as wave-particle duality, became a cornerstone of quantum physics.

The fundamental framework of quantum mechanics is encapsulated in the Schrödinger equation, which describes how the quantum state of a system evolves over time. Unlike Newtonian physics, where objects have definite trajectories, quantum systems are described by wave functions. A wave function provides the probabilities of a particle's position, momentum, and other properties. This probabilistic nature of quantum mechanics is central to its interpretation and introduces the concept of uncertainty.

Heisenberg's Uncertainty Principle

The uncertainty principle, formulated by Werner Heisenberg, states that certain pairs of physical properties, such as position and momentum, cannot be simultaneously measured with arbitrary precision. This limitation is not due to technological shortcomings but is intrinsic to the nature of quantum systems. The more precisely one property is known, the less precisely the other can be determined.

This principle challenges classical notions of determinism. In classical mechanics, knowing the initial conditions of a system allows for precise predictions of its future behavior. In contrast, quantum mechanics only provides probabilities, underscoring a fundamental randomness in nature.

Quantum Entanglement: Spooky Action at a Distance

Another profound concept in quantum mechanics is entanglement, where particles become interconnected in such a way that the state of one particle instantaneously influences the state of another, regardless of the distance between them. Albert Einstein famously referred to this phenomenon as "spooky action at a distance," as it seemed to violate the principle of locality, which states that objects are only influenced by their immediate surroundings.

Experiments, such as those conducted by Alain Aspect in the 1980s, have confirmed the existence of entanglement, leading to the violation of Bell's inequalities. These experiments demonstrated that quantum mechanics cannot be explained by any local hidden variable theory, deepening the mystery surrounding entanglement.

The Measurement Problem and Schrödinger's Cat

One of the most debated paradoxes in quantum mechanics is the measurement problem. According to quantum theory, particles exist in a superposition of states until they are observed or measured. The act of measurement "collapses" the wave function into a single state. But what constitutes a "measurement," and why does it cause the wave function to collapse?

Erwin Schrödinger illustrated this paradox with his famous thought experiment, known as Schrödinger's Cat. A cat is placed in a sealed box with a radioactive atom, a Geiger counter, and a vial of poison. If the atom decays, the Geiger counter triggers the release of the poison, killing the cat. According to quantum mechanics, until the box is opened and observed, the cat is simultaneously alive and dead—a superposition of states. This thought experiment highlights the absurd implications of applying quantum principles to macroscopic objects.

The Many-Worlds Interpretation

To address the measurement problem, physicist Hugh Everett proposed the Many-Worlds Interpretation (MWI). According to this interpretation, the universe splits into multiple branches whenever a quantum event occurs, with each branch representing a different outcome. In the Schrödinger's Cat scenario, one branch contains a live cat, while the other contains a dead one. These branches exist independently and are equally real.

While the MWI eliminates the need for wave function collapse, it raises philosophical questions about the nature of reality and the existence of parallel universes.

Critics argue that the lack of experimental evidence for other worlds makes the interpretation speculative, but its mathematical consistency keeps it a topic of active discussion.

Quantum Paradoxes and Realism

The paradoxes of quantum mechanics challenge traditional notions of realism—the idea that the universe exists independently of observation. Experiments involving quantum entanglement suggest that the universe may not adhere to the principles of locality and realism simultaneously, as upheld in classical physics. These findings have led to debates between proponents of objective reality and those who argue that reality is fundamentally observer-dependent.

Niels Bohr, a pioneer of quantum mechanics, advocated for the Copenhagen interpretation, which emphasizes the role of measurement and observer in defining physical reality. Einstein, on the other hand, rejected the idea of a fundamentally indeterminate universe, famously asserting, "God does not play dice with the universe." The tension between these perspectives remains unresolved, reflecting the philosophical depth of quantum mechanics.

Applications and Implications of Quantum Physics

Despite its paradoxes, quantum mechanics has revolutionized technology and science. It forms the foundation of modern electronics, including transistors, lasers, and quantum computers. Quantum cryptography promises unbreakable encryption, while quantum sensors enable unprecedented precision in measurement.

Quantum mechanics also has profound implications for our understanding of the universe. It underpins theories of particle physics, cosmology, and the early moments of the Big Bang. Yet, its reconciliation with general relativity, the theory of gravity, remains a major unsolved problem in physics.

Quantum mechanics is both a triumph and an enigma of modern science. Its principles, such as wave-particle duality, uncertainty, and entanglement, have transformed our understanding of nature at its most fundamental level. However, its paradoxes, from the measurement problem to quantum entanglement, continue to challenge our philosophical and scientific perspectives.

As physicists push the boundaries of quantum theory, exploring phenomena like quantum gravity and quantum field theory, the mysteries of the quantum realm may one day be unraveled. Until then, quantum mechanics remains a testament to the complexity and wonder of the universe, urging us to embrace uncertainty and rethink the fabric of reality itself.

<u>Understanding Entanglement and Interconnectedness</u>

Entanglement is one of the most intriguing and counterintuitive concepts in modern physics, suggesting that the universe is deeply interconnected at a fundamental level. It originates from quantum mechanics, the branch of physics that governs the behavior of the smallest particles of matter and energy. At its core, entanglement describes a phenomenon where two or more particles become so intricately linked that the state of one instantly influences the state of the other, regardless of the physical distance between them. This phenomenon not only challenges classical notions of locality and causality but also raises profound philosophical and scientific questions about the nature of interconnectedness in the universe.

Beyond its implications for physics, entanglement serves as a metaphor for understanding the interconnectedness of systems, people, and ideas. This essay delves into the science behind entanglement, its implications for our understanding of reality, and how it relates to broader notions of connection in various fields of thought.

The Science of Quantum Entanglement

Quantum entanglement was first theorized in the 1930s when Albert Einstein, Boris Podolsky, and Nathan Rosen proposed the Einstein-Podolsky-Rosen (EPR) paradox. In their view, quantum mechanics was incomplete because it allowed for what Einstein referred to as "spooky action at a distance." This was in direct conflict with the principle of locality, which states that objects can only be influenced by their immediate surroundings.

Entanglement arises when particles interact in such a way that their quantum states become intertwined. For instance, if two particles are entangled, measuring the spin, position, or polarization of one particle immediately determines the corresponding property of the other, no matter how far apart they are. This phenomenon has been experimentally verified through Bell test experiments, which demonstrated violations of Bell's inequalities, proving that no local hidden variable theory could fully explain quantum correlations.

A hallmark experiment conducted by Alain Aspect in the 1980s solidified the empirical foundation of entanglement. Aspect's team showed that entangled particles indeed exhibited correlations that defied classical explanations, confirming the predictions of quantum mechanics. This led to the recognition that entanglement is not a theoretical curiosity but a fundamental feature of the natural world.

Implications for Reality and Non-Locality

Entanglement challenges traditional views of reality and locality, suggesting that the universe may be more interconnected than previously believed. In classical physics, reality is considered deterministic and local, meaning events at one point in space cannot instantly affect events at another. Entanglement, however, defies this notion, implying that quantum systems exist in a state of non-locality, where the state of one particle is intrinsically linked to the state of another, regardless of distance.

This phenomenon raises questions about the nature of causality and the fabric of spacetime itself. Some interpretations of quantum mechanics, such as the Many-Worlds Interpretation, sidestep the issue by suggesting that every quantum event leads to a branching of parallel universes. Other interpretations, like the Copenhagen interpretation, embrace the probabilistic and observer-dependent nature of quantum states.

Entanglement also suggests that the universe operates as an interconnected whole rather than a collection of isolated parts. The interconnectedness revealed by entanglement resonates with ancient philosophical and spiritual traditions, which often emphasize unity and the interdependence of all things.

Applications of Entanglement

Entanglement is not just a theoretical concept; it has practical applications that are revolutionizing technology. In quantum computing, entanglement enables the creation of qubits, which can represent multiple states simultaneously, vastly increasing computational power. Quantum computers leverage entanglement to perform calculations that would be infeasible for classical computers, promising advancements in fields such as cryptography, materials science, and artificial intelligence.

Quantum entanglement is also the cornerstone of quantum cryptography, which ensures secure communication by making eavesdropping detectable. Quantum key distribution (QKD) protocols, such as BB84, rely on the principles of entanglement to create encryption keys that are virtually unbreakable.

Another emerging application is quantum teleportation, where entanglement is used to transfer quantum information between distant particles. While this does not involve the physical transportation of matter, it has significant implications for the development of quantum networks and the future of communication technologies.

Entanglement as a Metaphor for Interconnectedness

Beyond physics, entanglement serves as a powerful metaphor for understanding interconnectedness in other domains. In ecology, the concept of interconnectedness emphasizes how ecosystems are complex networks of interdependent species and processes. Just as entangled particles influence each other instantaneously, changes in one part of an ecosystem can have cascading effects throughout the system.

In sociology and psychology, interconnectedness highlights the interdependence of individuals within communities and societies. Human relationships, like entangled particles, often exhibit non-local characteristics—where actions and emotions can ripple through social networks in unexpected ways. Research in social sciences, for instance, has shown that happiness, stress, and even health behaviors can spread across social networks, demonstrating the profound interconnectedness of human lives.

The interconnectedness revealed by entanglement also resonates with philosophical and spiritual traditions. Many Eastern philosophies, such as Buddhism and Taoism, emphasize the interdependence of all phenomena. The concept of *dependent origination* in Buddhism, for instance, aligns with the idea that entities do not exist independently but arise through their relationships and interactions.

Challenges and Philosophical Implications

While entanglement has profound implications, it also raises philosophical challenges. For instance, if the universe is fundamentally interconnected, what does this mean for the concept of individuality? Are distinctions between objects and entities merely illusions arising from our limited perception.

These questions intersect with debates in metaphysics, where some philosophers argue for a holistic view of reality, suggesting that the universe is a single, interconnected entity. This perspective contrasts with reductionist approaches, which attempt to understand systems by breaking them into their constituent parts.

Moreover, entanglement challenges our understanding of time and space. If entangled particles can influence each other instantaneously, it suggests that spacetime is not a fundamental aspect of reality but an emergent phenomenon. This idea is explored in quantum gravity theories, such as string theory and loop quantum gravity, which seek to reconcile quantum mechanics with general relativity.

Understanding entanglement and interconnectedness provides profound insights into both the nature of the universe and the systems within it. At its core, entanglement reveals that the universe operates on principles that transcend classical notions of locality and separability. This interconnectedness is not confined to the realm of physics but extends to ecosystems, societies, and philosophical thought, emphasizing the unity and interdependence of all things.

As we continue to explore the mysteries of quantum mechanics, the lessons of entanglement remind us that the universe is more intricate and interconnected than we might imagine. Whether applied to advancing technology, deepening our understanding of ecosystems, or enriching our philosophical perspectives, the concept of entanglement offers a framework for appreciating the profound unity underlying the diversity of existence.

Quantum Principles: Inspiring New Ways of Viewing the World and Ourselves

Quantum physics, the branch of science that explores the behavior of matter and energy at the smallest scales, has revolutionized our understanding of the universe. Its principles challenge classical notions of reality, determinism, and separability, forcing us to confront the limits of human perception and intuition. Beyond its technical implications, quantum mechanics offers profound metaphors and frameworks for reimagining how we view the world and ourselves. By examining principles like superposition, uncertainty, and entanglement, we can find inspiration for addressing philosophical questions, navigating complexity, and embracing interconnectedness in our personal and collective lives.

The Principle of Superposition and Human Potential

In quantum mechanics, the principle of superposition states that particles can exist in multiple states simultaneously until observed or measured. For instance, an electron might occupy multiple energy levels at once, only collapsing into a single state when measured. This phenomenon defies the binary, either-or thinking of classical physics and opens the door to a richer understanding of possibility.

Superposition can serve as a metaphor for human potential. Just as particles exist in multiple states before observation, people often hold untapped potential that only becomes realized through action or self-reflection. This principle challenges us to see ourselves not as static beings confined by past choices but as dynamic entities capable of inhabiting multiple possibilities simultaneously. It reminds us that personal growth and transformation often involve embracing uncertainty and exploring diverse paths.

On a societal level, superposition invites us to reimagine how we approach problem-solving and decision-making. In a world characterized by complexity and rapid change, the ability to hold multiple perspectives and explore various possibilities simultaneously becomes invaluable. By rejecting rigid, deterministic models of thought, we open ourselves to innovation and creative solutions.

Uncertainty and Embracing the Unknown

The uncertainty principle, formulated by Werner Heisenberg, states that certain pairs of physical properties, such as position and momentum, cannot be simultaneously measured with absolute precision. This intrinsic limitation reflects the probabilistic nature of quantum systems, where outcomes are governed by probabilities rather than certainties.

The uncertainty principle offers a profound lesson about the nature of knowledge and the human experience. In a world often obsessed with control and predictability, it reminds us that uncertainty is not a flaw to be eliminated but a fundamental aspect of reality to be embraced. This shift in perspective encourages humility, adaptability, and a deeper acceptance of the unknown.

On a personal level, embracing uncertainty can lead to greater resilience and openness to change. Life, much like a quantum system, is inherently unpredictable, and attempts to control every aspect of it often lead to frustration and rigidity. By adopting a mindset that values curiosity and flexibility, we can navigate uncertainty with greater ease and creativity.

In broader societal contexts, the uncertainty principle challenges traditional paradigms of planning and governance. It suggests that policies and systems must account for unpredictability and adapt to evolving circumstances rather than relying on rigid, deterministic models. This perspective is particularly relevant in addressing global challenges like climate change, economic instability, and technological disruption.

Quantum Entanglement and Interconnectedness

Quantum entanglement, one of the most counterintuitive aspects of quantum mechanics, describes a phenomenon where particles become so deeply linked that the state of one instantly influences the state of the other, regardless of distance. This defies classical notions of separability and locality, suggesting that the universe operates as an interconnected whole.

Entangled   Sandra Ferreira

Entanglement offers a powerful metaphor for understanding human relationships and the interconnectedness of all life. Just as entangled particles are intrinsically linked, individuals and communities are deeply interconnected, with actions and events in one part of the world rippling across the global fabric. This perspective challenges the illusion of separateness and underscores the importance of empathy, cooperation, and collective responsibility.

On a philosophical level, entanglement invites us to reconsider the nature of identity. If the boundaries between particles—and by extension, between people—are not as clear-cut as they seem, then our sense of self may be more fluid and relational than traditionally understood. This idea resonates with Eastern philosophies like Buddhism, which emphasize the interdependence of all phenomena and the illusory nature of separateness.

In practical terms, the principle of interconnectedness inspires new approaches to solving global problems. Issues such as climate change, public health, and social inequality cannot be addressed in isolation; they require collaborative, systemic solutions that recognize the interdependence of ecological, economic, and social systems. By adopting a quantum-inspired perspective, we can foster a greater sense of shared responsibility and collective action.

Quantum Holism and Rethinking Systems

Quantum mechanics challenges reductionism—the idea that complex systems can be fully understood by breaking them down into their smallest components. Instead, it suggests a holistic view of the universe, where the properties of a system emerge from the relationships and interactions between its parts.

This shift from reductionism to holism has profound implications for how we understand systems in fields as diverse as biology, economics, and sociology. In ecosystems, for example, the health of the whole depends on the intricate interplay between organisms, habitats, and environmental factors. Similarly, in human societies, cultural, economic, and political systems are deeply intertwined, with changes in one area affecting the others in complex and often unpredictable ways.

Quantum holism also encourages us to view ourselves as part of larger systems. This perspective fosters a sense of belonging and purpose, as we recognize that our actions contribute to the well-being of the whole. It challenges the individualistic mindset prevalent in many modern societies and emphasizes the importance of collaboration, community, and collective effort.

Quantum Principles and Creativity

Quantum principles, with their emphasis on uncertainty, superposition, and interconnectedness, offer a rich source of inspiration for creativity and innovation. By challenging linear, deterministic thinking, they encourage us to explore new possibilities and embrace paradoxes.

Entangled   Sandra Ferreira

For artists, quantum mechanics provides a metaphorical framework for exploring themes of ambiguity, duality, and transformation. Writers, painters, and filmmakers have drawn on quantum concepts to challenge traditional narratives and create works that reflect the complexity and uncertainty of the human experience.

In science and technology, quantum principles inspire breakthroughs in fields like artificial intelligence, renewable energy, and biotechnology. By adopting a mindset that values exploration and experimentation, researchers and innovators can push the boundaries of what is possible.

Quantum physics is not merely a scientific framework for understanding the behavior of particles; it is a profound source of inspiration for reimagining how we view the world and ourselves. Its principles of superposition, uncertainty, entanglement, and holism challenge classical assumptions and invite us to embrace complexity, interconnectedness, and the unknown.

As we navigate an increasingly complex and interconnected world, the lessons of quantum mechanics can guide us toward greater creativity, empathy, and resilience. By adopting a quantum-inspired perspective, we can move beyond rigid, linear thinking and cultivate a deeper appreciation for the richness and interconnectedness of existence. In doing so, we not only deepen our understanding of the universe but also uncover new ways to thrive within it.

Chapter 10
Entanglement and Global Interconnection

Entanglement is the idea that particles can be intrinsically linked, regardless of distance—what happens to one affects the other. Similarly, global citizenship rests on the idea that actions in one part of the world ripple across continents, affecting people, environments, and economies in ways we might not initially perceive. This chapter explores how entanglement provides a powerful metaphor for understanding global interdependence.

Entanglement as a Model for Social and Environmental Impact

- Define "entanglement" from a quantum physics perspective.
- Extend the metaphor to interconnectedness in social and environmental systems.
- Present thesis: Understanding societal and environmental issues through the lens of entanglement can inspire holistic solutions and foster mutual accountability.

2. **Understanding Entanglement in Nature**
- Briefly explain the science behind quantum entanglement: particles remaining interconnected regardless of distance.
- Highlight examples of entanglement in ecosystems, such as predator-prey relationships and resource cycles.
- Emphasize the universal principle of interdependence.

3. **Entanglement in Social Systems**
- Discuss the interconnectedness of human societies: global economies, cultural exchange, and shared challenges like pandemics and climate change.
- Explore specific examples, such as supply chains and labor, where actions in one part of the world ripple globally.

4. **Environmental Impact and Responsibility**
- Analyze entanglement in the human-environment relationship.
- Examples: pollution crossing borders, deforestation affecting global climate systems, and oceanic interdependence.
- Argue that seeing humans as "entangled" with the environment can encourage sustainable practices.

5. **Toward a Holistic Approach to Change**
- Propose how the concept of entanglement can reshape policymaking and individual actions.
- Discuss multidisciplinary solutions: combining science, community engagement, and systemic reform.
- Reflect on shared responsibility and the necessity of collective action.
- Summarize the importance of viewing social and environmental challenges as entangled.

-     Reiterate how this model offers a framework for understanding and addressing global problems.

Entanglement as a Model for Social and Environmental Impact

Entanglement, a concept rooted in quantum physics, refers to the phenomenon where two particles become interlinked in such a way that the state of one directly influences the other, regardless of physical distance. Although this principle is often discussed in the context of subatomic particles, it offers a profound metaphor for understanding the interconnectedness of human societies and the natural world. Social systems and environmental processes are deeply intertwined, and the actions of one individual, community, or nation inevitably ripple across broader systems. By adopting entanglement as a conceptual model, we can develop a deeper understanding of the global impacts of our choices and foster approaches that emphasize shared accountability and collective well-being.

Understanding Entanglement in Nature

The principle of entanglement is not limited to the quantum realm; it resonates throughout natural ecosystems. In physics, entangled particles behave as a unified system, even when separated by vast distances. Similarly, ecosystems function through intricate networks of interdependence. For example, the survival of apex predators like wolves is entangled with the health of prey populations, vegetation growth, and even river ecosystems, as demonstrated in Yellowstone National Park after the reintroduction of wolves. This cascading relationship, known as a trophic cascade, illustrates how changes in one species affect the entire ecosystem.

Additionally, the water cycle exemplifies a form of environmental entanglement. Evaporation, precipitation, and groundwater flow link distant regions, ensuring that an event in one area—such as deforestation or pollution—can significantly impact water availability and quality elsewhere. These examples remind us that no component of nature operates in isolation. Recognizing these interdependencies can guide sustainable practices that prioritize the health of entire systems rather than individual components.

Entanglement in Social Systems

Just as ecosystems are interconnected, human societies are increasingly entangled in complex ways. The rapid globalization of trade, technology, and communication has created a web of interdependence that binds individuals, communities, and nations. For instance, the supply chain of a single smartphone involves raw materials from Africa, manufacturing in Asia, and consumers in Europe or the Americas. Each stage of production, consumption, and disposal generates social and environmental consequences, highlighting how actions in one region can have far-reaching effects.

This entanglement also manifests in shared global challenges. The COVID-19 pandemic underscored the interconnectedness of public health systems, economies, and information networks. A virus that originated in one city rapidly spread worldwide, revealing vulnerabilities in global healthcare systems and supply chains. Similarly, climate change demonstrates the shared consequences of human activities: carbon emissions from industrialized nations contribute to rising sea levels that threaten low-lying island nations. These examples illustrate that societal and environmental challenges cannot be addressed in isolation; they require a collective response that acknowledges their interconnected nature.

Environmental Impact and Responsibility

Human interactions with the environment are a profound example of entanglement, with consequences that transcend geographic and temporal boundaries. For instance, the burning of fossil fuels in one region contributes to greenhouse gas emissions that accelerate climate change globally. This warming trend leads to phenomena such as melting polar ice caps, rising sea levels, and extreme weather events that impact communities far removed from the original source of emissions. Similarly, ocean pollution, such as plastic waste, demonstrates the interconnectedness of human actions and ecological systems. Plastics discarded on one continent often end up in distant oceans, harming marine life and entering the global food chain.

Recognizing this entanglement shifts the narrative from assigning blame to embracing shared responsibility. If humanity is intrinsically connected to the environment, then protecting ecosystems becomes an act of self-preservation. This perspective encourages practices such as regenerative agriculture, renewable energy adoption, and circular economies, all of which prioritize long-term sustainability over short-term gains. Viewing environmental challenges through the lens of entanglement helps dissolve the illusion of separateness, fostering a mindset of mutual stewardship.

Toward a Holistic Approach to Change

To address the entangled nature of social and environmental issues, solutions must be holistic and multidisciplinary. Policies should reflect the interconnectedness of problems rather than treating them as isolated phenomena. For instance, combating climate change requires not only technological innovation but also community engagement, education, and international cooperation. Initiatives like the Paris Agreement emphasize the need for collective action, acknowledging that no single nation can solve the climate crisis alone.

On an individual level, understanding entanglement can inspire more conscious decision-making. Choices such as reducing waste, supporting ethical businesses, and advocating for systemic change demonstrate how personal actions ripple through larger systems. Meanwhile, collaborations between scientists, policymakers, and activists highlight the importance of integrating diverse perspectives to tackle complex challenges. This holistic approach aligns with the principle of entanglement, emphasizing unity and interdependence over fragmentation.

Entangled   Sandra Ferreira

Viewing social and environmental challenges through the lens of entanglement offers a powerful framework for understanding and addressing global problems. By recognizing the interconnectedness of ecosystems, societies, and economies, we can move beyond siloed thinking and embrace solutions that prioritize collective well-being. This perspective fosters a sense of shared responsibility, urging individuals and communities to act with an awareness of their impact on the broader system. In a world increasingly defined by complexity and interdependence, the model of entanglement reminds us that our fates are inexorably linked—and that by working together, we can build a more sustainable and equitable future.

Recognizing the Invisible Connections Between Our Actions and Global Consequences

In an increasingly interconnected world, the consequences of individual and collective actions often ripple far beyond their point of origin. These invisible connections—linking personal decisions to global outcomes—define the modern era, from the products we buy to the environmental footprint we leave behind. Often, these relationships are hidden in supply chains, ecological systems, and the broader socio-economic fabric. Yet, failing to recognize these invisible connections exacerbates global challenges such as climate change, economic inequality, and social unrest. This essay explores how our actions create far-reaching effects, why it is crucial to recognize these connections, and how doing so can inspire responsible, transformative behavior for a more sustainable and equitable future.

Understanding Invisible Connections

Invisible connections refer to the often-unseen relationships between cause and effect, particularly in complex systems. These links may span geographical, temporal, and systemic boundaries. For instance, when a consumer purchases a piece of clothing, they participate in a supply chain that includes the extraction of raw materials, manufacturing, and transportation. Along the way, hidden costs—such as environmental degradation from cotton farming or unfair labor conditions in factories—become entangled in the product's life cycle.

Similarly, ecological systems are replete with invisible connections. Cutting down a forest for agriculture, for example, may yield immediate economic benefits but also disrupts carbon sequestration, water cycles, and biodiversity. These disruptions, in turn, can contribute to global climate change and reduce ecosystem resilience, affecting communities thousands of miles away. Understanding these connections requires a systems-thinking approach, which considers how seemingly isolated actions can create cascading impacts across networks.

Global Consequences of Local Actions

The modern globalized world amplifies the reach of individual and local actions, creating consequences that are difficult to predict or control. One of the clearest examples of this phenomenon is climate change. Greenhouse gas emissions produced in industrialized countries affect the global climate system, resulting in rising sea levels, intensified weather events, and the loss of biodiversity. However, the most severe impacts often fall on vulnerable communities in developing nations, which contribute the least to emissions but lack the resources to adapt.

Economic systems also illustrate how local actions have global consequences. The rise of e-commerce, for instance, has revolutionized consumer habits, offering convenience and accessibility. Yet, the environmental toll of expedited shipping, overproduction, and increased packaging waste remains largely invisible to consumers. Similarly, food production systems demonstrate the interconnectedness of local choices and global outcomes. For example, the demand for inexpensive meat in developed countries drives deforestation in the Amazon rainforest to create grazing land, contributing to biodiversity loss and climate change.

These examples highlight the ethical and practical implications of failing to recognize invisible connections. When individuals, corporations, and governments ignore these links, they inadvertently perpetuate harm on a global scale. Recognizing these connections, on the other hand, can lead to more informed decisions that prioritize long-term sustainability over short-term gains.

Why Recognition Matters

Recognizing the invisible connections between actions and global consequences is essential for several reasons. First, it fosters accountability by making individuals and institutions aware of the broader implications of their choices. Awareness transforms seemingly insignificant decisions—such as reducing plastic use or choosing ethical brands—into meaningful contributions to global challenges.

Second, understanding these connections empowers people to advocate for systemic change. For instance, realizing that fast fashion contributes to both environmental degradation and worker exploitation can motivate consumers to demand transparency from companies and support sustainable alternatives. This shift in consumer behavior can, in turn, pressure industries to adopt ethical practices and reduce their ecological footprint.

Third, recognizing invisible connections promotes collaboration and shared responsibility. Global challenges like climate change, poverty, and pandemics require collective action across borders, industries, and disciplines. Acknowledging interconnectedness helps break down the silos that often hinder progress, encouraging partnerships that leverage diverse expertise and resources.

Finally, this recognition deepens our moral and emotional engagement with global issues. When people see themselves as part of an interconnected whole, they are more likely to empathize with others and act in ways that benefit the common good. This perspective can help bridge cultural and ideological divides, fostering a sense of unity in the face of shared challenges.

Strategies for Recognizing Invisible Connections

Recognizing invisible connections requires education, reflection, and systemic change. Education plays a critical role in unveiling these links, whether through formal curricula, public awareness campaigns, or community initiatives. Schools can integrate lessons on global systems, sustainability, and ethics to help students understand how their actions shape the world. Similarly, documentaries, books, and online resources can illuminate hidden connections for broader audiences.

Reflection is another vital strategy. By critically examining their consumption habits, lifestyle choices, and values, individuals can uncover the unseen consequences of their actions. Tools like carbon footprint calculators or supply chain transparency apps make these connections more tangible, empowering people to make informed decisions.

On a systemic level, governments and organizations can implement policies and practices that highlight and address invisible connections. For instance, mandating corporate social responsibility (CSR) reporting can reveal how businesses impact communities and ecosystems. Similarly, international agreements like the Paris Climate Accord underscore the shared responsibility of nations to mitigate global warming.

Finally, fostering dialogue and collaboration is key to recognizing and addressing invisible connections. Cross-sector partnerships between governments, businesses, and civil society can generate innovative solutions to complex challenges. For example, initiatives like the Fair-Trade movement demonstrate how collaboration can create equitable supply chains that prioritize both social and environmental well-being.

The Transformative Potential of Recognition

Recognizing invisible connections is not only a moral imperative but also a transformative opportunity. By embracing interconnectedness, individuals and societies can shift from reactive to proactive approaches in addressing global challenges. This paradigm shift aligns with emerging frameworks like the circular economy, which seeks to eliminate waste and regenerate natural systems by designing products and processes with their full life cycle in mind.

Moreover, recognizing invisible connections can inspire hope and resilience. While the scale of global challenges can feel overwhelming, understanding the power of collective action reminds us that small, meaningful changes can create far-reaching positive effects. For instance, community-led reforestation projects not only restore ecosystems but also empower local populations and mitigate climate change.

This perspective also challenges the notion of individual insignificance, reinforcing the idea that every action matters. By acknowledging the invisible threads that link personal choices to global outcomes, people can find purpose and agency in their efforts to build a better world.

The invisible connections between our actions and global consequences are integral to understanding the complexities of the modern world. From the products we consume to the policies we support, our choices reverberate through ecosystems, economies, and societies, often in ways we cannot immediately see. Recognizing these connections is essential for fostering accountability, driving systemic change, and cultivating a sense of shared responsibility.

As individuals and communities, we have the power to illuminate these hidden links and act in ways that honor our interconnectedness. By embracing this awareness, we can transform our relationship with the world, ensuring that our actions contribute to a more sustainable, equitable, and compassionate future. Recognizing invisible connections is not merely an intellectual exercise—it is a call to action, challenging us to see beyond the immediate and strive for a world where every choice aligns with the common good.

Interdependence in Action: Climate Change, Global Economics, and Human Rights

In today's interconnected world, interdependence defines the relationships between nations, communities, and individuals. Whether in addressing climate change, navigating the complexities of global economics, or upholding human rights, the actions of one group inevitably affect others. Interdependence underscores the reality that no issue exists in isolation; solving global challenges requires collective effort and cooperation. This essay explores practical examples of interdependence in three key areas—climate change, global economics, and human rights—demonstrating how these domains are deeply interconnected and why recognizing these links is essential for building a sustainable and equitable future.

Climate Change: A Shared Challenge

Climate change exemplifies global interdependence, as its causes and consequences transcend national borders. Greenhouse gas emissions produced in one country affect the entire planet, contributing to rising temperatures, extreme weather events, and environmental degradation. Addressing this crisis requires international cooperation, as no single nation can mitigate its impacts alone.

One practical example of interdependence in combating climate change is the Paris Agreement, a global treaty signed by nearly 200 countries. The accord acknowledges that limiting global warming to 1.5°C above pre-industrial levels depends on collective action. Countries commit to nationally determined contributions (NDCs), which outline their strategies for reducing emissions and transitioning to renewable energy. For instance, nations like Denmark and Germany have invested heavily in wind and solar power, setting an example for others and contributing to advancements in green technology. Meanwhile, developing countries such as Kenya have adopted renewable energy projects with the support of international funding, demonstrating how shared resources can drive progress.

Another example is the global response to deforestation in the Amazon rainforest. The Amazon plays a critical role in regulating the Earth's climate, absorbing vast amounts of carbon dioxide. However, deforestation driven by agriculture, logging, and mining threatens this vital ecosystem. Countries worldwide depend on the Amazon's ability to act as a carbon sink, highlighting the interconnectedness of environmental health and human activity. Organizations like the United Nations' REDD+ program (Reducing Emissions from Deforestation and Forest Degradation) promote collaboration between governments, indigenous communities, and private entities to conserve forests and ensure sustainable development.

Despite these efforts, climate change also highlights inequalities in interdependence. The countries most responsible for emissions, such as the United States and China, often face fewer immediate consequences than vulnerable nations like Bangladesh and Pacific Island states. This disparity underscores the need for stronger commitments to climate justice, where wealthier nations provide financial and technological support to those disproportionately affected. Recognizing the interconnected nature of the climate crisis is key to fostering a sense of shared responsibility and urgency.

Global Economics: A Web of Interconnected Markets

The modern economy is a testament to interdependence, with global supply chains linking producers and consumers across continents. From the coffee in a morning cup to the smartphone in a pocket, countless products rely on international cooperation and trade. While this interconnectedness has created unprecedented opportunities for growth and innovation, it also comes with challenges, such as economic inequality, environmental degradation, and vulnerability to global disruptions.

A clear example of economic interdependence is the production of electronics. Consider a smartphone: its raw materials, such as cobalt and lithium, are mined in countries like the Democratic Republic of Congo and Chile. Components are manufactured in places like China and South Korea, while final assembly may occur in countries such as Vietnam or India. The finished product is then sold worldwide. This intricate supply chain depends on cooperation between nations, corporations, and workers. However, it also reveals the vulnerabilities of interdependence, as disruptions in one part of the chain—such as a pandemic, labor strike, or resource shortage—can affect the entire system.

The COVID-19 pandemic starkly demonstrated this vulnerability. Lockdowns and restrictions disrupted global trade, causing shortages of essential goods, including medical supplies, food, and microchips. These disruptions highlighted the fragility of interconnected systems and underscored the need for resilience and collaboration. Governments and businesses have since sought to diversify supply chains and invest in regional production hubs to reduce dependence on single sources.

Economic interdependence also manifests in the realm of trade agreements and financial aid. Organizations like the World Trade Organization (WTO) and the International Monetary Fund (IMF) facilitate cooperation between nations to promote trade, reduce poverty, and stabilize economies. For instance, the African Continental Free Trade Area (AfCFTA) aims to boost economic integration across Africa, fostering growth through regional cooperation. These initiatives demonstrate how interdependence can drive prosperity while addressing shared challenges, such as unemployment and underdevelopment.

However, global economic interdependence is not without criticism. Critics point to exploitative labor practices, environmental harm, and unequal distribution of wealth as consequences of a system that prioritizes profit over sustainability and fairness. Fair trade movements and corporate social responsibility (CSR) initiatives have emerged as responses, advocating for ethical production and consumption practices. These efforts highlight the importance of balancing the benefits of economic interdependence with the need for equity and accountability.

Human Rights: A Universal Responsibility

Interdependence extends to the realm of human rights, where the protection and promotion of individual freedoms rely on collective action. Human rights violations in one part of the world often have far-reaching implications, affecting migration patterns, global security, and international relations. Recognizing the interconnected nature of human rights is essential for fostering global solidarity and accountability.

One practical example of interdependence in human rights is the global response to the Syrian refugee crisis. The civil war in Syria, which began in 2011, has displaced millions of people, creating one of the largest humanitarian crises in modern history. Neighboring countries like Turkey, Lebanon, and Jordan have borne the brunt of the influx, while European nations and other global powers have faced political and social challenges related to asylum seekers. This crisis highlights how conflicts and human rights abuses in one region can affect migration, security, and public opinion worldwide. International organizations like the United Nations High Commissioner for Refugees (UNHCR) and non-governmental organizations (NGOs) have stepped in to provide aid, demonstrating the necessity of collective responsibility.

Another example is the fight against modern slavery and human trafficking. According to the International Labour Organization (ILO), an estimated 50 million people worldwide are trapped in forced labor or forced marriage. These abuses often occur in industries tied to global supply chains, such as agriculture, textiles, and construction. Efforts to combat these practices involve governments, businesses, and civil society working together. Initiatives like the Ethical Trading Initiative and the Transparency in Supply Chains Act aim to hold corporations accountable and ensure that workers' rights are protected.

Finally, the global movement for gender equality illustrates the power of interdependence in advancing human rights. Campaigns like #MeToo have sparked conversations and policy changes across cultures and industries, demonstrating how shared experiences and collective action can challenge systemic injustices. International frameworks like the Convention on the Elimination of All Forms of Discrimination Against Women (CEDAW) provide a platform for collaboration, encouraging countries to adopt and enforce policies that promote gender equity.

Entangled   Sandra Ferreira

Interdependence shapes every aspect of the modern world, from environmental stewardship and economic cooperation to the protection of human rights. The examples of climate change, global economics, and human rights demonstrate how interconnected systems create shared challenges and opportunities. Recognizing this interdependence is crucial for fostering a sense of collective responsibility and driving meaningful action.

As the world becomes increasingly interconnected, embracing interdependence offers a path toward sustainability, equity, and resilience. By working together across borders, industries, and communities, humanity can address the complex challenges of the 21st century and create a future where all can thrive. Understanding and leveraging the power of interdependence is not merely a choice but a necessity for building a better world.

Chapter 11
Superposition and the Power of Choice

Superposition suggests that a quantum particle can exist in multiple states at once until observed. For global citizens, this principle can symbolize the multiple choices we hold at any given moment, each one leading to a different outcome. This chapter delves into the power of choice, exploring how our individual and collective actions can shape the future of our interconnected world.

Understanding Superposition and Its Implications for Potential Outcomes

Superposition, a concept rooted in quantum mechanics, has fundamentally reshaped our understanding of the physical universe and its inherent uncertainties. At its core, superposition refers to the ability of a quantum system to exist simultaneously in multiple states until measured or observed. This principle challenges classical notions of determinism and forces us to reconsider the relationship between observation and reality. Its implications extend beyond theoretical physics into fields such as computation, information theory, and even philosophy, offering new perspectives on potential outcomes in complex systems. This essay delves into the principle of superposition, its theoretical foundation, practical applications, and broader implications for understanding the nature of outcomes in an interconnected universe.

The Theoretical Foundation of Superposition

Superposition emerges from the foundational principles of quantum mechanics, particularly the wave-particle duality of matter and the probabilistic nature of quantum states. In classical physics, an object exists in a single state at any given time. For example, a ball rolling down a hill has a specific position and velocity that can be determined and predicted. However, in the quantum realm, particles such as electrons or photons exhibit dual behavior—they can act as particles or waves depending on the circumstances.

A hallmark of quantum mechanics is the Schrödinger equation, which describes the evolution of a quantum system's wave function over time. The wave function represents the probabilities of a particle's various potential states. In a state of superposition, the particle does not exist in any single, definite state but rather in a combination of all possible states. Mathematically, this is expressed as a linear combination of eigenstates, where each state has a specific probability amplitude.

A famous thought experiment illustrating superposition is Schrödinger's cat paradox. In this scenario, a cat in a box is linked to a quantum event (e.g., the decay of a radioactive atom) that determines its fate. Until the box is opened and the system is observed, the cat is said to be in a superposition of "alive" and "dead" states. This paradox underscores the non-intuitive nature of superposition and highlights the critical role of observation in collapsing a quantum system into a definite state.

Superposition and Potential Outcomes

The principle of superposition has profound implications for understanding potential outcomes, especially in systems governed by uncertainty. In classical systems, outcomes are deterministic, with well-defined cause-and-effect relationships. In contrast, quantum systems operate probabilistically, with multiple potential outcomes coexisting until measurement occurs.

This probabilistic nature can be visualized using the double-slit experiment. When particles such as electrons are fired through two slits, they produce an interference pattern on a screen, indicative of wave-like behavior. Remarkably, this pattern emerges even when particles are sent one at a time, suggesting that each particle exists in a superposition of passing through both slits simultaneously. However, when a measurement device determines which slit the particle passes through, the superposition collapses, and the particle behaves like a classical object, eliminating the interference pattern.

The implications of this phenomenon are vast. In quantum systems, the observer plays a critical role in determining which potential outcome manifests, a principle known as the observer effect. This challenges the classical notion of an objective reality independent of observation and introduces profound questions about the nature of existence and causality.

Applications of Superposition in Quantum Technology

Beyond its theoretical significance, superposition has practical applications in cutting-edge technologies, particularly in quantum computing and communication.

1. **Quantum Computing:**
Quantum computers leverage superposition to perform computations far beyond the capabilities of classical computers. Classical bits, the fundamental units of information, exist in one of two states: 0 or 1. In contrast, quantum bits, or qubits, can exist in a superposition of 0 and 1 simultaneously. This enables quantum computers to process vast amounts of information in parallel, making them exceptionally powerful for tasks such as cryptography, optimization problems, and simulating quantum systems. Algorithms like Shor's and Grover's exploit superposition to achieve exponential speed-ups in certain computations, illustrating its transformative potential.

2. **Quantum Communication:**
Superposition also plays a vital role in quantum communication technologies, such as quantum key distribution (QKD). QKD relies on the principles of superposition and entanglement to create secure communication channels. Any attempt to intercept the quantum states being transmitted disrupts their superposition, alerting the communicating parties to potential eavesdropping. This ensures unprecedented levels of security in data transmission.

3.   **Quantum Sensing**:

Superposition enhances the sensitivity and precision of quantum sensors, which are used in fields ranging from medical imaging to navigation. By exploiting quantum states, these devices can detect minute changes in physical quantities, such as magnetic fields or gravitational waves, with unparalleled accuracy.

Philosophical and Societal Implications

The concept of superposition extends beyond physics and technology, influencing philosophical discussions about reality, determinism, and free will. By suggesting that multiple potential outcomes coexist until observed, superposition challenges classical notions of a single, objective reality. This aligns with interpretations such as the many-worlds hypothesis, which posits that every potential outcome of a quantum event branches into a separate universe, creating an infinite multiverse.

Superposition also raises questions about the role of consciousness in shaping reality. The Copenhagen interpretation of quantum mechanics suggests that the act of observation collapses superpositions into definite states, implying a profound connection between the observer and the observed. While this remains a topic of debate, it underscores the interplay between human perception and the physical universe.

In a societal context, superposition serves as a metaphor for embracing uncertainty and potential. Just as quantum systems embody multiple possibilities, complex social, economic, and environmental systems may also harbor untapped potential for transformative outcomes. Recognizing this can inspire innovative approaches to problem-solving and decision-making in an increasingly interconnected world.

Superposition is a cornerstone of quantum mechanics that fundamentally challenges our understanding of reality and potential outcomes. From its theoretical underpinnings in wave-particle duality to its practical applications in quantum computing and communication, superposition exemplifies the power of embracing uncertainty and exploring multiple possibilities. Its implications extend beyond physics, shaping philosophical debates and offering new perspectives on complex systems in society. As we continue to harness the principles of superposition, we move closer to unlocking the mysteries of the quantum world and redefining our place within it.

The Importance of Conscious Decision-Making in a Globally Connected World

The world today is more interconnected than ever before, driven by rapid advancements in technology, globalization, and digital communication. As individuals, organizations, and nations interact on a scale never seen before, the choices we make have increasingly far-reaching consequences. This interconnectedness means that the impact of decisions is not confined to localized settings but ripples across borders, affecting distant regions and populations. In this globalized context, conscious decision-making—defined as the practice of being fully aware of the consequences and ethical implications of one's choices—is of paramount importance. This essay explores why conscious decision-making is crucial in a globally connected world, focusing on its effects on personal accountability, global challenges, technological advances, and the ethical considerations that arise in a networked society.

The Evolving Context of Decision-Making in a Globalized World

In a world that is rapidly shrinking due to digital connectivity, the scope of human decisions has expanded exponentially. With the advent of the internet, social media, and mobile technology, individuals can now communicate instantly with others across the globe. Business transactions, diplomatic agreements, and social movements unfold across vast distances in real-time, making the consequences of decisions more immediate and pervasive. Decisions that were once local now have the potential to reverberate globally, affecting economies, cultures, and environments.

Moreover, the issues that we face are increasingly global in nature. Climate change, pandemics, terrorism, and economic inequality are no longer problems that can be solved within the confines of national borders. These interconnected challenges demand a more holistic approach, where decision-makers must consider the global implications of their actions. As technology advances, many of these global issues are also influenced by decisions made at the personal, corporate, or governmental levels.

In this context, conscious decision-making becomes a critical skill. It involves more than just making the best choice for one's immediate interests or for one's community. It requires awareness of how our actions can affect others across the world, whether through environmental impact, economic shifts, or cultural influence.

Personal Accountability and the Global Impact of Choices

In a globally connected world, personal decisions—no matter how small—have the potential to influence a broader array of systems and individuals. The interconnected nature of global trade, digital platforms, and social media means that every individual has a degree of influence on the world around them. For example, purchasing habits directly impact the global supply chain, labor conditions, and environmental sustainability. Whether buying clothing, food, or technology, individuals are linked to distant workers and ecosystems, sometimes without realizing it.

Take the example of sustainable consumption. In the past, individual choices about what to purchase were largely limited to the local context. Today, however, consumer decisions about buying eco-friendly products, reducing waste, or supporting ethical companies have ripple effects that extend to global environmental and labor practices. The rise of social media and digital activism has made it possible for individuals to mobilize and demand accountability from large corporations, influencing corporate behavior in real-time.

Furthermore, conscious decision-making plays a significant role in personal relationships and social interactions. In an era where information travels quickly and misinformation can spread even faster, individuals must be thoughtful and deliberate about how they engage with others online. Decisions about what to share on social media, how to interact in digital spaces, and how to engage with people from different cultural backgrounds carry weight in fostering global empathy, understanding, and cooperation. By making conscious choices, individuals contribute to a more connected and empathetic global community.

The Role of Conscious Decision-Making in Addressing Global Challenges

Global challenges, such as climate change, poverty, and inequality, require decisions that reflect both ethical responsibility and an awareness of long-term consequences. In a globally connected world, the impacts of individual and collective actions are magnified, meaning that decision-makers—from government leaders to corporate executives—must consider not just their immediate interests, but the wider global ramifications of their choices.

1.   **Climate Change**:
One of the most pressing global challenges is climate change, which is driven by human activity, particularly fossil fuel consumption, deforestation, and industrial waste. Decisions made by individuals, corporations, and governments all have the potential to either mitigate or exacerbate the effects of climate change. A conscious decision to reduce one's carbon footprint, to advocate for policy changes that promote sustainable energy, or to invest in green technologies can contribute to positive environmental outcomes. Similarly, corporate decisions regarding supply chain management, energy consumption, and waste production also have significant environmental consequences. The interconnectedness of global economies means that a decision made in one part of the world can have environmental impacts in far-flung regions. For instance, the decision by a corporation to relocate production to a country with less stringent environmental regulations may result in environmental degradation that affects communities thousands of miles away.

2.   **Global Health**:
Pandemics like COVID-19 have illustrated the importance of collective, conscious decision-making in global health. Decisions about public health measures, vaccine distribution, and international cooperation can have far-reaching consequences. The global interconnectedness of economies, populations, and travel means that the health of one nation is intricately tied to the health of others. In this context, conscious decision-making involves understanding how choices, such as vaccination policies or social distancing measures, can either protect or harm not just local populations but the global community at large.

3.   **Economic Inequality**:
Global economic inequality has deepened in recent decades, with decisions made by multinational corporations and wealthy nations shaping the wealth distribution patterns across the globe. A conscious approach to decision-making in business, trade, and finance can help address inequality. Companies that prioritize fair wages, ethical labor practices,

and local empowerment can contribute to reducing the stark disparities between the Global North and South. Similarly, governments that engage in fair trade practices and invest in international development can create systems that uplift disadvantaged populations, breaking the cycle of poverty. In a connected world, decisions made by those with economic power can have significant effects on social mobility and wealth redistribution worldwide.

Technological Advances and the Ethics of Decision-Making

Advancements in technology have brought about profound changes in every aspect of life. While these advances offer unprecedented opportunities for progress, they also introduce new ethical dilemmas that require conscious decision-making. The development of artificial intelligence, for instance, brings with it the potential for significant improvements in medicine, transportation, and communication. However, it also raises concerns about privacy, job displacement, and inequality in access to technological resources.

The ethical use of technology is another area where conscious decision-making is essential. Decisions about how technologies are developed, deployed, and regulated can have lasting global consequences. For example, the decision to use data for targeted advertising or surveillance can undermine privacy rights and exacerbate existing inequalities. Similarly, decisions regarding the development of autonomous systems or genetic engineering need to consider not just the benefits to society but also the potential for harm. As the global interconnectedness of technology increases, so too does the need for ethical frameworks that guide decision-making in this space.

In an increasingly interconnected world, conscious decision-making is not only a personal responsibility but a global one. The choices we make—whether in our personal lives, in business, or in governance—have far-reaching consequences that extend well beyond our immediate surroundings. From environmental sustainability to global health and economic equity, the impact of our decisions is magnified in a networked world. As technology and globalization continue to shape the future, the importance of being aware of the ethical, social, and environmental consequences of our actions becomes ever more critical.

Conscious decision-making requires us to think beyond ourselves, to consider the long-term impacts of our choices, and to recognize our interconnectedness with people and places far from our own. By embracing a mindful approach to decision-making, we can create a more equitable, sustainable, and compassionate global society. In a world where our actions can affect others on the other side of the globe, being conscious of the outcomes of our choices is not just important—it is essential.

How Our Choices, Like Quantum States, Determine the Reality We Experience

The nature of reality and the factors that shape our experiences have long been subjects of philosophical debate and scientific inquiry. In recent decades, a unique perspective on how we might understand the creation of reality has emerged, drawing on insights from quantum physics and philosophy. Just as quantum mechanics suggests that particles exist in superposition, in a state of multiple possibilities until measured or observed, the choices we make in life can be viewed as determining which "reality" we experience. This essay explores the intriguing parallel between quantum states and human decision-making, suggesting that, much like particles in quantum mechanics, our choices collapse potential realities into the one we experience. By examining the role of free will, the power of consciousness, and the influence of decisions on our personal and collective reality, we will explore how, like quantum states, our choices shape the world around us and ultimately determine the fabric of our lived experience.

Quantum Mechanics and the Superposition of States

At the heart of quantum mechanics is the concept of superposition, which describes how quantum particles—such as electrons or photons—can exist in multiple states simultaneously. A particle, for instance, doesn't have a single position or momentum until it is measured. Instead, it exists in a superposition of all possible states, each with its own probability amplitude. The act of measurement collapses this superposition into one definite state. This phenomenon is famously illustrated by Schrödinger's cat thought experiment, where a cat in a box is simultaneously alive and dead until the box is open and an observer collapses the superposition into one observable state.

The principle of superposition has profound implications. It suggests that until an observation occurs, multiple outcomes or possibilities are coexisting. In essence, the quantum system is in all potential states until it is forced into a specific reality by the act of measurement. This brings us to an intriguing idea: what if the decisions we make in life similarly collapse a set of possibilities into the one reality we experience?

Human Choices as a Parallel to Quantum States

In the same way that quantum particles exist in superposition, the decisions we make in our lives can be seen as analogous to measurements that collapse various possibilities into a single, actualized reality. When we stand at a crossroads in life— whether in our careers, relationships, or personal endeavors—we are faced with a multitude of potential outcomes. The same event or choice can lead to different experiences depending on the decision we make, just as quantum particles exhibit different behaviors depending on how they are measured.

The idea that we have the power to determine the reality we experience through our choices is similar to the collapse of a quantum state. Each decision we make can be seen as a measurement that forces a potential outcome to manifest. The world of possibilities exists in an undetermined state until we act. For example, when faced with a decision to pursue one job over another, the choice we make collapses a range of potential futures into the one we ultimately experience. If we take one job, we may enter a career that brings fulfillment and success; if we choose another, we may face different challenges, but both paths are contingent on the specific decision we make.

Entangled   Sandra Ferreira

This concept mirrors quantum theory's assertion that, until measured, an electron exists in a state of multiple possibilities, each with a different probability. Similarly, before we make a decision, our life exists in a potential state of numerous outcomes, each one just as likely as the others, waiting for our choice to determine the path we will follow.

The Role of Consciousness and Free Will in Determining Reality

Central to the idea of choice and reality is the role of consciousness and free will. Quantum mechanics introduces the observer effect, which suggests that the act of observation affects the state of the system being observed. This has led some philosophers and physicists to speculate that consciousness itself plays a pivotal role in shaping the physical world. Similarly, our conscious choices have a direct impact on the reality we experience.

Free will, though a deeply philosophical and debated topic, plays a role in how we perceive and navigate the potential states of reality. While quantum mechanics does not provide an explicit answer to the question of free will, it hints at the idea that an observer's engagement with the system can influence its outcome. This concept can be paralleled in human behavior. Just as the act of observation collapses quantum states into specific realities, the choices we consciously make bring certain potential futures into existence. For instance, the choice to pursue an education can lead to a very different life compared to the decision to focus on work immediately after high school. In this way, free will is the mechanism through which we navigate the multiple potential futures available to us.

However, just as quantum mechanics suggests that probabilities govern the outcomes, not certainties, our choices are not always deterministic. The uncertainty inherent in both quantum mechanics and human decision-making highlights that while we shape our reality, we do not control every variable. Our choices may influence the direction of our lives, but they exist within a web of uncertainty and probability, which means the outcomes are never fully predictable.

The Intersection of Personal and Collective Realities

Our individual choices, though shaping our personal realities, also contribute to the collective reality we share with others. Just as quantum mechanics operates on both individual particles and the collective behavior of systems, the choices we make at an individual level influence the larger societal and global dynamics. The decisions of individuals and groups create a collective reality in the same way that the behavior of individual quantum particles leads to larger patterns, such as interference patterns in the double-slit experiment.

Consider, for instance, collective decisions made by a community or society. If a group of people chooses to focus on sustainability and conservation, the cumulative effect of their choices can lead to the manifestation of a reality where environmental concerns are addressed, and ecological balance is restored. Conversely, if the collective choice is to prioritize short-term economic gain at the expense of the environment, the reality of climate change becomes an inescapable part of the future. The collective will, much like the sum of individual quantum measurements, collapses a multitude of potential outcomes into one shared reality.

Similarly, in global events such as international politics, trade negotiations, and climate action, the choices made by leaders and organizations have the potential to affect millions of people across the world. These decisions, just like the quantum measurement of a particle, determine the global reality we experience. In this sense, the choices made on a small scale can create ripple effects that extend outward, shaping the broader world in a multitude of ways.

The Ethics of Choice and the Creation of Reality

The analogy between quantum states and human decision-making also brings with it ethical implications. If our choices truly determine the reality we experience, we must recognize the responsibility that comes with this power. In the quantum world, each measurement alters the system in some way, and similarly, our decisions shape the world around us, often in profound ways. Therefore, it is essential to approach decision-making with mindfulness and awareness, considering not only our immediate desires but also the long-term effects of our choices on ourselves and others.

Ethically, this perspective challenges us to consider the interconnectedness of our actions. Just as one quantum state can influence another, our decisions affect the fabric of reality for those around us. This interconnectedness requires us to make choices that foster collective well-being, promote sustainability, and consider the broader consequences of our actions. The ethical principle of "do no harm" aligns with the idea that we must be conscious of how our decisions contribute to the world around us.

Just as quantum mechanics suggests that particles exist in a superposition of possibilities until observed, our choices in life act as measurements that collapse a range of potential outcomes into the reality we experience. Our decisions—whether personal or collective—are the mechanisms through which we navigate the vast potentialities of life, determining the paths we take and the world we inhabit. While quantum theory offers a scientific framework for understanding probability and measurement, human decision-making mirrors this concept in the way our choices create the reality we live. In both realms, there is a deep interplay between possibility and observation, uncertainty and choice. Understanding the power of our decisions, and the potential for their ripple effects, can help us recognize the immense responsibility we bear in shaping the world we experience and, ultimately, the world we leave behind.

Chapter 12
Observation and Social Impact

In quantum mechanics, observation affects reality. On a societal level, this means that awareness and perception shape outcomes. When we witness social issues, engage in discussions, or learn about global crises, our "observation" becomes part of the social reality. This chapter examines the transformative power of awareness, media, and collective consciousness in creating a more engaged global society.

The Observer Effect and Its Relevance to Social Awareness

The observer effect, a term primarily associated with quantum physics, refers to the phenomenon in which the act of observation alters the behavior of the system being observed. This effect is commonly discussed in the context of experiments involving particles, where measuring or observing their position or momentum changes their state. Although the observer effect originates in the physical sciences, its implications extend beyond physics, providing a useful lens for understanding social behavior, human psychology, and societal dynamics. This essay will explore the observer effect's significance within the framework of social awareness, particularly how awareness or observation of individuals or groups influences their behavior and perception. By drawing connections between quantum mechanics and social interaction, this essay will show how the observer effect can deepen our understanding of societal issues, including the impact of surveillance, the role of media in shaping public opinion, and the evolution of social norms.

Understanding the Observer Effect in Physics

Before examining the broader implications of the observer effect in social contexts, it is essential to understand its roots in physics. In quantum mechanics, the observer effect refers to how the act of measuring or observing a quantum system (such as a subatomic particle) can alter its state. For instance, in the famous double-slit experiment, a particle like an electron behaves as both a wave and a particle. When no one observes the electron, it behaves like a wave, creating an interference pattern. However, when it is observed, the particle behaves as though it has gone through one slit, creating a particle-like distribution. This implies that the mere act of observing or measuring the particle influences its behavior, revealing that reality is not an independent, static entity, but one that is affected by the observer.

This concept has caused much debate and reflection among physicists, philosophers, and scientists alike. In particular, the observer effect in quantum mechanics suggests that consciousness or the act of measurement plays a fundamental role in shaping reality. The implications of this idea have extended into various interdisciplinary fields, including psychology, sociology, and even ethics, leading to new interpretations of how human observation shapes social behavior.

Social Awareness as an Extension of the Observer Effect

In a social context, the observer effect can be understood as the influence that individuals or groups experience when they are aware that they are being observed. Social psychology has long recognized that people alter their behavior when they know they are being watched, a concept closely linked to the idea of social awareness. The awareness of being observed is often referred to as the "spotlight effect," where individuals believe they are the center of attention and act accordingly. This behavior is seen in various contexts, such as in professional settings, public spaces, and social media platforms.

For example, research has shown that people are more likely to adhere to social norms and engage in prosocial behaviors (such as helping others or following rules) when they believe they are being observed. This effect is commonly utilized in settings like workplaces or educational institutions to encourage desirable behavior. Similarly, individuals may change their demeanor, appearance, or language in the presence of others, a phenomenon known as impression management. These changes in behavior, driven by the knowledge that others are observing, are a direct application of the observer effect in the social realm.

The Role of Surveillance in Social Behavior

One of the most prominent ways the observer effect influences social behavior today is through surveillance. With the advent of modern technology, surveillance has become ubiquitous in many societies, affecting individuals' daily lives in both public and private spheres. The presence of cameras, monitoring devices, and even the awareness of being tracked online all contribute to individuals altering their behavior. In many ways, surveillance acts as a constant "observer," prompting people to conform to certain behaviors out of fear of judgment, punishment, or social disapproval.

The famous social psychologist Erving Goffman explored the concept of the "total institution," where constant surveillance creates a sense of discipline and control over individuals. In modern society, similar mechanisms are at play through surveillance technologies. The knowledge that one is being observed can lead to heightened self-awareness, resulting in more conforming behavior. This dynamic is particularly evident in public spaces, where people may act more politely or adhere to societal expectations due to the presence of surveillance cameras or the assumption that they are being observed by others.

The implications of such widespread surveillance extend to political and social control. Governments, corporations, and institutions may use surveillance to monitor and regulate behavior, shaping public opinion and enforcing social norms. In democratic societies, debates over privacy and the ethics of surveillance often center on the balance between maintaining security and protecting individual freedoms. In these discussions, the observer effect is evident, as the act of being observed can either empower or constrain individuals, depending on the context.

Media and the Observer Effect in Shaping Public Opinion

Another significant area where the observer effect is relevant to social awareness is in the realm of media. The media plays a powerful role in shaping public perceptions, influencing attitudes, and guiding social behavior. Through the dissemination of news, entertainment, advertisements, and social media content, the media acts as an observer that constantly shapes how individuals see the world and how they believe others perceive them.

One way the media affects social behavior is through the creation of norms and expectations. For instance, the portrayal of beauty standards, gender roles, and societal values in advertisements and TV shows can lead individuals to modify their behavior to align with these representations. People, particularly adolescents and young adults, may adjust their appearances, aspirations, or lifestyles based on what they perceive as acceptable or desirable according to media portrayals. This is a direct manifestation of the observer effect: the awareness of being observed by the media leads individuals to conform to societal standards.

Furthermore, social media platforms, which are designed around the concept of constant visibility, exacerbate this effect. On platforms like Instagram, Facebook, and TikTok, individuals present curated versions of their lives, adjusting their behavior and appearances to gain likes, followers, or positive attention. The constant awareness that they are being observed, evaluated, and judged by their social networks drives individuals to behave in ways that conform to popular trends or expectations. In this sense, the observer effect amplifies the influence of social media in shaping personal identities and social behavior.

The Evolution of Social Norms and the Observer Effect

The observer effect also plays a crucial role in the evolution of social norms. As individuals become more aware of their behavior's impact on others, they may adjust their actions to align with changing societal values. Over time, this collective awareness can drive the transformation of social norms, as individuals collectively redefine what is considered acceptable or unacceptable. The observer effect here acts as a feedback loop, where behavior shifts in response to increased observation, and in turn, new norms emerge as society collectively adapts to new ways of being observed.

Consider the evolution of attitudes toward issues like gender equality, racial justice, and environmental sustainability. In the past few decades, increased awareness of these issues, often driven by social movements and media coverage, has led to significant changes in social norms. The act of observing and acknowledging social injustice has prompted widespread calls for reform, with individuals altering their behavior to reflect new understandings of fairness, inclusivity, and responsibility.

Social awareness and the observer effect are central to the process of social change. As society becomes more attuned to issues of inequality, discrimination, and injustice, the collective awareness that these issues are being observed often results in shifts in behavior, policy, and institutional practices. The observer effect, in this sense, not only reflects current social attitudes but also facilitates the evolution of social norms as individuals and groups adjust their behaviors to align with new values and expectations.

The observer effect, initially a concept rooted in quantum physics, has profound implications for understanding human behavior and social dynamics. Whether in the context of surveillance, media influence, or the evolution of social norms, the knowledge of being observed shapes how individuals act, think, and interact with others. In the realm of social awareness, the observer effect highlights the powerful role that observation and perception play in shaping societal behavior. As individuals become increasingly aware of their visibility in public and private spaces, their behavior adjusts accordingly, sometimes reinforcing existing norms and sometimes challenging them. Understanding the observer effect's relevance to social awareness can provide valuable insights into how we can navigate the complexities of modern society, promoting greater self-awareness, social responsibility, and collective change.

Knowledge and Awareness: Catalysts of Social Change

Throughout history, knowledge and awareness have been pivotal in driving social change. From the abolition of slavery to the civil rights movement, from environmental activism to gender equality, the power of understanding and being conscious of societal issues has sparked widespread reform. Knowledge—whether through education, experience, or revelation—helps individuals and communities recognize injustices, inequities, and the need for change. Awareness, on the other hand, connects that knowledge to action, driving collective efforts that seek to address these issues on a larger scale. This essay will explore how knowledge and awareness work together to propel social change by examining historical and contemporary examples, their psychological and sociological underpinnings, and the processes by which awareness transforms societies.

The Role of Knowledge in Social Change

Knowledge is the foundation of any meaningful social change. It serves as the starting point for individuals and groups to understand the status quo, identify problems, and envision potential solutions. In many cases, social progress has been catalyzed by the dissemination of knowledge—whether it is new scientific findings, historical research, or insights into societal issues. The accumulation of knowledge makes people aware of the shortcomings in their societies, pushing them to challenge existing power structures, norms, and institutions.

One example of knowledge driving social change can be found in the abolitionist movement in the 18th and 19th centuries. The Enlightenment era brought with it new philosophical ideas about human rights, liberty, and equality, which deeply influenced thinkers like John Locke, Voltaire, and Thomas Paine. These ideas laid the intellectual groundwork for the abolition of slavery. As knowledge of the brutality and inhumanity of slavery spread through literature, speeches, and the personal testimonies of former slaves, public awareness grew, and the moral case for abolition became undeniable.

Similarly, knowledge played a crucial role in the civil rights movement in the United States. The work of historians, sociologists, and political activists revealed the depth of racial inequality in the U.S. Through literature, speeches, and mass media, such as books like *Uncle Tom's Cabin* by Harriet Beecher Stowe, and later works like *The Autobiography of Malcolm X* and *Letter from Birmingham Jail* by Martin Luther King Jr., the broader public was made aware of systemic racism. These works exposed the contradictions in a society that proclaimed liberty and equality while perpetuating racial injustice. Knowledge of these inequalities led to greater social mobilization and the demand for legislative and cultural change.

Knowledge also plays a critical role in areas such as public health, where scientific discoveries have driven profound social transformations. The discovery of the germ theory of disease, for example, revolutionized medicine in the 19th century, leading to significant changes in public health practices, including sanitation, hygiene, and vaccination. Similarly, awareness of the dangers of smoking, and the subsequent research into its health impacts, led to widespread anti-smoking campaigns and policies aimed at reducing tobacco use.

The Power of Awareness in Social Change

While knowledge is essential, it is awareness that motivates action. Awareness of a problem or issue enables individuals and communities to recognize their responsibility in addressing it. Social change often occurs when large groups of people become conscious of issues that may have previously been ignored or accepted as part of the status quo. Once people become aware of societal problems, they begin to question the structures and systems that perpetuate those issues, which can drive both individual and collective actions.

One of the most notable examples of awareness driving social change is the environmental movement, particularly the rise of global concern over climate change. The publication of Rachel Carson's *Silent Spring* in 1962 raised awareness about the environmental damage caused by pesticide use. It illuminated the interconnectivity of ecosystems and the ways in which human activities could have a devastating impact on the natural world. Carson's work, along with the increasing evidence of pollution and its effects on human health, led to the formation of environmental organizations and the passage of key legislation such as the Clean Air Act and the Clean Water Act in the United States. The growing awareness of environmental issues over time has spurred movements for renewable energy, conservation, and international agreements to address climate change.

Another example of how awareness leads to social change is the feminist movement. In the late 19th and early 20th centuries, women began to raise awareness about gender inequality, advocating for women's suffrage, property rights, and access to education and employment. The knowledge of how women were systematically oppressed in various domains, paired with growing awareness of the possibility of gender equality, led to the first wave of feminism. As the feminist movement evolved, awareness of issues such as reproductive rights, workplace discrimination, and sexual violence brought attention to ongoing struggles for gender equality, sparking legislative changes and cultural shifts. Today, awareness of gender-based violence, the gender pay gap, and intersectionality continues to drive social activism.

The LGBTQ+ rights movement provides another example of how awareness has driven change. Historically marginalized, the LGBTQ+ community began to organize in the mid-20th century, raising awareness of issues related to discrimination, healthcare, and marriage equality. The 1969 Stonewall riots in New York City marked a pivotal moment in the LGBTQ+ rights movement, drawing public attention to the mistreatment of LGBTQ+ individuals. Since then, growing awareness of the social, legal, and economic challenges faced by LGBTQ+ individuals has led to significant legal and cultural changes, including marriage equality in many countries, anti-discrimination laws, and broader social acceptance.

The Psychological Mechanisms Behind Knowledge and Awareness

To understand how knowledge and awareness drive social change, it is important to consider the psychological mechanisms that underlie these processes. One of the key concepts here is cognitive dissonance—the psychological discomfort that arises when there is a discrepancy between a person's beliefs or attitudes and their actions. When individuals become aware of social injustices or contradictions in their society, they may experience cognitive dissonance if their actions or the actions of others do not align with their new understanding.

For example, if someone becomes aware of the environmental damage caused by their consumption habits, they may feel discomfort if they continue to engage in behaviors that contribute to pollution. This discomfort can motivate them to change their actions, whether by reducing waste, supporting environmentally friendly policies, or participating in environmental activism. Similarly, awareness of social injustices, such as racial inequality or gender discrimination, may lead individuals to reevaluate their own behaviors and attitudes, promoting empathy, solidarity, and activism.

Another psychological factor is social identity, which plays a role in how individuals engage with social change. As people become more aware of societal problems, they often find that they identify with others who share similar concerns. This collective identity can provide the social support needed to mobilize and sustain efforts for change. For instance, movements like Black Lives Matter and #MeToo have been driven by the collective awareness of systemic issues and the shared sense of injustice experienced by individuals within those communities.

Awareness and Action: From Knowledge to Policy Change

Awareness does not always immediately lead to action, but it is a crucial step toward effecting change. The transformation of awareness into concrete action—whether through grassroots organizing, political lobbying, or mass protest—is the critical next stage in the process of social change. Knowledge without action may remain theoretical, but when awareness sparks collective action, it can challenge and alter the status quo.

For instance, the awareness generated by the #MeToo movement, which exposed the widespread prevalence of sexual harassment and assault, led to significant cultural shifts and legislative changes. The movement prompted public figures to be held accountable, led to changes in workplace policies, and influenced political discourse around sexual harassment. Similarly, climate change awareness has spurred international agreements such as the Paris Climate Accord, which aims to curb global warming and reduce greenhouse gas emissions.

The intersection of knowledge and awareness also plays a crucial role in advocacy and policy reform. Social change is often achieved through the coordinated efforts of activists, organizations, and policymakers who use knowledge to raise awareness, mobilize communities, and create lasting change. The combination of awareness and action provides the necessary momentum for movements to succeed, whether through legal reforms, cultural shifts, or changes in individual behavior.

Knowledge and awareness are two critical drivers of social change. Knowledge equips individuals with the understanding necessary to identify problems and recognize injustice, while awareness connects this knowledge to action by prompting individuals and communities to act in pursuit of social betterment. Throughout history, social movements have been sparked by the spread of knowledge and the awakening of awareness. From the abolition of slavery to the fight for gender equality, from the environmental movement to LGBTQ+ rights, the power of knowledge and awareness has fundamentally transformed societies. As we face new global challenges, such as climate change, racial injustice, and political polarization, the continued interplay between knowledge and awareness will be essential in shaping a more just, equitable, and sustainable future.

The Role of Media, Education, and Public Engagement in Shaping Global Outcomes

In the increasingly interconnected world of the 21st century, the forces shaping global outcomes are diverse and multifaceted. Media, education, and public engagement play fundamental roles in influencing societal attitudes, public policy, and international relations. These tools help shape public opinion, spread knowledge, and mobilize action on critical issues such as climate change, social justice, and global health. This essay will explore how these three elements interact to shape global outcomes by examining their influence on public perception, policy development, and the overall process of social change. By exploring both the positive and negative impacts of media, education, and public engagement, this essay will highlight their critical roles in addressing global challenges and advancing collective goals.

The Role of Media in Shaping Global Outcomes

The media serves as a primary source of information in contemporary societies, acting as a bridge between events occurring globally and the general public. As a tool for shaping global outcomes, media not only informs but also influences public perception, behavior, and policy. In particular, the rise of digital media platforms has revolutionized the way people receive information, engage with news, and participate in global dialogues.

Media's influence on shaping global outcomes is perhaps most evident in its coverage of major global crises, such as the COVID-19 pandemic, climate change, and political conflicts. For example, the role of media in disseminating information about the COVID-19 virus was crucial in shaping public response, government action, and the global response to the pandemic. Through television, radio, newspapers, and social media, information about the virus's spread, government regulations, and safety measures reached billions of people worldwide. Media campaigns were also essential in promoting vaccination, managing public health messaging, and combating misinformation.

Furthermore, media plays a critical role in framing global issues in particular ways, influencing how the public perceives them. For example, media coverage of climate change can either emphasize the urgency of taking action or downplay the threat, depending on the narratives promoted by specific outlets. In recent decades, the role of media in promoting environmental awareness has been pivotal in mobilizing global action on climate change. Documentaries like *An Inconvenient Truth* and *Before the Flood* have brought widespread attention to the issue, influencing public opinion and encouraging political leaders to prioritize climate action.

Similarly, media has been instrumental in highlighting issues of social injustice, such as racial inequality and gender discrimination. The Black Lives Matter movement, for example, gained global traction largely due to the power of social media and its ability to quickly disseminate information and organize protests. Hashtags like #MeToo and #BlackLivesMatter have helped bring attention to systemic inequalities, influencing both public attitudes and policy decisions in numerous countries. Media, particularly social media, has thus become a crucial tool in shaping not only public perception but also driving grassroots movements and international calls for reform.

However, the media is not without its challenges. The proliferation of misinformation and the rise of "fake news" have complicated the media's role in shaping global outcomes. Social media platforms, while enabling the rapid spread of information, have also facilitated the spread of disinformation, conspiracy theories, and polarized views. The challenge of navigating the vast array of media sources and discerning truth from falsehood has become a pressing issue in the digital age. Consequently, while media plays a powerful role in shaping global outcomes, it also requires critical engagement to ensure that its influence is constructive and beneficial.

The Role of Education in Shaping Global Outcomes

Education is another critical force in shaping global outcomes. As a fundamental institution, education equips individuals with the knowledge, skills, and values necessary to navigate the world and contribute to societal development. The impact of education on global outcomes can be seen both in the personal development of individuals and in the broader social, political, and economic progress of nations.

On a global scale, education is key to addressing issues such as poverty, inequality, and human rights. For example, education has long been recognized as a critical tool in reducing poverty and improving living standards. The United Nations' Sustainable Development Goal (SDG) 4, which aims to ensure inclusive and equitable quality education and promote lifelong learning opportunities for all, underscores the importance of education in fostering global progress. By providing individuals with access to education, societies empower their citizens to contribute to economic development, innovation, and the reduction of poverty.

Moreover, education can shape global outcomes by promoting values such as human rights, equality, and environmental stewardship. Global educational initiatives, such as the integration of sustainability into school curricula and the promotion of gender equality, help to cultivate a generation of individuals who are more aware of and engaged with pressing global issues. For instance, the incorporation of climate education in schools is fostering a generation of students who understand the complexities of environmental challenges and are better equipped to advocate for climate action.

Higher education institutions also play a key role in shaping global outcomes by driving research and innovation. Universities and research centers contribute to the development of new technologies, scientific advancements, and policy solutions to address global challenges. For example, research on renewable energy sources, public health, and disease prevention often originates in academic institutions and is crucial in shaping global strategies to address these challenges.

Despite its transformative potential, education systems around the world face significant challenges. Disparities in access to quality education, especially in developing countries, hinder progress toward global equality. The digital divide also presents barriers to education, particularly as more learning is shifting online. For education to fully realize its potential in shaping global outcomes, it must be accessible, inclusive, and equitable.

The Role of Public Engagement in Shaping Global Outcomes

Public engagement refers to the active participation of citizens in political, social, and community activities. It encompasses a wide range of activities, from voting and attending protests to participating in community service and advocacy work. Public engagement is essential in shaping global outcomes because it enables individuals to influence decision-making, hold governments and corporations accountable, and drive collective action on global issues.

One of the most significant ways public engagement shapes global outcomes is through political participation. Elections, referendums, and policy debates are all forms of public engagement that allow individuals to shape the political landscape. In many countries, the right to vote is seen as a key mechanism for citizens to influence government policy and ensure that their voices are heard on issues such as healthcare, education, and climate change. When large segments of the population become engaged in political processes, they can drive significant policy changes that affect global outcomes.

Public engagement also plays a crucial role in social movements. Throughout history, social movements have been instrumental in advocating for change and shaping global outcomes. For example, the civil rights movement in the United States was propelled by the active engagement of individuals and communities demanding an end to racial segregation and discrimination. Similarly, the global movement for LGBTQ+ rights has seen significant progress, with many countries legalizing same-sex marriage and enacting anti-discrimination laws, largely due to the tireless work of activists and public engagement in these issues.

In addition to formal political processes and social movements, public engagement is also critical in driving collective action on global challenges. For example, the global response to climate change has been fueled by public pressure on governments and corporations to adopt more sustainable practices. Movements such as Fridays for Future, led by youth activist Greta Thunberg, have galvanized millions of people around the world to demand urgent climate action. Similarly, public engagement in areas such as human rights, refugee support, and global health has helped shape international policies and foster global cooperation.

However, public engagement can also face barriers, such as political apathy, misinformation, and disillusionment with institutions. In many cases, individuals may feel disconnected from the political process or may lack access to the resources necessary to participate in public life. Ensuring that all individuals have the opportunity and the means to engage in societal issues is crucial for achieving positive global outcomes.

Media, education, and public engagement are essential forces in shaping global outcomes. Each of these elements has the power to influence public opinion, mobilize action, and drive social, political, and economic change. Through the media, people are informed about critical global issues and can participate in global conversations. Education provides the knowledge and values necessary to address global challenges and advance societal progress. Public engagement empowers individuals to actively shape the world around them through political participation, activism, and collective action. Together, these forces are instrumental in shaping a more just, equitable, and sustainable global future. However, for them to be fully effective, they must be accessible, inclusive, and driven by a commitment to positive change.

Chapter 13
Probability, Uncertainty, and Ethical Responsibility

Quantum physics deals with probabilities rather than certainties. The Heisenberg Uncertainty Principle teaches us that some aspects of reality are inherently unknowable. This chapter explores the parallels between quantum uncertainty and the ethical responsibility of a global citizen in a complex, unpredictable world. It encourages embracing uncertainty with curiosity and compassion, recognizing that we cannot predict every impact, but we can act responsibly.

The Uncertainty Principle and Its Application to Ethical Decision-Making

The **Uncertainty Principle**, formulated by the physicist Werner Heisenberg in 1927, asserts that there are fundamental limits to the precision with which certain pairs of physical properties, such as position and momentum, can be known simultaneously. This principle has been one of the cornerstones of quantum mechanics, challenging classical physics' belief in deterministic laws of nature. At its core, the Uncertainty Principle suggests that the act of measurement itself disturbs the system being measured, implying that the more accurately one property is known, the less accurately the other can be determined.

While the Uncertainty Principle is often considered purely a concept within the realm of physics, its philosophical implications extend far beyond the confines of science. In particular, it can be applied to the field of ethics, where decision-making is often marked by ambiguity, incomplete information, and unpredictability. Ethical dilemmas frequently arise when individuals or groups must make decisions in uncertain contexts, where the full consequences of their actions are unknown and the stakes are high. By exploring the Uncertainty Principle in the context of ethical decision-making, we can better understand how uncertainty shapes moral choices and how it should be navigated in complex moral landscapes.

This essay will explore the Uncertainty Principle, examining its scientific origins and then considering how the underlying concept of uncertainty can inform and influence ethical decision-making. We will explore how uncertainty affects moral judgment, the implications for ethical theories, and how individuals and organizations might navigate ethical dilemmas in the face of unknown outcomes.

The Uncertainty Principle in Physics

To understand the philosophical implications of the Uncertainty Principle, it is important first to grasp its basic formulation in quantum mechanics. The principle is mathematically expressed through Heisenberg's inequality:

Here, represents the uncertainty in position, represents the uncertainty in momentum, and is the reduced Planck constant. This inequality shows that there is a fundamental limit to how precisely the position () and momentum () of a particle can be simultaneously known. The more precisely one of these values is known, the greater the uncertainty in the other. This is not due to limitations in measurement technology, but a fundamental feature of the nature of particles at the quantum level.

In classical physics, the position and momentum of objects could be measured with arbitrary precision, and the future state of a system could, in theory, be predicted based on these measurements. However, quantum mechanics defies this deterministic approach, introducing inherent uncertainty into the fabric of nature. This principle undermines the classical notion of a fully predictable universe and suggests that uncertainty is an intrinsic part of reality at the quantum scale.

While Heisenberg's Uncertainty Principle initially pertained to the behavior of subatomic particles, its implications extend to broader philosophical and theoretical considerations. For instance, it challenges the assumption that reality is fully knowable and that knowledge can always lead to absolute certainty. This challenge to certainty is something that can also be explored within the domain of ethics, where moral decision-making often occurs in the presence of incomplete information and competing values.

The Nature of Ethical Decision-Making

Ethical decision-making involves choosing between competing values, principles, or actions in situations where the right course of action is not immediately clear. Many ethical dilemmas involve uncertainty, where individuals or groups must navigate ambiguity in both the available information and the potential consequences of their choices.

For example, a healthcare professional may have to decide whether to allocate limited resources (such as life-saving medication) to one patient over another. The decision might be complicated by uncertainty about the patient's prognosis, the likely outcomes of treatment, and the broader social or ethical implications of the choice. The healthcare provider may have access to incomplete or conflicting information, such as differing medical opinions or ambiguous ethical guidelines, making the decision even more difficult.

The concept of **moral uncertainty** refers to situations in which individuals are unsure about the moral correctness of various courses of action. This uncertainty can arise for a variety of reasons, including the complexity of the situation, the lack of clear ethical guidelines, or the unpredictable consequences of different actions. In such cases, individuals must make choices based on imperfect knowledge, with the recognition that their decision could have unintended or unforeseen consequences.

Like the Uncertainty Principle in quantum mechanics, moral uncertainty implies that ethical decision-making is not always about choosing between absolute rights and wrongs. Instead, moral decisions are often made in contexts where the ethical dimensions are not fully knowable, and outcomes may be influenced by factors beyond the decision-maker's control.

The Uncertainty Principle and Ethical Theories

The application of the Uncertainty Principle to ethical decision-making challenges several dominant ethical theories. These theories often operate under assumptions of certainty, clear guidelines, and predictable consequences. For example, **utilitarianism**, which advocates for the greatest good for the greatest number, often assumes that one can predict the outcomes of actions with sufficient clarity to maximize overall happiness. However, the inherent uncertainty in the consequences of any action complicates this calculation.

Deontological ethics, which emphasizes duty and adherence to moral rules, may also struggle with uncertainty, as it assumes that one can apply fixed moral principles to every situation. However, in cases where the implications of following a rule are unclear or ambiguous, decision-makers may find themselves caught in a conflict between adhering to a duty and addressing unforeseen consequences.

The **virtue ethics** approach, which focuses on the development of moral character and the cultivation of virtues, might offer a more flexible framework for navigating uncertainty. Since virtue ethics emphasizes the role of practical wisdom (phronesis) and judgment in moral decision-making, it allows for more adaptability in the face of uncertainty. Virtue ethicists recognize that good decision-making requires considering context, uncertainty, and the complexities of human life.

The **precautionary principle**, often used in environmental ethics, is another example of an ethical framework that embraces uncertainty. This principle suggests that in the face of uncertainty about the potential risks of an action (particularly with respect to long-term environmental or societal consequences), one should err on the side of caution. In this way, the precautionary principle explicitly integrates the acknowledgment of uncertainty into the ethical decision-making process.

Thus, the Uncertainty Principle does not just challenge deterministic views of ethics but also enriches the conversation about how to make responsible and morally sound decisions in the face of the unknown.

Practical Implications: Navigating Uncertainty in Ethical Decision-Making

Understanding uncertainty in ethical decision-making has profound practical implications. First, it encourages humility and openness in the decision-making process. Acknowledging uncertainty means recognizing that one's knowledge is limited, and that absolute certainty is rarely attainable. Decision-makers who embrace uncertainty may be more willing to engage in dialogue, seek advice, and revise their decisions as new information becomes available.

Second, ethical decision-making in the context of uncertainty requires flexibility. Rather than adhering rigidly to a single ethical framework, individuals and organizations must be able to adapt their approach depending on the circumstances. This may involve balancing competing values, weighing short-term and long-term consequences, and acknowledging the possibility of unintended outcomes. It also involves recognizing that even well-intentioned decisions can have negative or unforeseen consequences.

Third, the acknowledgment of uncertainty may foster a more compassionate and empathetic approach to ethical decision-making. Understanding that others, too, are navigating uncertainty can encourage a more understanding and cooperative environment. For instance, in a healthcare context, providers might empathize with patients' uncertainty and fears, recognizing that their own decisions are based on incomplete information.

The Uncertainty Principle, though originally a scientific concept, offers valuable insights into ethical decision-making. Just as Heisenberg's principle reveals the limits of knowledge in quantum mechanics, it highlights the limits of certainty in moral decision-making. Uncertainty is an inherent part of both physical and ethical realities, shaping our understanding of what is possible and what is morally acceptable.

In ethical contexts, uncertainty requires decision-makers to exercise judgment, adaptability, and humility. The recognition that knowledge and outcomes are often incomplete or unpredictable leads to a more nuanced approach to moral choices. Ethical theories that account for uncertainty—such as virtue ethics and the precautionary principle—offer useful frameworks for making responsible and compassionate decisions when the future is unclear.

As our world continues to grow more complex and interconnected, the Uncertainty Principle reminds us that ethical decision-making is rarely straightforward. Embracing uncertainty, rather than fearing it, can lead to more thoughtful, reflective, and ethical choices in the face of an unpredictable world.

Embracing Uncertainty as a Global Citizen

In an increasingly interconnected world, the notion of global citizenship has gained considerable prominence. It refers to the idea that individuals should identify not just with their local or national communities, but with humanity as a whole, taking responsibility for issues that transcend borders—such as climate change, global health, economic inequality, and human rights. Global citizens are expected to be informed, empathetic, and engaged with the wider world, recognizing the complexities and interdependencies that shape our global community.

One of the central challenges faced by global citizens today is the pervasive nature of **uncertainty**. From geopolitical instability and climate change to the rapid pace of technological advancement and global health crises, uncertainty is now a defining feature of contemporary life. Embracing this uncertainty, rather than succumbing to fear or disengagement, is essential for meaningful participation in the global community. This essay will explore why embracing uncertainty is crucial for global citizens, how uncertainty shapes our worldview, and what it means to take responsible action in the face of global challenges. By reflecting on uncertainty, we can better understand how to navigate the complexities of being a global citizen in a world marked by unpredictability.

Understanding Uncertainty in a Globalized World

Uncertainty, in its most basic sense, refers to the inability to predict future events or outcomes with absolute precision. The globalized world is characterized by dynamic and interconnected systems—social, economic, political, and environmental—that often make predictions difficult. Political upheavals, climate disasters, the spread of infectious diseases, and the potential for technological disruptions all contribute to a sense of instability and unpredictability. In this context, uncertainty is not a temporary or isolated phenomenon but rather a permanent feature of the global landscape.

A key area where uncertainty manifests is in **geopolitics**. Global political dynamics are increasingly shaped by complex and competing interests—nations striving to maintain power and influence, multinational corporations pursuing economic gain, and non-state actors such as NGOs and grassroots movements pushing for social change. International relations are increasingly defined by shifting alliances, economic sanctions, trade wars, and diplomatic negotiations. The unpredictability of these relations creates uncertainty not only for governments but also for ordinary people who are impacted by decisions made at the global level.

The **climate crisis** represents another source of profound uncertainty. While scientists agree that climate change is a real and imminent threat, predicting the exact effects of global warming, such as specific regional impacts or the timing of ecological breakdowns, remains uncertain. The pace of climate change, its consequences for ecosystems, and the ability of nations to mitigate or adapt to these changes are all difficult to forecast. As a result, global citizens are left to confront an uncertain future where the choices made today will have long-term consequences for the planet and future generations.

The recent **COVID-19 pandemic** also highlighted the uncertainty that defines global health. Despite advanced medical technology, the speed at which the virus spread, the variations in infection rates, and the development of effective vaccines were all shaped by unpredictable factors. Global citizens had to navigate these uncertainties, making decisions about personal behavior, public health policy, and societal responses based on incomplete and changing information.

This uncertainty—spanning politics, environment, technology, and health—calls for a new approach to global citizenship that does not shy away from unpredictability but rather embraces it as an opportunity for growth, resilience, and collective action.

Why Global Citizens Must Embrace Uncertainty

To be a global citizen in today's world requires not just an awareness of these global uncertainties but also an active commitment to confronting them with open-mindedness, resilience, and compassion. Embracing uncertainty is essential for several reasons.

1.   **Facilitating Adaptation and Innovation**: In an uncertain world, adaptation is a key skill. Embracing uncertainty allows global citizens to remain flexible, open to new ideas, and ready to adjust to changing circumstances. Rather than being paralyzed by fear of the unknown, global citizens who embrace uncertainty are better able to respond creatively to challenges, whether it be through innovation, social change, or collaborative problem-solving. For example, during the pandemic, countries that

embraced uncertainty and acted swiftly—albeit with imperfect information—were able to mitigate the spread of the virus and save lives.

2.   **Building Resilience**: Resilience is the ability to recover from setbacks, adapt to challenges, and continue to move forward despite adversity. The ability to embrace uncertainty fosters resilience because it encourages global citizens to acknowledge and accept that outcomes are not always predictable. Resilient individuals and communities can better cope with shocks, such as natural disasters or economic crises, because they are prepared to adapt, rethink strategies, and rebuild in the face of adversity. By accepting uncertainty, we cultivate a mindset of resilience that is essential for navigating an unpredictable global landscape.

3.   **Promoting Collaboration and Empathy**: Embracing uncertainty helps foster empathy, as it encourages individuals to recognize that everyone faces the unknown in different ways. Global challenges such as poverty, conflict, and climate change affect different regions and communities differently. Understanding and accepting this uncertainty allows global citizens to approach others with empathy and a willingness to collaborate. Rather than assuming that there is a single "correct" solution to a global problem, empathetic global citizens appreciate the diversity of experiences and perspectives that exist and are open to collective problem-solving.

4.   **Encouraging Ethical Responsibility**: As global citizens, we have a moral responsibility to take action in the face of uncertainty. Ethical decision-making often involves making choices with imperfect or incomplete information. Global citizens who embrace uncertainty are better equipped to make responsible decisions, knowing that the consequences of their actions may not be immediately clear. This responsibility includes recognizing our shared global vulnerabilities—whether in the form of climate change, human rights violations, or the global economy—and taking action even when the outcomes are uncertain. In this way, embracing uncertainty becomes an ethical commitment to the well-being of future generations, global justice, and environmental sustainability.

Navigating Global Challenges with Uncertainty

How can global citizens effectively navigate the challenges posed by uncertainty? Several strategies are essential for turning uncertainty into an opportunity for positive change.

1.   **Critical Thinking and Information Literacy**: In an age where misinformation and disinformation are rampant, global citizens must develop the ability to critically assess sources of information. Embracing uncertainty requires recognizing that knowledge is often fragmented or evolving. Critical thinking allows individuals to make informed decisions despite incomplete or conflicting data. Additionally, information literacy—understanding how to evaluate and verify information—helps global citizens avoid the trap of false certainty, making it easier to engage with global issues responsibly.

2.   **Collaborative Decision-Making**: Embracing uncertainty in global citizenship also means working together to address complex challenges. Global problems, such as climate change and the refugee crisis, require cooperation across borders, sectors,

and disciplines. By embracing uncertainty, global citizens can move beyond national or ideological boundaries and engage in collaborative decision-making processes that prioritize collective well-being. This may involve working with international organizations, local communities, businesses, and governments to develop solutions that are adaptable and flexible in the face of uncertainty.

3.　　　　**Mindfulness and Emotional Intelligence**: Global citizenship also requires emotional intelligence—being aware of one's emotions and the emotions of others—and practicing mindfulness. In uncertain times, emotional intelligence helps individuals regulate stress, anxiety, and frustration, which are common responses to instability. By developing emotional intelligence, global citizens can approach difficult decisions with a clearer mindset and greater empathy, improving the quality of their interactions and actions in the global sphere.

4.　　　　**Long-Term Thinking**: While uncertainty makes it difficult to predict short-term outcomes, global citizens can embrace a long-term perspective when making decisions. Long-term thinking encourages decision-makers to consider the potential consequences of their actions over decades or even centuries. For instance, investing in sustainable development, renewable energy, or global education can lead to positive outcomes in the future, even though the immediate results may be unclear. Long-term thinking can help mitigate the effects of uncertainty and create a more resilient and sustainable global community.

In a world characterized by rapid change, political instability, environmental degradation, and technological advancement, embracing uncertainty is no longer optional for global citizens—it is essential. Uncertainty is an inherent part of the human experience, and by embracing it, global citizens can become more adaptable, resilient, empathetic, and responsible in their actions. Rather than retreating from the unknown, embracing uncertainty empowers individuals to actively engage with global challenges and contribute to the creation of a more just and sustainable world.

The process of embracing uncertainty is not about abandoning hope or certainty, but about fostering the skills, mindset, and compassion necessary to navigate an unpredictable future. By doing so, global citizens can move beyond fear and hesitation, becoming agents of positive change in an uncertain world.

Balancing Knowledge and Humility in Approaching Complex Global Issues

The world today is facing an unprecedented array of complex global challenges, including climate change, economic inequality, geopolitical instability, and the rise of new technologies. These issues are interconnected, multifaceted, and often difficult to predict, requiring thoughtful responses from governments, businesses, civil society, and individuals. As global citizens, we are called to contribute to solutions to these problems. However, in our efforts to tackle such vast challenges, we must balance the acquisition of knowledge with a healthy sense of humility. Knowledge alone is not enough to solve global problems; without humility, we risk overconfidence, tunnel vision, and unintended consequences.

This essay will explore the importance of balancing knowledge and humility when addressing complex global issues. It will argue that knowledge provides the foundation for understanding and action, but that humility allows us to recognize the limitations of our understanding and the need for collaboration, empathy, and adaptability. We will examine how knowledge and humility interact in different contexts, including policymaking, climate action, and the fight against global inequality. By maintaining this balance, we can create more effective, sustainable, and ethical responses to the world's most pressing challenges.

The Role of Knowledge in Addressing Global Issues

Knowledge, in the context of global challenges, refers to the understanding of the issues at hand, including their causes, effects, and potential solutions. In our increasingly interconnected world, knowledge is crucial for several reasons. First, it provides a framework for identifying problems and formulating strategies to address them. Second, it allows us to evaluate the effectiveness of different approaches, ensuring that we are taking the best possible action in any given situation. Finally, knowledge equips global citizens and leaders with the tools needed to make informed decisions and navigate the complexities of a rapidly changing world.

In addressing complex issues like **climate change**, for example, scientific knowledge is essential. Understanding the mechanisms behind global warming, the impact of greenhouse gases, and the ways in which human activity contributes to environmental degradation is fundamental to designing effective policies and interventions. Knowledge of renewable energy technologies, carbon capture methods, and sustainable practices can guide efforts to reduce emissions and mitigate the worst effects of climate change.

Similarly, in tackling **global health crises**, such as pandemics, the role of knowledge cannot be overstated. From understanding the biology of diseases to the logistics of vaccine distribution, knowledge underpins every aspect of the response. The COVID-19 pandemic demonstrated the importance of scientific expertise in both preventing the spread of the virus and developing treatments. Epidemiologists, virologists, and public health experts play critical roles in identifying the source of a disease, predicting its trajectory, and devising effective public health strategies.

However, while knowledge is essential, it can also create blind spots, especially when applied without caution. This is where the need for humility becomes evident.

The Importance of Humility in Global Problem-Solving

Humility, in the context of global challenges, involves acknowledging the limits of one's knowledge and recognizing that no single individual or group can fully grasp the complexities of a global issue. Humility allows us to accept that our understanding is often incomplete, that our solutions may have unintended consequences, and that the perspectives of others are just as valuable as our own. It is essential for navigating the uncertainty and unpredictability inherent in complex global issues.

One of the key elements of humility is the recognition of uncertainty. Global issues are inherently complex, and the future is difficult to predict. For example, while scientists have a good understanding of the basic principles of climate change, the precise impacts on specific regions, ecosystems, and economies are still uncertain. The outcomes of various interventions—such as the transition to renewable energy or carbon pricing—cannot be predicted with absolute certainty. Humility in this context means acknowledging that our knowledge may be incomplete and that our best efforts may not always produce the expected results.

Humility also encourages **collaboration**. Complex global issues cannot be solved by individuals or even single countries. Addressing climate change, for example, requires the collective efforts of nations, businesses, and civil society. Humility means being open to the ideas and perspectives of others, recognizing that no one has all the answers. When global leaders, scientists, and activists collaborate across borders and cultures, they can share insights and expertise, create more inclusive solutions, and build consensus on difficult issues. This humility-driven approach can lead to more equitable and sustainable outcomes.

Moreover, humility involves empathy—the ability to understand and share the feelings of others. Many global challenges, such as poverty and inequality, have deeply human consequences. Approaching these issues with empathy allows us to consider the lived experiences of others, particularly those who are marginalized or disenfranchised. It reminds us that solutions to global problems should be rooted in compassion, fairness, and respect for human dignity.

Balancing Knowledge and Humility in Practice

Balancing knowledge and humility requires an awareness of when each is needed and how they complement one another. In practice, this balance plays out in several critical areas:

1.   **Policy-Making and Governance**: Effective governance requires a solid foundation of knowledge—about economics, environmental science, social systems, and more. However, the application of knowledge in policymaking must be tempered with humility. Political leaders must acknowledge the limits of their understanding and be willing to learn from others. For example, when drafting climate policies, leaders should listen to scientists, economists, and communities that will be most affected by climate change. They must also be willing to adjust policies as new information becomes available. A humble approach to governance recognizes that policies will need to evolve over time, and that feedback from affected communities should shape the decision-making process.

2.   **Climate Action**: Climate change provides a compelling example of how knowledge and humility must work together. On the one hand, knowledge about climate science, renewable energy, and sustainable practices is crucial for informing effective climate action. However, because the effects of climate change are geographically uneven and often unpredictable, humility is essential. Solutions must take into account regional differences, respect local knowledge, and consider the needs of vulnerable populations. For instance, the implementation of renewable energy solutions may not be as straightforward in low-income countries without access to the necessary infrastructure.

Humility ensures that solutions are context-specific and inclusive, rather than one-size-fits-all approaches.

3.   **Global Health**: The COVID-19 pandemic underscored the importance of both knowledge and humility in addressing global health challenges. The rapid spread of the virus demonstrated the need for scientific knowledge in diagnosing, treating, and containing the disease. At the same time, humility was crucial in managing public health responses. Early in the pandemic, uncertainty regarding the virus's transmission and the effectiveness of different interventions led to varying public health strategies. The willingness of governments and health organizations to change policies based on evolving evidence and to engage in international cooperation demonstrated humility in action. Humility also involves recognizing that health disparities exist both within and between countries, and that global health responses must be equitable.

4.   **Social and Economic Inequality**: Addressing global inequality requires a deep understanding of economic systems, historical injustices, and the structures that perpetuate poverty. However, humility is essential when considering the perspectives of marginalized communities. In many cases, those who are most affected by inequality may have insights that academic research or top-down policies do not fully capture. By embracing the humility of listening to local voices and respecting the lived experiences of those facing poverty and marginalization, policymakers can design more effective, community-driven solutions.

The Dangers of Imbalance

While both knowledge and humility are necessary for addressing global issues, an imbalance between the two can lead to problems. When knowledge is applied without humility, it can result in **over confidence**. Experts may believe they have all the answers, leading to rigid, top-down solutions that ignore local contexts or human factors. This overconfidence can result in **unintended consequences**, such as environmental degradation, economic dislocation, or social unrest.

Conversely, an excess of humility without sufficient knowledge can lead to **inaction** or **indecision**. Humility is important in recognizing uncertainty and limits, but it should not lead to paralysis. Global challenges require informed action, even in the face of uncertainty. A failure to act because of an overemphasis on humility can worsen global problems and lead to missed opportunities for progress.

The most effective way to approach complex global issues is by balancing knowledge with humility. Knowledge provides the foundation for informed decision-making, while humility reminds us that our understanding is always partial, and that we must remain open to learning from others and adapting our strategies as new information emerges. In addressing global challenges such as climate change, global health, and inequality, the balance between these two elements is essential for creating solutions that are sustainable, ethical, and effective. As global citizens, we must cultivate both knowledge and humility to navigate the complexities of our interconnected world and contribute to building a more just, equitable, and resilient global community.

Chapter 14
Non-Locality and Global Solidarity

Non-locality suggests that particles can be connected in ways that transcend space. For global citizens, non-locality becomes a call to build solidarity across distances, fostering compassion for people we may never meet and places we may never visit. This chapter examines how technology, empathy, and shared goals can create a "non-local" solidarity that bridges cultures and continents.

Non-locality as a Foundation for Solidarity in a Globalized World

In an increasingly interconnected and globalized world, the concept of solidarity has gained prominence as a vital force for addressing shared challenges and promoting justice, equality, and peace across borders. At its core, solidarity involves the recognition of the interconnectedness of human beings, both in moments of crisis and in the everyday conditions of life. However, in a world where people are more physically separated than ever—divided by national borders, economic disparities, and technological divides—the question arises: how can we foster a sense of solidarity across these vast distances? One potential answer lies in the idea of non-locality, a concept derived from quantum physics but increasingly applied in social, political, and philosophical discussions. This essay explores how non-locality can serve as a foundation for solidarity in a globalized world, emphasizing its potential to transcend geographical, cultural, and political boundaries in the pursuit of collective well-being.

The Concept of Non-locality

At its most fundamental level, non-locality refers to a phenomenon in quantum mechanics where particles appear to be instantly connected to each other, regardless of the distance that separates them. This behavior contradicts classical notions of causality and space-time, suggesting that the universe is far more interconnected than previously understood. In simple terms, non-locality suggests that the boundaries of space and time may not be as rigid as they seem, and that actions in one place can have immediate effects on distant locations.

The most famous example of non-locality in quantum mechanics is *entanglement*. When two particles become entangled, the state of one particle instantly influences the state of the other, regardless of the distance between them. This phenomenon challenges our classical understanding of physical reality, implying that the universe is much more interconnected than it might appear on the surface.

While quantum physics primarily explores the behavior of subatomic particles, the principles of non-locality can be metaphorically applied to social and political contexts. In these domains, non-locality suggests that the fates of individuals, communities, and nations are interconnected in ways that transcend physical distance. Just as entangled particles influence one another across vast distances, human beings are interconnected in ways that are not always visible, and yet can profoundly affect one another's lives.

Solidarity in a Globalized World

Solidarity, in its simplest form, refers to the sense of unity and mutual support that arises among individuals or groups, particularly in times of struggle or need. It embodies the idea that people share a common humanity and have a responsibility to act in support of one another, even when they are separated by great distances.

In the context of globalization, solidarity takes on an expanded significance. The modern world is characterized by the rapid movement of goods, information, and people across borders, making it increasingly clear that the challenges faced by one community can have far-reaching effects on others. Environmental crises, economic instability, public health threats, and political conflicts are no longer confined to one nation or region; they spill over into other areas, demanding collective responses. In this environment, solidarity becomes essential for tackling global challenges such as climate change, poverty, human rights violations, and the rise of authoritarianism.

The challenge, however, lies in cultivating a sense of solidarity across the many divisions that persist in our world. People often remain disconnected from those living in distant parts of the world, primarily due to the physical, cultural, and political boundaries that separate them. Moreover, the structures of globalization, such as multinational corporations and international organizations, can perpetuate inequalities rather than promote solidarity. As a result, fostering genuine solidarity in a globalized world requires overcoming these barriers and recognizing the interdependence of all people, regardless of their location.

Non-locality as a Framework for Global Solidarity

Non-locality provides a compelling framework for understanding and fostering solidarity in the globalized world. Just as quantum entanglement challenges traditional ideas of separation and distance, non-locality suggests that human beings, too, are fundamentally interconnected, regardless of geographic or political boundaries. In this sense, non-locality serves as a metaphor for how global solidarity might function.

1.   **Shared Humanity Beyond Borders**
The idea of non-locality reminds us that human beings are not isolated individuals, but rather part of a vast, interconnected web of life. Despite the physical separation that exists between us, we share a common fate. The actions and decisions made in one part of the world can affect individuals thousands of miles away. For example, the environmental destruction caused by deforestation in one region can contribute to climate change, which in turn affects people living in distant places. Similarly, economic policies enacted in wealthy countries can have far-reaching effects on the lives of the poor and marginalized

in the Global South. Non-locality, in this sense, challenges the notion that we are isolated from one another, urging us to recognize that our destinies are intertwined.

By embracing the concept of non-locality, we can begin to see solidarity not as a localized or bounded phenomenon, but as a universal force. The struggles faced by individuals and communities in different parts of the world are not isolated; they are part of a larger, interconnected system. This recognition can inspire a sense of shared responsibility and compassion, leading to more meaningful and effective global cooperation.

2.   Technological Connectivity and Non-locality

In the digital age, the world has become more interconnected than ever before. The internet, social media, and other forms of communication allow people to share information, ideas, and experiences in real-time, regardless of geographic location. This technological connectivity mirrors the non-local nature of quantum entanglement, as it enables individuals and groups to influence one another across vast distances.

Social movements and campaigns that promote global solidarity have flourished in this environment, as people use technology to connect with others who share their values and goals. For instance, movements like #MeToo, Black Lives Matter, and Fridays for Future have transcended national borders, demonstrating the power of collective action in addressing issues such as gender inequality, racial injustice, and climate change. These movements show that solidarity is not confined to local contexts; it can be global in scope, driven by the recognition of shared struggles and aspirations.

Technology also allows for the rapid dissemination of information, making it easier for people to understand the challenges faced by others around the world. This has the potential to cultivate empathy and solidarity, as people are more likely to support causes they understand. Non-locality, in this sense, is made tangible through the interconnectedness of the digital world, which helps break down the physical and cultural barriers that often impede solidarity.

3.   Global Justice and the Ethics of Interconnection

Non-locality also has important ethical implications. If we accept that we are all interconnected, then it follows that we have a responsibility to care for one another, regardless of where we are located. This idea is central to the concept of global justice, which argues that individuals and nations have an ethical obligation to address the needs of others, especially those who are marginalized or suffering.

Non-locality invites us to rethink traditional notions of justice, which are often confined to the nation-state. Instead, it calls for a broader, more inclusive understanding of justice—one that recognizes the interdependence of all human beings. This can manifest in various ways, from advocating for fair trade and international human rights.

Chapter 15
Entropy and Social Evolution

Entropy is the tendency toward disorder, a principle that applies to both thermodynamics and social structures. Just as quantum systems evolve, so does society—often through periods of chaos and reorganization. This chapter looks at how global citizens can navigate social and environmental challenges, using entropy as a metaphor for transformation and adaptation.

Entropy, in both quantum physics and social evolution, is a concept that expresses the degree of disorder or unpredictability in a system. However, its applications in these fields diverge greatly due to the distinct nature of physical versus social systems. In quantum physics, entropy is a measure of uncertainty and information content within a system, playing a critical role in the second law of thermodynamics and the understanding of quantum states. On the other hand, entropy in social evolution is more metaphorical, often used to describe the increasing complexity, unpredictability, or dissolution of social structures over time. Both of these fields, despite their differences, employ the notion of entropy to explore the transition from order to disorder and the limits of predictability, yet they do so within very different frameworks. This essay will explore how entropy manifests in these two fields, drawing connections between quantum theory's rigorous physical principles and the more abstract, evolving processes within human society.

1. Entropy in Quantum Physics

Entropy in quantum physics is a measure of uncertainty, disorder, or lack of information about the state of a system. In thermodynamics, entropy is classically understood as a measure of the disorder in a system, with higher entropy corresponding to greater randomness or disorder. In quantum mechanics, this classical interpretation is extended and refined to address the uncertainties inherent in quantum states, where the properties of particles cannot be known with absolute certainty, but only in terms of probabilities.

1.1 The Second Law of Thermodynamics

The second law of thermodynamics states that the total entropy of an isolated system can never decrease over time. This law reflects the natural tendency of isolated systems to evolve toward a state of maximum disorder. In a quantum context, the second law still holds, but its implications are slightly more subtle due to the probabilistic nature of quantum states. The concept of quantum entropy is often discussed in terms of the *von Neumann entropy*, which is a quantum analog of the classical entropy. For a quantum system, entropy measures the degree of uncertainty about the system's state when described by a density matrix rather than a specific wave function.

For example, in quantum thermodynamics, the state of a system can evolve in such a way that even if the system is not physically "disordered" in the classical sense, the probability distribution of its states can become increasingly complex, thus increasing the entropy. This relates to how quantum information behaves—quantum entropy accounts for the uncertainty in quantum systems, considering the probabilistic nature of quantum measurement.

1.2 Entropy and Quantum Information Theory

Quantum entropy plays a crucial role in quantum information theory, which combines quantum mechanics with information theory. The famous *Shannon entropy* measures the uncertainty of information, and its quantum counterpart, the *von Neumann entropy*, serves to quantify uncertainty in quantum systems. In quantum information theory, entropy is closely tied to the concept of quantum entanglement, which describes how quantum particles can become correlated in ways that are not possible in classical systems.

For example, in a quantum computing system, the entropy can help quantify the potential for information to be processed. The more entangled the system, the greater the quantum entropy, reflecting the complexity of the information that can be extracted from the system. Thus, entropy is central to understanding how quantum systems behave and how they can be utilized in the processing and transmission of information.

1.3 The Arrow of Time and Entropy

In both classical and quantum physics, entropy provides a direction for the passage of time. The "arrow of time" is the concept that time has a preferred direction, from past to future, and entropy plays a fundamental role in this. As entropy increases, systems tend to evolve toward more probable states, which are often more disordered, providing a time asymmetry that defines the directionality of events. In the quantum realm, this concept remains valid, though quantum systems can exhibit behaviors that defy classical expectations, such as quantum tunneling or entanglement, complicating the relationship between entropy and time.

2. Entropy in Social Evolution

In the context of social evolution, entropy is often used metaphorically to describe the processes by which societies become more complex, unpredictable, and less ordered over time. Unlike the strictly defined physical laws of quantum mechanics, entropy in social evolution does not refer to a quantifiable measure of disorder, but rather to the metaphorical "disorder" arising from the increasing complexity and unpredictability in human societies.

2.1 The Evolution of Social Structures

Just as physical systems evolve from lower entropy states to higher entropy states, societies evolve over time from simple to complex structures. Early human societies, for example, were less complex and more homogeneous, but as societies developed, they grew more complex, with the emergence of diverse social roles, institutions, and political systems. This increasing complexity is often viewed as a form of increasing social entropy.

Social entropy in this sense reflects the ways in which human societies move from simple, egalitarian structures to more hierarchical and differentiated forms. As societies expand, they face greater challenges in managing social relations, resources, and power structures. This growing complexity often results in less predictability in social behaviors, just as quantum systems become more uncertain as their entropy increases. However, while quantum entropy can be quantified, social entropy is inherently subjective and depends on the context and perspective of the observer.

2.2 The Breakdown of Social Order

Entropy in social evolution can also refer to the dissolution of established social orders. Societies that have reached a certain level of complexity may begin to fragment or lose cohesion, leading to a breakdown of previously stable structures. For example, the collapse of empires or the decline of institutions can be seen as an increase in social entropy, where the previously orderly systems give way to chaos or transformation.

In this sense, social entropy does not always imply a mere increase in disorder but can represent a shift toward a new kind of order. As in physical systems, the transition from one state to another may not be entirely random but instead can be driven by underlying forces such as economic pressures, technological advancements, or ideological shifts. This view of entropy in social evolution acknowledges that societies may go through periods of upheaval that lead to the creation of new, more sustainable forms of social order.

2.3 The Unpredictability of Social Evolution

A key feature of social entropy is the inherent unpredictability of social evolution. As societies evolve, they encounter unforeseen challenges and develop new forms of organization that were not anticipated in their earlier stages. This mirrors the quantum concept of uncertainty, where the behavior of a system can only be predicted probabilistically. In social systems, predictions about the future trajectory of a society are similarly fraught with uncertainty due to the many variables involved, including human behavior, cultural shifts, and external influences such as environmental changes.

For instance, the rapid technological advancements of the 21st century have introduced new complexities into social systems, resulting in greater uncertainty about the future of work, politics, and culture. Just as quantum mechanics describes the probabilistic nature of particles, the future of human societies can be seen as a set of potential outcomes, each with varying degrees of likelihood, but none of them entirely predictable.

3. Connecting Entropy in Quantum Physics and Social Evolution

Despite the vast differences between quantum physics and social evolution, there are interesting parallels between entropy in these fields. Both concepts of entropy are tied to the idea of systems evolving toward states of greater complexity or disorder, and both highlight the limits of predictability and control. Quantum physics provides a mathematical framework for understanding entropy, while social evolution uses entropy as a metaphor to describe the increasing complexity and unpredictability of human societies.

3.1 Order and Disorder

In both realms, entropy represents a transition from order to disorder, whether that be the increasing randomness in the quantum state of a particle or the breakdown of social institutions. In the case of quantum systems, the increased entropy corresponds to a system's evolution toward a higher probability state. In social systems, the "disorder" of entropy may signify a breakdown of old structures and the emergence of new ones, creating new forms of organization that may be unpredictable.

3.2 Information and Uncertainty

Another parallel between quantum and social entropy lies in the role of information. In quantum physics, entropy quantifies the amount of uncertainty about a system's state. Similarly, in social systems, entropy can be seen as a measure of the uncertainty and unpredictability inherent in social evolution. As societies become more complex, the number of variables and interactions increases, making predictions more difficult and reflecting an increase in "social entropy."

3.3 Emergence and Complexity

Both quantum physics and social evolution are characterized by emergent behaviors. In quantum systems, the complex interactions between particles can lead to phenomena like entanglement, where the system exhibits behaviors that are not reducible to the individual parts. In social evolution, emergent properties manifest as new social norms, ideologies, and technologies that arise from the interaction of individuals within the society. These emergent phenomena are often unpredictable, contributing to the overall entropy of the system.

Entropy serves as a powerful conceptual tool for understanding the behavior of both quantum systems and human societies. In quantum physics, it provides a rigorous measure of uncertainty, disorder, and the probabilistic nature of the universe. In social evolution, it functions more metaphorically to describe the increasing complexity, unpredictability, and dissolution of social order. Despite these differences, both interpretations highlight the movement of systems from simpler to more complex states and the inherent uncertainty that arises in such processes. Whether applied to particles or societies, entropy reveals the limitations of prediction and control, emphasizing the fundamental unpredictability that characterizes both the physical and social worlds.

Recognizing Periods of "Disorder" as Opportunities for Growth

Disorder, often perceived as a period of confusion, instability, or decline, has historically been regarded as a challenge to overcome. In both personal and societal contexts, disorder is usually seen as a negative force, associated with failure or collapse. However, a deeper and more nuanced understanding of disorder reveals that it can, in fact, be an opportunity for growth and transformation. Whether it is in the form of personal upheaval, societal disruptions, or organizational changes, moments of disorder often carry within them the seeds of creativity, resilience, and renewal. This essay explores how recognizing periods of disorder as opportunities for growth—rather than setbacks— can lead to positive outcomes in individual lives, social structures, and organizations. Drawing upon examples from various domains of life, the essay will argue that disorder, when approached with the right mindset, can catalyze significant growth.

1. The Nature of Disorder

Disorder can be understood in various ways depending on the context. In its simplest form, disorder refers to a lack of order or predictability, and it can manifest as chaos, confusion, or disruption. In personal life, it may emerge as unexpected challenges, emotional turmoil, or life transitions. In the context of society, disorder can take the form of social unrest, economic instability, or political upheaval. Organizationally, it may be seen in the restructuring of companies or shifts in business models due to market changes.

Despite its often negative connotations, disorder is not inherently detrimental. It is, in fact, a natural and unavoidable part of life. The universe, human history, and individual lives all experience phases of change, instability, and disarray. The key to transforming disorder into an opportunity for growth lies in our perception and response to these periods. By embracing disorder and adopting a growth-oriented mindset, we can unlock new potentials for creativity, adaptation, and resilience.

2. Personal Growth Through Disorder

At the individual level, periods of disorder are frequently catalysts for personal transformation. When a person encounters unexpected challenges, such as the loss of a job, the end of a relationship, or a health crisis, they are forced to confront feelings of vulnerability and uncertainty. While such events may initially appear as setbacks, they can serve as powerful opportunities for self-discovery, learning, and growth.

2.1 The Role of Adversity in Building Resilience

Psychological research consistently shows that individuals who navigate periods of adversity often emerge stronger and more resilient. This phenomenon, known as post-traumatic growth, refers to the positive psychological changes that can occur following difficult or traumatic experiences. These changes may include a renewed sense of purpose, increased emotional strength, and a deeper appreciation for life.

Adversity forces individuals to reevaluate their values, goals, and perspectives. For example, someone who has experienced a health scare might become more mindful of their lifestyle choices, leading to improved physical and emotional well-being. Similarly, someone who has faced a personal or professional failure may reassess their priorities and make adjustments that lead to greater fulfillment in the long term. In this sense, disorder is not just a challenge to endure but a powerful teacher that encourages growth through reflection and adaptation.

2.2 Learning Through Failure and Mistakes

Failure is often perceived as the ultimate form of disorder, yet it is through failure that many people learn the most. In personal development, failure provides critical insights into what does not work, allowing individuals to adjust their strategies, try new approaches, and ultimately succeed. Thomas Edison's famous quote, "I have not failed. I've just found 10,000 ways that won't work," reflects this mindset: failure, or disorder, is simply a step on the path to success.

By reframing disorder as an opportunity to learn, individuals can develop greater perseverance and a stronger sense of agency. Instead of avoiding mistakes, they can embrace them as integral components of their personal evolution. Disorder, when approached with a growth mindset, encourages individuals to innovate, take risks, and challenge themselves, ultimately leading to self-improvement and success.

3. Disorder as an Opportunity for Social and Collective Growth

On a societal scale, periods of disorder—such as social unrest, political revolutions, and economic crises—can also be powerful drivers of growth and change. While such disruptions may seem threatening or destabilizing in the short term, history shows that they often lead to significant advancements in social, political, and economic structures.

3.1 Social Unrest and Cultural Shifts

History is replete with examples of social movements that arose during times of disorder, often sparking profound cultural and societal changes. The civil rights movement in the United States during the 1960s, for instance, emerged during a period of social and political turmoil. While the unrest of the time seemed chaotic, it catalyzed important reforms that continue to shape the social landscape today, including the expansion of civil rights and greater awareness of racial inequality.

Similarly, global movements for gender equality, LGBTQ+ rights, and environmental justice have emerged in response to systemic inequalities and injustices. In these cases, disorder in the form of protests, strikes, and social upheaval has spurred changes in laws, policies, and societal norms, leading to greater inclusivity and fairness in society. These examples demonstrate that social disorder, rather than being a force of destruction, can be a force of transformation, pushing societies toward more equitable and progressive futures.

3.2 Economic Crises and Innovation

Economic downturns, such as the Great Depression of the 1930s or the 2008 global financial crisis, are typically seen as periods of great disorder. Yet, these crises often lead to structural changes in the economy and the emergence of innovative solutions. For example, the Great Depression catalyzed the development of the New Deal, a series of programs and reforms that helped rebuild the U.S. economy and provided a model for future economic policies.

Similarly, the 2008 financial crisis spurred innovations in technology, finance, and business models. The rise of fintech, the sharing economy, and online platforms can be traced back to the disruptions caused by the crisis. While the immediate effects of economic disorder were painful, they ultimately led to the development of more resilient and adaptable economic systems. This illustrates that economic disorder, when coupled with creative thinking and adaptability, can foster innovation and long-term growth.

4. Organizational Growth Through Disorder

In the world of business and organizations, periods of disorder, such as mergers, restructuring, or shifts in market conditions, are often seen as crises to be avoided or managed. However, these periods can also serve as opportunities for reinvention, creativity, and organizational growth.

4.1 Innovation and Adaptation in Response to Change

Organizations that embrace disorder rather than fear it are often better equipped to navigate change and adapt to new realities. For example, companies that are able to pivot in response to market disruptions or technological innovations are often the ones that thrive in the long term. Consider the rise of companies like Netflix or Amazon, which revolutionized their respective industries by adapting to the shifting landscapes of media and retail.

When organizations face periods of disorder, they are forced to reassess their business models, streamline operations, and think creatively. This process can lead to the discovery of new opportunities, the refinement of products and services, and a more agile, resilient organizational culture. By recognizing disorder as an opportunity for growth, organizations can turn challenges into stepping stones for long-term success.

4.2 Leadership and Transformation

Effective leadership is critical in periods of organizational disorder. Leaders who can maintain a vision while navigating through disruption are often able to guide their organizations through turbulent times and emerge stronger. Transformational leaders understand that disorder can be a springboard for growth, using it as an opportunity to inspire innovation, encourage collaboration, and push the organization toward its next phase of development.

For instance, companies undergoing restructuring or downsizing often face internal chaos. However, leaders who communicate clearly, support their teams, and encourage new ways of thinking can help employees find purpose and focus amid the uncertainty. By fostering an environment that embraces change, leaders can turn disorder into an opportunity for collective growth and transformation.

Disorder, whether it occurs at the individual, societal, or organizational level, is often seen as a force to be feared or avoided. However, by recognizing periods of disorder as opportunities for growth, we can unlock their potential to drive positive change. Whether through personal resilience, social transformation, or organizational innovation, disorder presents a unique opportunity to reimagine the status quo and build something better. By reframing our understanding of disorder from a negative force to a catalyst for growth, we can cultivate a mindset that embraces change, adapts to challenges, and fosters long-term success. Embracing disorder as an opportunity for growth is not only a path to personal development but also a key to societal progress and organizational evolution.

Resilience and Adaptability as Essential Traits for Global Citizens

In the face of an increasingly interconnected world marked by rapid technological advancements, climate change, political instability, and shifting global power dynamics, the ability to adapt and remain resilient has never been more important. Global citizenship today demands individuals who can navigate these challenges while maintaining empathy, understanding, and commitment to shared human values. Resilience and adaptability are two fundamental traits that equip global citizens to effectively confront these challenges. Resilience is the ability to bounce back from adversity, while adaptability is the capacity to adjust to new conditions or environments. These traits are essential not only for personal growth but also for fostering positive social change, sustainability, and global cooperation. This essay explores why resilience and adaptability are crucial for global citizens, examining how these traits can help individuals and communities thrive in an ever-changing world.

1. The Concept of Global Citizenship

Global citizenship is an evolving concept that transcends national borders, emphasizing the importance of interconnectedness, mutual respect, and collective responsibility. It involves recognizing the shared challenges humanity faces, from environmental degradation to social inequality, and acting in ways that promote the well-being of all people. A global citizen is not bound by parochial loyalties or national interests but is instead concerned with the broader welfare of the planet and its inhabitants. This outlook calls for individuals who are informed, compassionate, and capable of understanding different perspectives and cultures.

At its core, global citizenship requires a willingness to embrace diversity and work collaboratively to address common problems. Given the complexity and unpredictability of today's world, resilience and adaptability are indispensable traits for global citizens. These qualities enable individuals to navigate global challenges and contribute to positive social, economic, and environmental change.

2. The Role of Resilience in Global Citizenship

Resilience, in the context of global citizenship, refers to the ability to recover from setbacks, overcome adversity, and continue pursuing personal and collective goals despite challenges. In a world marked by rapid changes and global crises, resilience is an essential trait for individuals who aim to contribute meaningfully to their communities and the world.

2.1 Resilience in the Face of Global Crises

Humanity is currently grappling with numerous crises, from climate change to pandemics and conflicts. Global citizens who possess resilience are better equipped to cope with the consequences of these challenges. For instance, during the COVID-19 pandemic, people around the world were forced to adapt to new ways of living, working, and interacting. Communities with resilient populations—those who could quickly adjust to changing circumstances—were better able to navigate the emotional, economic, and social disruptions caused by the pandemic.

In addition to personal resilience, collective resilience is equally crucial. Communities that come together to support one another during difficult times, whether through mutual aid networks, government support, or social solidarity, are better able to recover from crises. A resilient society fosters not only the well-being of its members but also the ability to collaborate and rebuild in the face of adversity.

2.2 Mental and Emotional Resilience in Global Citizens

Resilience also involves mental and emotional strength. For global citizens, this means the ability to maintain hope and motivation even when facing difficult circumstances. In a world that is often marked by inequality, conflict, and environmental degradation, it is easy to become overwhelmed or disillusioned. However, resilient global citizens remain committed to improving the world, even in the face of setbacks or seemingly insurmountable challenges.

The development of mental and emotional resilience can be facilitated by cultivating skills such as emotional intelligence, mindfulness, and problem-solving. These abilities allow individuals to stay grounded, think clearly in times of stress, and recover from setbacks. For global citizens, such resilience is not merely about survival; it is about maintaining a sense of agency and purpose in the face of adversity.

3. The Role of Adaptability in Global Citizenship

Adaptability refers to the ability to adjust to new conditions or environments. In a globalized world that is constantly evolving, adaptability is an essential trait for individuals who wish to engage with different cultures, navigate shifting political landscapes, and contribute to the global community. Adaptability enables global citizens to respond effectively to change, whether in their personal lives, professional careers, or broader societal contexts.

3.1 Navigating Cultural and Social Diversity

One of the most important aspects of global citizenship is the ability to navigate cultural and social diversity. Global citizens must be able to engage with people from different backgrounds, respecting their values, traditions, and ways of life. This requires an openness to learning and an ability to adjust one's perspective to accommodate different viewpoints.

Adaptability in this context involves the willingness to step outside of one's comfort zone, engage in cross-cultural dialogue, and build relationships with people from diverse cultures. It is through this process of adaptation that individuals become more empathetic, inclusive, and capable of fostering global solidarity.

For example, global citizens working in international development or diplomacy must adapt to the social, political, and economic realities of the regions they work in. They must adjust their strategies and approaches to suit local contexts while still adhering to universal human rights and ethical standards. This level of cultural adaptability is crucial for fostering cooperation and mutual understanding in a globalized world.

3.2 Adapting to Technological Change

Another domain in which adaptability is crucial for global citizens is in responding to technological advances. Technology is reshaping almost every aspect of human life, from communication to healthcare, education, and governance. Global citizens must be able to understand and embrace new technologies in order to stay engaged in the modern world.

For instance, the rise of digital technologies has created new opportunities for global collaboration. Tools like video conferencing, social media, and digital platforms have enabled people to connect across borders, work together on global projects, and mobilize around social causes. Global citizens who are adaptable are better equipped to utilize these technologies in ways that promote positive social change.

However, the rapid pace of technological change also presents challenges, such as issues of digital literacy, cybersecurity, and privacy. Adaptable global citizens are able to navigate these challenges, ensuring that technology is used ethically and responsibly while remaining open to new advancements that can improve global well-being.

3.3 Adapting to Environmental Change

The impact of climate change is one of the most pressing global challenges today. As natural disasters become more frequent and ecosystems face unprecedented pressures, individuals and communities must adapt to the changing environment. Global citizens must embrace sustainable practices and adjust their lifestyles to reduce their environmental footprint. Whether it is adopting renewable energy sources, reducing waste, or supporting climate action policies, adaptability plays a critical role in addressing environmental issues.

Furthermore, adaptability in the face of environmental change involves fostering resilience at the community level. For example, communities in coastal areas vulnerable to rising sea levels must develop adaptive strategies, such as building flood defenses or relocating populations. Global citizens who understand the urgency of environmental issues are better equipped to engage in these efforts and advocate for meaningful change.

4. The Interconnection Between Resilience and Adaptability

While resilience and adaptability are distinct traits, they are deeply interconnected. Resilience provides the mental and emotional fortitude to withstand challenges, while adaptability enables individuals to adjust to changing circumstances. Together, they form a powerful toolkit for global citizens who must navigate a world marked by uncertainty and rapid change.

In the context of global citizenship, resilience allows individuals to remain committed to their values and goals in the face of adversity, while adaptability ensures that they can adjust their strategies and actions to meet evolving needs. Both traits are essential for engaging with the complexities of the modern world and contributing to the creation of a more just, sustainable, and peaceful global society.

For example, a global citizen working on international development projects may encounter unexpected obstacles, such as political resistance or resource limitations. Resilience enables them to stay focused on their mission, while adaptability allows them to find alternative solutions and adjust their approach to fit new circumstances.

Resilience and adaptability are essential traits for global citizens in the 21st century. As the world becomes more interconnected and complex, individuals must be able to bounce back from adversity and adjust to new realities in order to contribute meaningfully to global issues. Whether facing personal challenges, cultural differences, technological disruptions, or environmental crises, global citizens who possess these traits are better equipped to engage with the world in a constructive and compassionate way.

By cultivating resilience and adaptability, individuals can not only enhance their own well-being but also contribute to the creation of a more equitable, sustainable, and interconnected world. These traits are not just about survival; they are about thriving in an ever-changing world and working collaboratively to address the shared challenges humanity faces. In a time when the future is uncertain and the stakes are high, resilience and adaptability are the cornerstones of effective global citizenship.

Chapter 16
Quantum Field Theory and the Power of Collective Action

In quantum field theory, particles and forces interact through fields that extend across space and time. In the same way, the collective actions of global citizens create "fields" of influence that impact societies worldwide. This chapter explores how grassroots movements, environmental efforts, and human rights campaigns create momentum across borders, forming a "field" of collective action.

The concept of quantum fields originates from the realm of quantum physics, a discipline that delves into the most fundamental components of matter and the forces that govern their interactions. Quantum fields represent the underlying fabric of reality, from which particles, forces, and energy emerge. The term "field" in quantum physics does not just refer to the space between objects, as it does in classical physics, but to an all-pervasive entity that influences everything at the quantum level. In a similar vein, collective influence refers to the ways in which groups, societies, or networks of individuals shape the actions, attitudes, and outcomes of their members. The metaphor of quantum fields can provide valuable insight into understanding the invisible, pervasive, and interconnected ways in which collective influence operates within human societies. Just as quantum fields permeate all of space, collective influence spreads across social networks, shaping individual and group behavior. This essay will explore the metaphor of quantum fields in the context of collective influence, illustrating the ways in which society, like the quantum world, operates through complex, non-local interactions that affect individuals in profound and often invisible ways.

Quantum Fields: A Brief Overview

To understand the metaphor of quantum fields, we first need a basic overview of the concept. In quantum physics, the idea of fields has been central since the development of quantum field theory (QFT) in the early 20th century. The theory combines quantum mechanics and special relativity, postulating that particles are not distinct, standalone entities but are excitations or disturbances in quantum fields. Every type of particle is associated with a corresponding field, such as the electron field, the photon field, or the Higgs field. These fields extend throughout all of space and time, and the interactions between these fields give rise to the particles and forces we observe. Crucially, these fields are not confined to any specific location; they exist everywhere and influence everything in the universe simultaneously.

A key feature of quantum fields is their non-locality. The interactions within these fields are not limited by distance, as in classical physics, where effects are felt only through direct contact or at a defined range. Quantum fields can interact with distant regions instantaneously, an effect known as "quantum entanglement." This interconnectedness is a hallmark of quantum systems and stands in stark contrast to classical understandings of physics, where objects are seen as separate and influenced only by their immediate surroundings.

Collective Influence: Social Networks and Shared Experiences

When examining collective influence, we turn to the dynamics of human interaction, where individuals and groups are constantly shaping one another's behaviors, beliefs, and outcomes. Collective influence refers to the ways in which the behaviors, opinions, or attitudes of individuals are influenced by those around them. This influence can be both direct—such as a leader directing a group or a peer persuading another—and indirect, as when the norms of a society shape individual behaviors without explicit interaction.

Social networks, both online and offline, serve as prime examples of the mechanisms of collective influence. Through shared experiences, mutual reinforcement, and subtle cues, individuals within a group can significantly alter their thoughts and actions. This influence often operates below the level of conscious awareness, much like the unseen influence of quantum fields. Individuals may believe they are acting independently, but their behaviors and decisions are frequently shaped by the social networks they inhabit. These networks, in turn, are influenced by external forces, from the media to cultural norms, which act as pervasive fields in their own right.

The notion of "social fields" has been explored in various ways by sociologists and psychologists. The idea that individuals are interconnected through networks of influence mirrors the way quantum fields bind particles together. Just as a disturbance in a quantum field can propagate and affect distant parts of the system, so too can a change in one part of a social network ripple out, influencing individuals far removed from the initial source. This connection between individuals is not always direct; rather, it operates through multiple layers of relationships, much like the interconnected layers of quantum fields influencing particles across space.

Non-locality and Interconnectedness in Social Influence

The non-locality of quantum fields provides a powerful metaphor for understanding collective influence. In the quantum world, particles are not isolated; their properties are deeply interdependent, and they can influence each other over vast distances, even without direct contact. Similarly, in the realm of social influence, actions and attitudes can spread rapidly across a population, even when individuals are not directly interacting with one another. This is especially evident in phenomena such as viral trends, social movements, and the spread of ideas.

Consider the example of social media. A tweet or video posted by one individual can rapidly spread to millions of others, even those who are geographically distant or have no direct connection to the original poster. In a sense, the individual is an excitation in the broader social field, and their actions ripple through the network, influencing others far removed from the source. This non-locality mirrors the behavior of quantum fields, where an interaction in one part of the field can lead to consequences in other, distant regions without the need for any direct physical connection.

Moreover, just as quantum entanglement allows particles to instantaneously affect one another across great distances, collective influence can manifest through subtle, indirect channels that transcend individual actions. For example, cultural trends, societal norms, and mass media can shape the behaviors of individuals, even if they are not directly exposed to specific messages or interactions. The influence of these overarching fields on individual behavior is profound, as people unconsciously conform to patterns and expectations established by the broader social system.

Emergence and Collective Behavior

Another key feature of quantum fields is the concept of emergence—the idea that complex phenomena arise from the interaction of simpler components. In the case of quantum fields, particles emerge from the underlying field when certain conditions, such as energy input or disturbances, are met. Similarly, collective behaviors emerge from the interactions of individuals within a group. These behaviors can be observed at the group level, even though they are not necessarily predictable from the actions of any single member of the group.

This is seen in phenomena such as crowd behavior, collective decision-making, or the dynamics of social movements. A group of individuals acting in concert may produce results that would be impossible for any single individual to achieve. Just as a collective excitation in a quantum field can manifest as a particle, so too can collective action in a social field manifest as societal change or a shift in public opinion. The individual actions of people—while significant—are often just part of a larger, emergent pattern that reflects the influence of the broader social field.

In the context of social movements, for example, individuals may initially join based on personal convictions or localized connections. However, as the movement gains momentum, it becomes a collective force, shaping the behaviors and beliefs of others who might not have been directly involved in the initial stages of the movement. The movement itself becomes a kind of "field" that influences its members and even those outside it, much as a disturbance in a quantum field can spread and influence the larger system.

The Role of the Observer: Consciousness and Social Influence

One of the most fascinating aspects of quantum mechanics is the role of the observer. In quantum theory, the act of observation can collapse a quantum wave function, determining the outcome of a potential event. In a similar vein, the collective actions of individuals in society can be influenced by the awareness, attention, or consciousness of the group. As social beings, individuals are constantly observing and reacting to one another, and the very act of attention or awareness can influence the behaviors and decisions of the group as a whole.

Entangled　　　　　　　　　　　　**Sandra Ferreira**

In a quantum field, the observer's presence influences the system's behavior. Similarly, in a social field, the collective attention of a group can alter the trajectory of the group itself. For example, the rise of a leader or the formation of a social consensus can shift the behaviors of individuals within the group, shaping the overall direction of the collective. This concept is especially relevant in the age of mass media, where the attention of millions can be directed by a few key figures or events, influencing societal norms, behaviors, and beliefs on a massive scale.

Quantum fields and collective influence, while originating from vastly different domains, share many similarities in their principles of interconnectedness, non-locality, emergence, and the role of observation. Just as quantum fields govern the behavior of particles in ways that are often invisible and indirect, so too does collective influence shape the actions and behaviors of individuals in a society. Both are characterized by complex interactions that defy easy categorization or prediction, with consequences that ripple through systems in subtle and profound ways.

By using quantum fields as a metaphor for collective influence, we gain a deeper appreciation for the invisible forces that shape our lives. In both the quantum world and the social realm, interactions are not confined to local, direct relationships but instead operate through a network of interconnected fields, influencing individuals in ways that transcend immediate boundaries. This metaphor allows us to conceptualize society not as a collection of isolated individuals but as a dynamic, interconnected system, where every individual is part of a larger web of influence, shaping and being shaped by the collective.

Through this lens, we can better understand the power of social networks, media, and cultural norms in shaping behavior, highlighting the importance of awareness and intentionality in navigating the forces of collective influence. Just as in quantum physics, where the observer plays a role in determining outcomes, so too can individuals and groups influence the broader social field through conscious attention, collective action, and shared purpose. Thus, the metaphor of quantum fields offers a rich and insightful way to explore the invisible and powerful forces of collective influence in our world.

Grassroots Movements and Their Global Ripple Effects

In recent decades, grassroots movements have become an increasingly significant force in shaping social, political, and environmental landscapes worldwide. These movements, often initiated by local communities, seek to address issues that affect individuals at the most basic levels of society. They are distinguished by their bottom-up approach, relying on the collective efforts of ordinary people rather than political elites, institutions, or external powers. While grassroots movements often begin as localized efforts to address specific issues, their impact can extend far beyond the initial scope, creating ripple effects that reverberate across national borders and spark global change. This essay explores the nature of grassroots movements, their origins, the mechanisms through which they generate ripple effects, and their transformative power in shaping global social, political, and environmental landscapes.

Entangled   Sandra Ferreira

The Nature of Grassroots Movements

Grassroots movements are typically characterized by their organic, decentralized structure. They arise from the communities directly affected by a particular issue, driven by the belief that change must come from the people themselves rather than being imposed from above. These movements often begin with small groups of activists or concerned citizens who recognize a common problem and organize to raise awareness, mobilize others, and demand change. Key issues may include social justice, human rights, environmental sustainability, economic inequality, and political reform.

Unlike top-down movements, which are usually led by political leaders, elites, or institutions, grassroots movements emphasize collective action and local engagement. The grassroots model fosters a sense of ownership and empowerment among participants, enabling them to take action in ways that reflect their unique experiences and needs. The nature of these movements is inherently diverse, with strategies ranging from peaceful protests and civil disobedience to grassroots advocacy and community organizing. This local focus, however, does not prevent these movements from achieving global reach, as the issues they address often resonate with people across the world.

The Emergence of Grassroots Movements: Case Studies

While grassroots movements can arise in response to a wide range of issues, several prominent movements provide insight into how they begin, grow, and achieve global influence.

One notable example is the environmental movement, which began in the 1960s and 1970s with small local initiatives aimed at raising awareness about pollution, conservation, and sustainability. In its early stages, environmentalism was focused on specific issues such as clean air and water or protecting endangered species. Over time, however, these efforts coalesced into a broader, more global movement advocating for climate change action, renewable energy, and the protection of natural resources. Grassroots organizations such as Greenpeace and the Sierra Club played pivotal roles in raising public awareness and pressuring governments to adopt more environmentally friendly policies. The rise of global environmental summits, such as the 1992 Rio Earth Summit and the 2015 Paris Climate Agreement, demonstrates the far-reaching impact of grassroots activism, which transformed environmental concerns from localized issues to global imperatives.

Another powerful example is the civil rights movement in the United States, which began as a local movement advocating for the rights of African Americans in the southern states. Figures like Rosa Parks and Martin Luther King Jr., alongside countless other activists, helped catalyze the movement through acts of resistance, boycotts, and marches. Their efforts were driven by local communities but gained national and international attention, culminating in landmark legislative changes like the Civil Rights Act of 1964 and the Voting Rights Act of 1965. The ripple effects of the U.S. civil rights movement inspired similar struggles for racial equality and justice worldwide, particularly in South Africa during the apartheid era and in other nations grappling with racial discrimination.

Grassroots movements are also central to global social justice causes. The feminist movements, for example, began with local efforts to secure voting rights, reproductive rights, and workplace equality for women. Over time, these movements evolved to address global gender inequality, leading to the creation of international bodies such as the United Nations Women's Agency and the ratification of global treaties like the Convention on the Elimination of All Forms of Discrimination Against Women (CEDAW). Feminist activism and campaigns like #MeToo have transcended national boundaries, fostering global solidarity among women and challenging systemic misogyny worldwide.

The Mechanisms of Ripple Effects

The ripple effects of grassroots movements arise from a combination of strategies, networks, and opportunities that allow local movements to resonate on a global scale. Several mechanisms help facilitate these effects.

1.   **Social Media and Digital Connectivity**: The rise of the internet and social media platforms has revolutionized the ability of grassroots movements to amplify their message and connect with supporters across the globe. Platforms like Twitter, Facebook, and Instagram allow activists to share information, organize events, and mobilize people instantaneously, regardless of geographic location. The global reach of social media enables grassroots movements to transcend national borders, drawing attention to issues that may otherwise remain invisible on the global stage. For example, movements like the Arab Spring in 2010-2011, which started as protests in Tunisia, spread rapidly across the Middle East and North Africa, fueled in part by social media's ability to connect people and amplify messages of resistance.

2.   **Transnational Networks and Alliances**: Grassroots movements often extend beyond national borders by forming transnational networks and alliances. These networks connect local groups with international organizations, human rights advocates, and other movements that share similar goals. One example is the global labor movement, which began with local strikes and worker protests but grew into a larger international movement advocating for fair wages, workers' rights, and social protections. Transnational organizations such as the International Labour Organization (ILO) and global trade unions have been instrumental in shaping labor standards worldwide, often in response to grassroots pressure.

3.   **Globalization and Shared Struggles**: The global interconnectedness of the modern world has created an environment where local issues often have broader global implications. Climate change, for instance, is a problem that originates in local environmental degradation but affects the entire planet. Grassroots movements addressing environmental issues, such as those led by Indigenous groups or local farmers, have the potential to spur global action by connecting their struggles to global concerns about sustainability, resource depletion, and climate justice. As a result, these movements can

generate global solidarity, with activists from different countries collaborating to advocate for systemic change.

4.   **Cultural Diffusion**: Grassroots movements also influence the world through the diffusion of culture and ideas. For example, the cultural shift brought about by LGBTQ+ advocacy in one country can inspire similar movements in others. The global visibility of Pride marches and the eventual acceptance of same-sex marriage in various countries reflects the cultural impact of grassroots movements. These movements often begin in specific regions but gain momentum as they resonate with people in different cultural contexts, eventually sparking global debates about human rights, justice, and equality.

The Impact of Grassroots Movements on Global Change

The ripple effects of grassroots movements can lead to substantial, far-reaching changes in various domains.

1.   **Political Change**: Grassroots movements have historically been instrumental in driving political change, both at the national and international levels. From the civil rights movement in the United States to the pro-democracy protests in Hong Kong, grassroots activism has challenged entrenched political systems, demanded accountability, and pushed for reforms. These movements often serve as a counterbalance to powerful political elites, holding governments accountable for injustices and pushing for greater representation, rights, and freedoms.

2.   **Social Transformation**: Grassroots movements can also trigger social transformation, shifting societal values and norms. The feminist movement, for instance, has influenced not only laws but also cultural attitudes towards gender roles, sexual harassment, and women's rights. Similarly, the environmental movement has helped shift global perceptions of sustainability, encouraging individuals, businesses, and governments to adopt more environmentally responsible practices. These social transformations are often driven by local activism that resonates with larger global trends, making the social changes feel interconnected and universal.

3.   **Environmental Impact**: Grassroots movements are particularly effective in advocating for environmental change. Local efforts to combat pollution, deforestation, or water contamination often inspire larger global efforts to address climate change. The work of organizations like Greenpeace, which started as a small grassroots initiative in Canada, has had profound global environmental impacts, raising awareness about issues like whaling, pollution, and climate change.

Grassroots movements, originating from local concerns and struggles, have the remarkable ability to create ripple effects that transcend national borders and ignite global change. Through social media, transnational alliances, and the increasing interconnectedness of the world, these movements can influence political, social, and environmental transformations on a scale previously unimaginable. The local efforts of ordinary people, united by a shared cause, have the power to challenge entrenched systems, promote justice, and foster solidarity across cultures and nations. As we continue to face global challenges, the importance of grassroots activism in shaping the future cannot be overstated.

How Individuals Can Control Collective Action for Meaningful Change

In an interconnected world where societal challenges increasingly transcend national and local boundaries, collective action has emerged as a critical vehicle for effecting meaningful change. The success of social movements, political campaigns, environmental activism, and community organizing often hinges on the ability of individuals to mobilize others toward a common goal. However, the process of controlling or directing collective action to bring about tangible, meaningful change is complex and multifaceted. While individual efforts can sometimes seem insignificant in the face of entrenched systems, history has shown that individuals who understand the dynamics of collective action can harness the power of the group to create lasting societal transformation. This essay explores how individuals can control collective action by fostering leadership, building networks, framing issues, leveraging resources, and sustaining momentum. By understanding and strategically navigating these elements, individuals can play a decisive role in directing collective efforts toward meaningful and lasting change.

The Power of Individual Leadership in Collective Action

At the heart of many successful collective actions lies a leader or a group of leaders who are able to galvanize others around a shared cause. While leadership within collective action movements is often decentralized, individual leaders often serve as catalysts for larger social transformations. Leaders do not always need to have formal positions of authority; instead, their ability to inspire, communicate effectively, and rally people toward a common purpose can significantly influence the trajectory of a movement.

Consider the example of figures like Martin Luther King Jr., Mahatma Gandhi, and Malala Yousafzai, whose personal leadership and vision were central to major social movements in the United States, India, and Pakistan, respectively. These individuals were able to control the direction of collective action by articulating a compelling vision of change and motivating people to work toward it. King's leadership in the American Civil Rights Movement and Gandhi's role in the Indian independence struggle exemplify how individuals can control collective action by providing moral clarity and a unifying goal.

One key aspect of individual leadership is the ability to inspire a sense of shared purpose. When individuals feel connected to a movement and understand how their personal actions contribute to a larger goal, collective action becomes more powerful and effective. Leaders are often able to craft a narrative or message that resonates with the emotions and values of the broader population, encouraging widespread participation and commitment to the cause.

Building Networks and Alliances

While individual leadership is crucial, it is often the ability to build networks and alliances that determines the scale and impact of collective action. Individuals who seek to control collective action must recognize the importance of collaboration and coalition-building. A single person or small group may not have the resources or influence to bring about large-scale change, but by building alliances with like-minded individuals, organizations, and even international networks, they can amplify their efforts.

In the case of climate change activism, for example, individuals like Greta Thunberg and organizations like 350.org have been able to mobilize millions of people around the world. Thunberg's personal commitment to the cause and her ability to connect with youth worldwide through social media helped form a global network of activists who participate in the Fridays for Future movement. While Thunberg's personal actions were key in sparking the movement, the broader collective action that followed was made possible through the networks she and others built, allowing the cause to grow into a global phenomenon.

Building these networks requires individuals to be strategic in identifying and forming partnerships with other groups or movements that share similar goals. A focus on shared values and a willingness to compromise on less critical issues allows individuals to form coalitions that can work together toward a common objective. These alliances enable a diverse group of people to contribute their unique skills, knowledge, and resources, expanding the capacity of the movement to create change.

Framing Issues and Shaping Public Perception

Another powerful way individuals can control collective action is by framing the issues they are addressing in a way that resonates with the public. The ability to shape how an issue is perceived and understood plays a pivotal role in determining whether collective action will be successful. The framing of a problem can influence public opinion, inspire action, and create a sense of urgency.

For example, the LGBTQ+ rights movement has successfully reframed issues of discrimination as matters of civil rights and human dignity. Leaders like Harvey Milk in the United States and groups such as ACT UP (AIDS Coalition to Unleash Power) have reframed the conversation about LGBTQ+ rights, focusing not just on individual rights but on collective well-being, equality, and health. By framing the LGBTQ+ struggle as a human rights issue rather than a niche concern, these movements were able to draw broad support from individuals and communities outside the LGBTQ+ population, enabling collective action to extend far beyond the confines of a specific interest group.

Similarly, the environmental movement has successfully framed climate change as not just an environmental issue, but a moral and existential challenge that affects all living beings, especially the most vulnerable. By presenting environmental activism as an urgent call to action that transcends national borders and affects future generations, individuals have been able to motivate millions to join the cause, from school children to world leaders. The language used to frame an issue is crucial, as it influences both the level of public support and the willingness of people to take action.

Leveraging Resources for Collective Action

While leadership and messaging are key to influencing collective action, individuals can also control the course of social movements by effectively leveraging resources. Resources—whether financial, human, or informational—are essential for sustaining collective action and driving it toward meaningful change. A leader's ability to strategically mobilize resources, secure funding, and create effective campaigns can determine the extent to which a movement can influence policy or shift societal norms.

One example of this is the #MeToo movement, which, while initiated by Tarana Burke in 2006, gained global momentum due to the strategic use of social media and the resources provided by supporters, including major celebrities and organizations. By using platforms like Twitter and Instagram, Burke and others were able to give voice to countless survivors of sexual violence and harassment. The #MeToo movement tapped into the power of social media networks to spread awareness, advocate for legal reform, and encourage societal change, effectively harnessing resources to bring attention to systemic issues of sexual abuse and inequality.

In addition to financial and informational resources, individuals seeking to control collective action must also be skilled in organizing volunteers, recruiting activists, and mobilizing the people needed to sustain momentum. By leveraging the enthusiasm and energy of those who believe in the cause, individuals can ensure that movements continue to grow and have the necessary reach to make an impact.

Sustaining Momentum and Overcoming Challenges

One of the greatest challenges in controlling collective action is maintaining momentum over time. While movements often begin with an initial surge of energy, sustaining that energy over weeks, months, or even years requires careful planning, commitment, and adaptability. Individuals who want to control collective action must be prepared to overcome setbacks, manage conflicts within the movement, and navigate external opposition.

The civil rights movement, for example, faced significant opposition from political and social elites, as well as internal divisions among different factions. However, leaders like Martin Luther King Jr. were able to maintain momentum through strategic decision-making, nonviolent resistance, and a long-term vision of equality. The ability to sustain collective action despite challenges is crucial for ensuring that progress is not only achieved but also institutionalized.

In the modern era, the internet and social media have also created new challenges, including the spread of misinformation and the potential for fragmentation within movements. Leaders must therefore be adept at using technology to unite rather than divide, ensuring that the core message remains clear and that activists remain focused on common goals.

Individuals play a pivotal role in controlling collective action for meaningful change. Through effective leadership, building strong networks, framing issues in ways that resonate with the public, and leveraging resources, individuals can steer movements toward lasting transformation. Additionally, the ability to sustain momentum in the face of challenges and opposition is crucial for ensuring that the collective effort remains focused and successful over time. Ultimately, the power of collective action lies in the ability of individuals to recognize and harness the potential of the group, directing it toward a shared vision of justice, equality, and societal betterment. By understanding the dynamics of collective action, individuals can catalyze change not just within their communities, but on a global scale.

Chapter 17
Becoming a Quantum Citizen

What does it mean to live as a "quantum citizen"? This chapter synthesizes the scientific and philosophical principles explored in earlier chapters into practical advice for becoming a mindful, compassionate, and proactive global citizen. Through exercises, reflections, and real-world examples, readers will learn how to cultivate empathy, awareness, and resilience as they navigate an interconnected, ever-evolving world.

Practical Steps to Integrate Quantum Thinking into Daily Life

Quantum thinking refers to a way of processing information that is based on the principles of quantum mechanics, the fundamental theory in physics that explains how subatomic particles behave. Unlike classical mechanics, which deals with deterministic and predictable systems, quantum mechanics is inherently probabilistic, interconnected, and non-local. These characteristics—such as superposition, entanglement, and uncertainty—offer a new lens through which to view the world. While quantum mechanics may seem like an abstract or highly technical field, its principles can offer profound insights into how we approach problem-solving, decision-making, and interpersonal relationships in daily life.

Integrating quantum thinking into our daily routines is not about mastering complex physics but about adopting a mindset that embraces uncertainty, interconnectedness, and creative possibilities. This essay will explore practical steps for integrating quantum thinking into everyday life, with a focus on fostering adaptability, increasing awareness, and encouraging innovative problem-solving approaches.

I. Embracing Uncertainty: The Power of Flexibility

One of the core tenets of quantum mechanics is the idea of uncertainty. The Heisenberg Uncertainty Principle suggests that we cannot simultaneously know both the position and momentum of a particle with complete precision. In everyday life, this principle can be applied to how we approach decisions and navigate the unknown.

1. Cultivate an Open-Minded Approach to Uncertainty

Rather than seeking absolute certainty in all situations, embracing uncertainty can lead to more flexible, adaptive thinking. This might involve:

- **Letting go of rigid expectations:** In the same way that quantum particles can exist in multiple states at once (superposition), we can allow ourselves to hold multiple possibilities for the future without needing to lock into a single outcome.
- **Reframing fear of the unknown:** Many decisions in life come with ambiguity. By recognizing that uncertainty is not inherently negative, but a space for

creativity, we can become more comfortable in ambiguous situations, such as job changes, relationships, or new projects.

2. Practice Mindfulness and Presence

Quantum thinking encourages an awareness of the present moment, where the future is not predetermined. By practicing mindfulness—whether through meditation, conscious breathing, or simply paying attention to your surroundings—we can train our minds to focus on the "now," which can help reduce anxiety about future outcomes. Being present allows for more fluid thinking and decision-making, much like the wave-particle duality in quantum physics, where particles are observed as both waves and particles depending on the situation.

II. Interconnectedness: Seeing the Bigger Picture

Quantum mechanics reveals that everything in the universe is interconnected through a phenomenon called entanglement. Entangled particles remain connected, regardless of the distance between them, meaning that a change in one particle can instantly affect the other. This can serve as a metaphor for understanding how our actions and choices have far-reaching consequences, even in ways we may not immediately understand.

1. Recognize the Interconnectedness of People and Events

Incorporating quantum thinking into daily life requires an acknowledgment that our actions affect others. This can be applied in various ways:

- **Mindful Communication:** Just as particles in quantum entanglement influence each other, our words and actions influence those around us. By practicing active listening, empathy, and constructive feedback, we can foster better relationships.
- **Long-Term Perspective:** Understanding the ripple effect of decisions can help us make choices that align with our values and long-term goals. Whether in business, personal finances, or relationships, acknowledging the interconnectedness of all things encourages more thoughtful decision-making.

2. Collaborative Problem-Solving

Quantum thinking highlights the idea that systems are rarely isolated. Solutions to problems are often found through collaboration and collective intelligence. We can apply this to our daily interactions by:

- **Seeking Diverse Perspectives:** Whether at work or in personal matters, asking for input from people with different backgrounds, expertise, and viewpoints can reveal solutions that we may not have considered on our own.
- **Engaging in Group Problem-Solving:** Quantum systems are often best understood through collaboration—similar to how collective brainstorming or teamwork can yield better results than solo efforts. Being open to working with others and pooling resources can lead to more innovative solutions.

III. Superposition: Navigating Multiple Possibilities

In quantum mechanics, superposition refers to the ability of a quantum system to exist in multiple states simultaneously, only collapsing into one state when observed. This concept can be applied to our daily decision-making processes, where we are often faced with multiple options, each with different outcomes.

1. Keep Multiple Options Open

Rather than committing to a single course of action, quantum thinking encourages keeping multiple possibilities in mind. For instance:

- **Explore Diverse Pathways:** When faced with a decision, such as choosing a career path or making an investment, consider the potential benefits of keeping multiple options open rather than locking into a single choice. Allow yourself the freedom to explore different possibilities.
- **Avoid Overcommitting:** Superposition teaches us that it's okay to hold space for uncertainty and multiple outcomes. We don't need to decide everything immediately or be certain about every choice, as the future is not predetermined.

2. Embrace Creativity and Innovation

Superposition can also be a powerful tool for creativity. Just as particles can exist in multiple states, we can adopt a mindset that embraces creative thinking by exploring different angles for a solution to a problem. Rather than thinking in binary terms—right or wrong, yes or no—consider multiple perspectives and approaches.

- **Brainstorming with "What If" Scenarios:** When tackling a challenge, ask yourself "what if" questions. What if this situation could play out in several ways? This can help us think outside the box and identify solutions that may not be immediately obvious.

IV. Quantum Mindset in Decision-Making: Embracing Probability

Quantum thinking emphasizes the role of probability in understanding outcomes. In classical physics, outcomes are typically seen as deterministic, whereas in quantum mechanics, the future is probabilistic. This shift can help us better understand the role of chance and likelihood in our decisions.

1. Reframe Risk as Probability

In many aspects of life, we face situations that involve risk—be it financial investments, career decisions, or personal endeavors. By embracing quantum thinking, we can reframe risk as probability rather than certainty. For instance:

- **Risk as Opportunity:** Understand that life involves probabilities, and while the future is uncertain, we can make educated guesses based on available data. Rather than avoiding risk, look at it as a series of probabilities, and assess the potential outcomes to make informed decisions.

- **Accepting Failures as Part of the Process:** Just as quantum mechanics involves inherent uncertainty and unpredictability, we can approach failure as part of the learning process. A failed attempt is simply one possible outcome in a range of potential results, and it does not negate future successes.

2. Using Intuition as a Guide

Quantum thinking also acknowledges the importance of intuition. Intuition can be seen as a tool that helps us navigate the complex and uncertain terrain of our daily lives. By listening to our inner voice and integrating it with rational analysis, we can make decisions that align with both our logical and intuitive senses.

V. Harnessing Quantum Thinking for Personal Growth

The principles of quantum thinking not only influence our interactions with the world but also our personal development. By applying quantum ideas to our growth, we can expand our potential and cultivate a greater sense of self-awareness.

1. Self-Reflection and Awareness

Quantum thinking encourages self-awareness and introspection, as it emphasizes the fluidity and interconnectedness of all aspects of life. Taking time to reflect on our behaviors, thoughts, and feelings allows us to better understand how we fit into the broader context of the world.

- **Journaling:** Regular self-reflection through journaling can help individuals track their thoughts and emotions, identifying patterns and areas for growth.
- **Mindful Awareness of Thought Patterns:** By becoming aware of our thoughts, we can better understand how they shape our reality and decide whether to embrace or challenge them.

2. Pursuing Personal Evolution

Quantum thinking suggests that personal growth is not a linear process but one that involves multiple potential pathways. Embrace the idea that you are always evolving and that new possibilities and opportunities are available for exploration.

Integrating quantum thinking into daily life is not about mastering complex scientific theories but about adopting a mindset that embraces uncertainty, interconnectedness, creativity, and flexibility. Whether through reframing our understanding of uncertainty, recognizing the interconnectedness of people and events, or embracing the fluidity of multiple possibilities, quantum thinking can provide valuable insights into how we approach decision-making, problem-solving, and personal growth. By weaving these principles into our everyday experiences, we can foster greater resilience, creativity, and innovation in our lives.

Exercises for Fostering Global Awareness and Empathy

Fostering global awareness and empathy has never been more crucial. Global awareness involves understanding the issues, cultures, and perspectives of people from around the world, while empathy refers to the ability to understand and share the feelings of others. These two qualities are essential in navigating the challenges of a diverse and complex world. Cultivating them can lead to more harmonious relationships, greater social responsibility, and a more peaceful global community.

This essay will explore various exercises that can be used to develop global awareness and empathy. These activities can be applied in educational settings, workplaces, communities, and personal development practices. They range from experiential learning activities to reflective exercises that help individuals see the world through the eyes of others. The goal of these exercises is to create a more inclusive, understanding, and compassionate world by nurturing empathy and awareness on a global scale.

I. Engaging with Diverse Cultures

One of the most effective ways to foster global awareness and empathy is by immersing oneself in different cultures. This can be done through direct experiences or by engaging in activities that allow individuals to learn about the customs, values, and perspectives of others.

1. Cultural Exchange Programs

Participating in cultural exchange programs, whether physical or virtual, is a powerful way to experience the customs, languages, and daily lives of people from different countries. These exchanges can take place through travel, work-study programs, or even online platforms. Direct interaction with people from different cultures fosters mutual understanding and helps to break down stereotypes.

- **Example Exercise:** Students or employees from different countries can engage in virtual exchange sessions where they share their cultural practices, challenges they face, and their views on global issues. Participants can also swap daily life routines, meals, and language lessons to further connect on a personal level.

2. Hosting or Attending Cultural Events

Local cultural festivals, international food fairs, and language meet-ups provide an excellent opportunity to experience global cultures without leaving home. By attending these events, individuals can learn about the art, food, music, and history of different cultures, which cultivates a deeper understanding and appreciation of global diversity.

- **Example Exercise:** Organize a global awareness day where participants learn about and celebrate a different country or culture through food, music, fashion, and storytelling. The event can include guest speakers from the represented culture to provide firsthand insights.

II. Reading and Storytelling from Different Perspectives

Reading books, watching films, and consuming other media from various parts of the world is an excellent way to foster empathy and global awareness. This allows individuals to see the world through different lenses, understand the struggles faced by others, and appreciate the diversity of human experiences.

1. Reading Global Literature

Literature offers a window into the emotional lives and experiences of people from different cultures. Novels, short stories, and poetry written by authors from various countries can help readers understand the complexities of global issues, such as poverty, migration, gender equality, and environmental concerns. This exercise can open the mind to different perspectives, giving voice to those who are often marginalized.

- **Example Exercise:** Organize a book club focused on global literature. Each month, participants can read a book written by an author from a different country or region. Afterward, they can discuss the themes of the book, how it relates to global issues, and what personal insights they gained from the experience.

2. Sharing Personal Stories

Storytelling is an ancient practice that allows people to connect on an emotional level. When people share personal stories of hardship, resilience, or hope, it fosters a deeper understanding of others' experiences and builds empathy. Whether through writing, art, or spoken word, storytelling helps bridge the gap between cultures and histories.

- **Example Exercise:** Create a platform or safe space for individuals to share their personal experiences related to global issues. This could take the form of an open-mic night, a storytelling workshop, or an online forum where people from different backgrounds share their stories of overcoming challenges and fostering change in their communities.

III. Volunteering and Service Learning

Volunteering in communities that face different challenges—whether locally or internationally—provides hands-on experience in understanding the needs and struggles of others. Service learning programs, in which individuals engage in volunteer work while reflecting on the cultural and social implications of their work, are a particularly effective tool for building empathy and global awareness.

1. Volunteering Abroad or at Local Organizations

Traveling abroad to volunteer offers direct exposure to global issues, such as poverty, healthcare, and education. Similarly, volunteering with local immigrant communities or refugees helps individuals develop an understanding of the challenges faced by newcomers, including language barriers, cultural adjustment, and discrimination.

- **Example Exercise:** Volunteer with a local organization that supports refugees or immigrants. Through this experience, volunteers can learn about the cultural, social, and economic factors that influence the lives of refugees, while offering support through language tutoring, community building, or advocacy efforts.

2. Participating in Global Service Projects

Organizations such as Habitat for Humanity, the Peace Corps, and Global Vision International offer opportunities for individuals to participate in service projects worldwide. These projects are an opportunity to contribute to local communities while learning about the broader socio-political and economic issues that shape those communities.

•   **Example Exercise:** Plan a group service project that focuses on addressing a global issue, such as climate change, hunger, or education. Participants can work together to raise awareness, fundraise, and physically contribute to the cause. This exercise fosters a sense of global responsibility and the desire to make a difference in the world.

IV. Engaging in Discussions and Debates on Global Issues

Open discussions and debates about global issues, such as climate change, inequality, or human rights, can deepen understanding and encourage individuals to see the world from multiple perspectives. By engaging in thoughtful, respectful conversations, participants can challenge assumptions, broaden their views, and cultivate empathy for others who may be directly affected by these issues.

1. Global Issue Debates
Participating in debates on global topics encourages critical thinking and the exploration of different viewpoints. Whether discussing international politics, environmental policies, or humanitarian efforts, debates allow individuals to articulate their beliefs while considering the experiences and needs of others.

•   **Example Exercise:** Host a debate or discussion on a pressing global issue. Assign participants different roles—representing different countries, perspectives, or stakeholders—to help them understand the complexity of the issue. This exercise will encourage participants to think beyond their personal beliefs and develop a more comprehensive understanding of global challenges.

2. Global Awareness Workshops
Workshops focused on specific global issues can serve as educational platforms for raising awareness. These workshops can cover topics such as human trafficking, environmental sustainability, or social justice. Facilitators can invite experts to share their knowledge, followed by group discussions and interactive activities that allow participants to explore these issues on a deeper level.

•   **Example Exercise:** Organize a series of workshops that focus on different global issues. After each session, participants can reflect on how these issues are interconnected and what actions they can take to contribute to a solution, either locally or globally.

V. Practicing Reflection and Mindfulness

Empathy and global awareness are not only cultivated through active engagement but also through quiet reflection. By practicing mindfulness and reflecting on one's own biases, assumptions, and privileges, individuals can develop a deeper understanding of their place in the world and how they relate to others.

1. Journaling on Global Issues

Journaling offers a private space for reflection on global issues and personal growth. Individuals can use journaling to explore their thoughts on cultural differences, international conflicts, or their personal role in addressing global challenges. This exercise helps individuals connect their internal thoughts and beliefs with the broader global context.

- **Example Exercise:** Encourage individuals to keep a global awareness journal where they reflect on their experiences with diversity, current events, and interactions with people from different cultures. Writing about these experiences helps individuals gain clarity on their attitudes and how they might need to change in order to become more empathetic.

2. Practicing Empathy Meditation

Empathy meditation is a practice that helps individuals develop compassion for others by imagining themselves in another person's shoes. This practice involves sitting in a quiet space, focusing on the breath, and visualizing someone from a different background or culture. By contemplating their struggles and experiences, individuals can deepen their empathy.

- **Example Exercise:** Lead a guided empathy meditation in which participants are asked to envision the life of a person living in a different country, experiencing a different set of challenges. This practice cultivates a sense of connectedness and emotional resonance with people from diverse backgrounds.

Fostering global awareness and empathy is an ongoing journey that involves active participation, reflection, and engagement with people and cultures beyond our own. By engaging in exercises such as cultural exchanges, volunteering, reading diverse literature, and participating in global discussions, we can begin to break down the barriers that divide us and build a more compassionate, understanding world. These exercises not only help us understand the global community but also cultivate the empathy necessary to navigate our interconnected world with kindness and respect. Through these practices, we can develop a deeper appreciation for the richness of the human experience and contribute to a more inclusive, peaceful global society.

Strategies for Staying Engaged in Global Issues While Cultivating Personal Wellbeing and Mental Health

The modern world is filled with interconnected global challenges—climate change, poverty, inequality, political instability, and human rights violations. With the rise of social media and constant access to news, it has become increasingly difficult to avoid exposure to these issues. While remaining engaged with global concerns is essential for fostering positive change, it can also take a toll on personal wellbeing and mental health.

The emotional burden of constantly absorbing information about crises, suffering, and injustice can lead to feelings of helplessness, burnout, and anxiety.

Finding a balance between staying informed about global issues and preserving mental and emotional health is critical. It is possible to contribute to meaningful causes and maintain a sense of purpose without compromising personal wellbeing. This essay will explore various strategies that individuals can use to stay engaged with global issues while cultivating mental resilience and emotional health. These strategies will focus on emotional regulation, establishing boundaries, seeking support, engaging in positive action, and practicing mindfulness.

I. Emotional Regulation: Managing Emotional Responses to Global Events

One of the greatest challenges when engaging with global issues is managing the emotional responses they can provoke. Constant exposure to negative news can lead to emotional overwhelm, frustration, sadness, or anger. Developing emotional regulation skills is crucial in maintaining a healthy balance between being informed and caring for one's mental health.

1. Acknowledging Emotions Without Becoming Overwhelmed

It is natural to feel emotions such as sadness or anger when learning about global injustices or crises. However, acknowledging these emotions without allowing them to consume us is important for maintaining mental health. Emotional regulation involves recognizing feelings, allowing oneself to process them, and then finding ways to cope constructively.

- **Strategy:** Whenever you feel overwhelmed, practice naming the emotion you're experiencing (e.g., "I feel sad about the situation in X country") and take a step back to reflect on the bigger picture. Recognize that your feelings are valid, but they do not define your entire reality.

2. Developing Healthy Coping Mechanisms

In moments of emotional distress, it is important to have healthy coping strategies that help calm the mind. This could include physical activities such as exercise, creative outlets like painting or writing, or practicing relaxation techniques like deep breathing and progressive muscle relaxation. Coping mechanisms can help process difficult emotions without suppressing them or allowing them to escalate.

- **Strategy:** Develop a personal toolkit for emotional regulation. When overwhelmed by global news, take a break and engage in activities that ground you, such as taking a walk, journaling, or spending time in nature. These practices help reset your emotional state.

II. Establishing Boundaries: Managing Media Consumption

Constant exposure to global news can lead to information fatigue and a sense of helplessness. Setting clear boundaries around media consumption is one of the most effective strategies for staying engaged without compromising mental health.

1. Limiting News Intake

While it is important to stay informed, overconsumption of distressing news can contribute to anxiety and burnout. Establishing a healthy routine for consuming news, such as limiting time spent reading or watching global news, can help reduce the emotional impact.

- **Strategy:** Set specific times during the day for consuming news, and commit to not checking the news outside of those hours. Use tools such as news apps with "quiet hours" or set alarms to remind yourself when to stop consuming news for the day.

2. Curating Sources and Media

It is also essential to curate the sources of information to avoid sensationalist or overwhelming content. Consuming news from reliable, balanced sources can ensure that information is accurate and does not contribute to unnecessary fear or panic.

- **Strategy:** Subscribe to newsletters, websites, or social media channels that provide balanced and informative perspectives. Avoid constantly refreshing your social media feed or scrolling through news outlets that sensationalize or focus on the most traumatic aspects of global events.

III. Seeking Support: Connecting with Like-Minded Individuals

Caring about global issues can sometimes feel isolating, especially when it seems that others are not as engaged or aware. Building a supportive community with like-minded individuals can help combat feelings of loneliness and provide a space for mutual understanding and shared action.

1. Joining Activist Groups and Communities

Finding groups or organizations dedicated to global causes can provide a sense of camaraderie and collective purpose. Being part of a community working towards positive change can reduce feelings of helplessness, as it shifts focus from individual problems to collective efforts.

- **Strategy:** Participate in local or online activist groups that align with your values and passions. Whether through environmental organizations, human rights initiatives, or social justice movements, working alongside others provides emotional support and shared motivation.

2. Talking to Friends or Professionals

Sharing your thoughts, emotions, and concerns with friends, family, or mental health professionals is an important way to alleviate the burden of global issues. Having open conversations allows for the expression of complex emotions and can offer new perspectives or coping strategies.

- **Strategy:** Schedule regular check-ins with friends or loved ones where you can discuss global issues in a safe, supportive space. Additionally, if news-related anxiety becomes overwhelming, consider speaking to a mental health professional who can help you develop strategies to manage distress.

IV. Engaging in Positive Action: Contributing to Change

Engaging in meaningful action toward solving global problems can help individuals feel more empowered, reduce feelings of helplessness, and create a sense of purpose. Taking proactive steps, whether through volunteering, advocacy, or charitable contributions, can give individuals a tangible way to address the global challenges they care about.

1. Volunteering Locally or Globally

Volunteering offers a direct way to contribute to global or local causes. Whether helping in one's own community or participating in international volunteer efforts, this form of engagement fosters a sense of connection to a broader purpose while simultaneously benefiting others.

- **Strategy:** Commit to regular volunteer work that aligns with your values, whether it's working with a local nonprofit, organizing community events, or supporting causes related to global issues such as climate change or human rights.

2. Advocacy and Awareness Campaigns

Raising awareness about critical global issues, such as climate change, poverty, or gender inequality, is another way to make an impact. Advocacy can be done through social media, writing to lawmakers, participating in protests, or supporting petitions.

- **Strategy:** Dedicate a specific amount of time each week to advocacy work, whether it's sharing educational posts on social media, signing petitions, or participating in letter-writing campaigns. Small acts of advocacy contribute to larger systemic change.

V. Practicing Mindfulness and Self-Care: Nurturing Inner Peace

Practicing mindfulness and self-care is essential in maintaining mental and emotional health while staying engaged with global issues. Mindfulness allows individuals to stay grounded in the present moment, reducing anxiety and fostering emotional resilience. Self-care practices are also important for replenishing emotional energy and preventing burnout.

1. Mindfulness Meditation

Mindfulness meditation is a powerful tool for cultivating awareness and emotional regulation. It involves focusing on the present moment, observing thoughts and feelings without judgment, and cultivating compassion for oneself and others. Regular mindfulness practice can help individuals detach from overwhelming emotions tied to global issues.

- **Strategy:** Set aside time each day for mindfulness meditation. Apps like Headspace, Calm, or Insight Timer offer guided sessions that focus on reducing stress and increasing emotional resilience. Even just a few minutes of mindful breathing can help reset emotional balance.

2. Physical Self-Care

Engaging in regular physical activities—such as exercise, yoga, or outdoor activities—supports mental and emotional health by releasing endorphins, reducing stress, and promoting overall well-being. Physical self-care nurtures the body and mind, helping individuals recharge so they can remain engaged in global issues without burning out.

• **Strategy:** Incorporate physical self-care practices into your routine, whether it's a morning yoga session, regular walks in nature, or hitting the gym. Ensure that physical activity is something you enjoy, as this will make it easier to maintain consistency.

Staying engaged in global issues while cultivating personal wellbeing and mental health requires a delicate balance. By practicing emotional regulation, setting boundaries around media consumption, seeking support from others, engaging in positive action, and prioritizing mindfulness and self-care, individuals can contribute meaningfully to global change without sacrificing their emotional and mental health. These strategies help maintain a sense of empowerment and purpose while ensuring that personal resilience is nurtured in the process. In a world that can often feel overwhelming, it is possible to stay connected to global causes while also fostering inner peace and well-being.

Conclusion
A Quantum Vision for a Global Future

In the final chapter, we envision a future where humanity collectively embraces the principles of quantum citizenship—a framework that unites clinical psychology, sociology, spirituality, and economic innovation under the shared banner of global interconnectedness. This vision invites us to reimagine our roles as individuals and communities in a deeply interwoven world.

From the perspective of clinical psychology, embracing global citizenship fosters mental well-being by reducing isolation and cultivating empathy. Understanding our interconnectedness promotes a sense of belonging and purpose, which are vital for psychological resilience. When individuals perceive themselves as part of a global network, they are more likely to develop emotional intelligence and adopt healthier coping strategies, creating a foundation for collective mental health.

Sociologically, global citizenship can transform societies by bridging cultural divides and fostering mutual respect. It shifts the focus from competition to collaboration, inspiring systemic solutions to shared challenges such as inequality, climate change, and public health crises. By valuing diversity as a strength, societies can evolve toward inclusivity, leveraging the power of diverse perspectives to drive innovation and social cohesion.

Spiritually, quantum citizenship resonates with principles of interconnectedness found in many traditions, encouraging a deeper awareness of our shared humanity. By cultivating mindfulness and compassion, individuals can transcend divisions of race, nationality, or creed. This spiritual awakening inspires a commitment to the greater good, aligning personal growth with global progress and nurturing a collective consciousness rooted in love and respect.

Economically, the principles of global citizenship offer innovative pathways for sustainable development. By prioritizing equitable resource distribution and ethical practices, businesses and governments can create economies that benefit all rather than a select few. Global citizenship encourages investments in education, clean energy, and technology, empowering communities while addressing systemic disparities. This shift not only stabilizes economies but also generates shared prosperity, fostering a global marketplace grounded in mutual benefit.

By approaching life with the curiosity of a quantum physicist and the compassion of a global citizen, we can contribute to a world that values unity over division, complexity over simplicity, and shared purpose over isolated interests. A quantum vision for the future is not just a hopeful ideal but a practical roadmap for individual and collective transformation. It is a call to action for humanity to rise to its greatest potential—living with intention, embracing diversity, and co-creating a thriving, interconnected world.

Final Thoughts
The Journey of Entanglement

The journey of global citizenship, much like quantum mechanics, involves uncertainty, connection, and potential. This book is a starting point—a lens to view the world with greater depth, empathy, and understanding. The principles of quantum physics remind us that we are all interconnected in ways we may never fully understand. Yet, in embracing this mystery, we unlock the potential to live more meaningful, impactful lives.

Welcome to the journey of entangled citizenship. May it inspire you to see yourself as a vital, connected part of the quantum world and the global society alike.

BIBLIOGRAPHY

Books

1.   Barad, Karen. *Meeting the Universe Halfway: Quantum Physics and the Entanglement of Matter and Meaning.* Durham, NC: Duke University Press, 2007.

2.   Bohm, David. *Wholeness and the Implicate Order.* London: Routledge, 1980.

3.   Bourdieu, Pierre. *Distinction: A Social Critique of the Judgment of Taste.* Cambridge, MA: Harvard University Press, 1984.

4.   Erikson, Erik H. *Childhood and Society.* New York, NY: W. W. Norton & Company, 1950.

5.   Frankl, Viktor E. *Man's Search for Meaning.* Boston, MA: Beacon Press, 1946.

6.   Geertz, Clifford. *The Interpretation of Cultures: Selected Essays.* New York, NY: Basic Books, 1973.

7.   Goffman, Erving. *The Presentation of Self in Everyday Life.* New York, NY: Anchor Books, 1956.

8.   LeVine, Robert A. *Culture, Behavior, and Personality: An Introduction to the Comparative Study of Psychosocial Adaptation.* New York, NY: Aldine, 1973.

9.   Nussbaum, Martha C. *Political Emotions: Why Love Matters for Justice.* Cambridge, MA: Harvard University Press, 2013.

10.   Rovelli, Carlo. *Reality Is Not What It Seems: The Journey to Quantum Gravity.* New York, NY: Riverhead Books, 2016.

11.   Stiglitz, Joseph E. *The Price of Inequality: How Today's Divided Society Endangers Our Future.* New York, NY: W. W. Norton & Company, 2012.

12.   Tylor, Edward B. *Primitive Culture: Researches into the Development of Mythology, Philosophy, Religion, Language, Art, and Custom.* London: John Murray, 1871.

13.   Turner, Victor W. *The Ritual Process: Structure and Anti-Structure.* Ithaca, NY: Cornell University Press, 1969.

14.   Isin, Engin F. *Citizenship in Flux: The Figure of the Activist Citizen.* London: Zed Books, 2008.

Articles

15.   Isin, Engin F., and Bryan S. Turner. "Investigating Citizenship: An Agenda for Citizenship Studies." *Citizenship Studies* 11, no. 1 (2007): 5–17.

16.   Lloyd, Seth. "A Quantum of Natural Rights." *Nature Physics* 7, no. 10 (2011): 841–844.

17.   Barad, Karen. "Quantum Entanglements and Hauntological Relations of Inheritance: Dis/continuities, SpaceTime Enfoldings, and Justice-to-Come." *Derrida Today* 3, no. 2 (2010): 240–268.

Chapters in Edited Volumes

18.   Haraway, Donna. "Situated Knowledges: The Science Question in Feminism and the Privilege of Partial Perspective." In *Feminism and Science*, edited by Evelyn Fox Keller and Helen Longino, 249–263. Oxford: Oxford University Press, 1996.

19.   Wendt, Alexander. "Quantum Mind and Social Science." In *Quantum Physics and Political Science: Entanglements and Implications*, edited by David Chandler and Julian Reid, 87–106. London: Routledge, 2017.

Reports and Papers

20.   United Nations. *Human Rights and Quantum Computing: A Framework for Global Citizenship*. Geneva: UN Human Rights Office, 2020.

Online Resources

21.   Physics World. "Quantum Citizenship: The Intersection of Science and Society." *PhysicsWorld.com*, accessed December 8, 2024. www.physicsworld.com.

22.   The Quantum Citizenship Project. "Exploring Identity and Entanglement in the Digital Age." Accessed December 8, 2024. www.quantumcitizen.org.

www.ingramcontent.com/pod-product-compliance
Lightning Source LLC
Chambersburg PA
CBHW061040250726
48653CB00001B/179